D1243186

A Quest for the Post-Historical Jesus

A Quest for the Post-Historical Jesus

William Hamilton

Continuum · New York

1994
The Continuum Publishing Company
370 Lexington Avenue
New York NY 10017

ISBN 0–8264–0641–6

Library of Congress Catalog Card Number 93–073822

Printed and bound in Great Britain by
Mackays of Chatham PLC, Chatham, Kent

As the sexual union of horse and donkey produces two different hybrids, the mule and the hinny, so the mixture of historical writing and fiction gives rise to different products which, under the common designation of 'historical novel', sometimes want to be appreciated as history, sometimes as novel. They derive their interest, in fact, from history, but their intent is that of the novel; they want to affect the emotions. Others among these literary creations function in quite the opposite way. They do not hesitate to invent persons and even events in order to describe the special character of a period, but first and foremost they aspire to historical truth despite the admitted fiction. Others even manage to a large extent in reconciling the demands of artistic creation with those of historical fidelity. How much fiction, contrary to the intentions of the historian, still creeps into his presentation, requires little further comment.

(Sigmund Freud, unpublished introduction to *Das Mann Moses*, dated 8 September 1934. Translated by Yosef H. Yerushalmi, *Freud's Moses*, 17)

Contents

I

Beyond Belief

1. *The summer of 1990*

This is a book about Jesus of Nazareth. I'll come to 'post-historical' presently, but first I want to note that my primary concern is how what I am calling 'the poets'[1] (and I will define them in a moment) have portrayed Jesus in our century, and why they have done what they have done.

My interest in the poets on Jesus has both a personal and a theological context. I suspect that the theologians and the historians have less and less to teach us about Jesus, and so I feel justified in adding the non-traditional half-truths of the poets to the traditional half-truths we already think we know. This examination of the poets may also help locate my own relationship to the Christian tradition. My poets will turn out to be inside, outside, and partly inside and partly outside that tradition, and thus they may help me define the way I may be inside, outside, or partly in and partly out. I will be asking the poets to help me locate a place that is beyond belief, neither belief nor unbelief.

First, a brief autobiographical note. Two things – a lecture I read and a movie I saw – in the summer of 1990 served as triggers for this book. The lecture is called 'Is Nothing Sacred?' and it was written by Salman Rushdie as the Herbert Read Memorial Lecture and read by Harold Pinter at the Institute of Contemporary Arts, London, on 6 February 1990. The movie, written and directed by Denys Arcand, is 'Jesus of Montreal'.

Rushdie's lecture does in non-fictional form what *The Satanic Verses* does as fiction: it provides a way, both angry and loving, for the author to define himself and his relationship to the Muslim tradition. In the lecture, Rushdie admits that until recently he was confident that the answer to the question 'Is Nothing Sacred?' should be a simple 'yes'. After all, he says, I am a novelist and between religion and the novel there is a fixed and unbridgeable gulf.

> Between religion and literature, as between politics and literature, there is a linguistically based dispute. But it is not a dispute of simple opposites. Because whereas religion seeks to privilege one language above all others, one set of values above all others, one text above all others, the novel has always been *about* the way in which different languages, values and narratives quarrel, and about the shifting relations between them, which are relations of power. The novel does not seek to establish a privileged language, but it insists upon the freedom to portray and analyse the struggle between the different contestants for such privileges.[2]

This is an eloquent and convincing description of what the modern novel does, but Rushdie is careful not to claim that the novel desacralizes life or replaces religion. He sees himself as a religious writer, and admits that throughout his whole life he has asked: 'Can the religious mentality survive outside of religious dogma and hierarchy?' Can art replace the sacred – or, more exactly – is there a way through art to a secular definition of the sacred or the transcendent?

Students of American literature will find themselves on familiar ground as they ponder Rushdie's inability either to sacralize or secularize his life and work. One thinks of that unforgettable meeting of Hester Prynne and Dimmesdale in the forest outside of town portrayed in Nathaniel Hawthorne's *The Scarlet Letter*. They are speaking of the sexual act that conceived Pearl. Hester whispered:

> What we did had a consecration of its own. We felt it so! We said it to each other! Hast thou forgotten it?

Dimmesdale, unable to acknowledge Pearl before the world, not only acknowledges her to Hester, but accepts her sexual-secular understanding of the sacred.

Hush, Hester . . . No! I have not forgotten.[3]

A little more than ten years after *The Scarlet Letter*, Abraham Lincoln at Gettysburg confronted the same problem: what can be sacred for us, today, in this place? He begins by declaring that they are assembled to 'dedicate' a portion of the battlefield. Then he steps back from that definition.

> But, in a larger sense, we cannot dedicate – we cannot consecrate – we cannot hallow – this ground.

Conventional piety (never Lincoln's strong suit) would agree. *We* cannot consecrate anything. Only God, or someone ordained by him, can do so. But Lincoln does not say that.

> The brave men, living and dead, who struggled here, have [already] consecrated it far above our poor power to add or detract.

The soldiers have already done whatever consecrating was necessary: northern, southern, black, white, killed, wounded, unhurt. War itself (even in the service of evil), blood itself, courage, even death – all these become Lincoln's secular forms for the sacred. If Jonathan Edwards cannot help the nineteenth century define what is sacred, perhaps Hester Prynne and President Lincoln can.

Rushdie does not say that because he is a novelist he cannot be religious. He wants religion without, as he puts it rather lamely, dogma or hierarchy. He will not have us moving to a time of no religion at all. We were foolish to believe that we could do without religion. What has failed us is not religion but 'the idea that men and women could ever define themselves in terms that exclude their spiritual needs'.[4]

We must be religious, Rushdie argues, for three reasons. We need a way to articulate our imperfect experiences of wonder and awe. We need answers to unanswerable questions – where are we from (creation) and where are we going (eschatology)? And we need some way of answering the question about how to live.

Just as we expect him to say that art (the new sacred) can provide what Islam (and Christianity) cannot, he fortunately edges away from that banality. (Banal even when Dostoevsky cried out that beauty alone can save us.) In Rushdie's world – the world of Beckett's tramps and Joyce's wanderers – there are neither rules nor answers. Beckett himself embodied and defined the roadblock that modernism erected between art and the sacred: 'Ever tried. Ever failed. Never mind. Try again. Fail better.'

Rushdie insists in this address, and this is where I find him of greatest help, that the great religions are now engaged in the task of keeping us from religion. They must not be allowed to succeed. Even if there are no more privileged languages, we must remain or become religious men and women, and we need to find – inside and/or outside our inherited or discovered religious worlds – something to interpret and order that religiousness. For Rushdie, the artist (or what I am naming the 'poets') may be of help in locating rules that are not rules, answers that are not answers.

In the summer of 1990 I not only read a lecture by Rushdie, I saw a movie written and directed by the Quebec film-maker Denys Arcand. If the lecture suggested the possibility of relocating my own religiousness with the help of the artists, 'Jesus of Montreal' shows how a gifted artist can point an admiring finger towards Jesus in a world in which non-fundamentalist Christianity is collapsing.

The film's device is not a new one. Kazantzakis used it, rather turgidly, in *The Greek Passion*: 'What happens when a bunch of people get together and put on a passion play?' In this film, something like Jesus comes to Montreal.

A decent but timid older priest invites a young actor, Daniel Coloumbe (but why is he named for the third person of the Trinity and not the second?) to prepare a new version of an outdated and traditional 'seven stages of the Cross' pageant-drama for a Montreal church and shrine. Coloumbe brings together four other actors, and we watch them preparing the script, moving from rehearsal to performance, and slowly becoming caught up in the story they are learning to tell.

There is nothing outrageous or avant-garde about Coloumbe's script: it is neither passover plot nor reactionary Vatican piety. It is, in fact, a good pastiche of the best mainstream New Testament scholarship, a touch more uncertain about the historical Jesus than

Dodd, Bornkamm or Küng; less sceptical than Bultmann or John Knox.

The two actresses in the troupe differ significantly in their responses to the experiences of the play. Constance, a single mother working at a soup kitchen between jobs, is truly the constant one: serene, unselfish, once-born. She really doesn't need redemption. She is the regular bed-partner of the priest, and she beautifully expresses her loving decency: 'it gives him so much pleasure, and me so little pain'. Mireille is a beautiful young model valued by the world of television commercials only for her body. Working with Daniel and the others gives her a confidence she had never known. More than any others in the group, Mireille is radically and tragically transformed by the encounter with the passion of Jesus.

The revised passion play is wildly successful, pushed and praised by local radio and television broadcasters. A lawyer, looking out on Montreal from a high-rise office building, assures Daniel that the city could be his if he only exploited his success properly: did a book, do the talk shows, and so on. Daniel is untempted and untemptable.

The film's *peripeteia* comes when Daniel accompanies Mireille (who is beginning to fall in love with him) to an audition for a beer commercial directed by Mireille's former lover. She is asked to remove her sweat-shirt, and she replies that she has nothing on under it. She is again asked; the clients (beer company officers) wish to see her breasts. She begins to comply, and Daniel tells her very quietly not to. With a deliberate fury, Daniel destroys a camera and overturns a table holding a TV monitor and assorted refreshments. The studio where commercials are filmed becomes the temple of the late twentieth century. Daniel comes to Mireille's defence partly because he 'is' Jesus and partly because as a man and a friend he does not believe that actresses should be so demeaned. The actors had simply come to care for each other as they worked together on the play. Daniel is brought to court for his destruction of property, and Arcand himself appears as the knowing judge at the hearing.

The priest is distressed by the message of the revised passion play (with its lesson that all religious institutions are corrupt) as well as by its success. He has the church authorities close the show.

The extended and tragic climax begins when the church's security forces try to stop the play during performance. In the fracas, the audience defends the performers and takes on the security forces. The cross, with Daniel hanging on it, falls to the ground, crushing him. He is mortally injured, and the remainder of the film is about the death of Daniel Coloumbe.

Actually, there are four deaths of Daniel Coloumbe and, just possibly, a resurrection.

1. Daniel's first death is the death of Jesus that he so vividly re-enacts, night after night, in the play. The details of the fixing of the body to the cross, the nailing, the blood, the nakedness, are depicted with force and simplicity. In the play, Jesus is asked by Pilate to explain his message. Jesus answers with John 15.13: 'Greater love has no man than this, that a man lay down his life for his friends.' This is just what Daniel does in the film, probably to no avail.

2. The second death of Daniel is the injury which the cross inflicts on him in the fight caused by the church's attempt to stop the play. Daniel is rushed to St Mark's Hospital. But St Mark's received him not; the emergency room is crowded and chaotic, unable to help him. He recovers enough strength to leave the hospital and to continue in a kind of half-life (a risen life?) for a few hours. Constance and Mireille help him out of the hospital to a subway station. His voice has strangely changed. He is no longer Daniel; he has become the Christ of the Little Apocalypse, warning those in the station of a judgment to come, predicting the advent of false Christs (himself?), murmuring partly to himself and partly to the others of the desperate unhappiness of his (Daniel's? Jesus'?) life.

3. The third death is Daniel's collapse in the subway station. Constance goes for an ambulance while Mireille cradles the head of the dying Daniel in her lap, as the two of them become a kind of Pietà in the now deserted station.

4. The fourth death is the actual death of Daniel Coloumbe. This time the ambulance does not take him to St Mark's (neither the gospel nor the church of that name could receive him), but to the Jewish Hospital, where he receives swift and expert attention. His own finally did receive him, but it was too late. The actual

cross, the passion play, the heartless bureaucracies of both the Catholic Church and the Catholic hospital, all conspired to bring about the fourth death. At the end, only the Jewish doctors and Daniel's friends cared. In Daniel's play, a corrupt high priest persuades a cynical Pilate to give him this one little crucifixion, while outside the play the courageous Jewish doctors lose in their fight for Daniel's life.

Is there anything after this quadruple crucifixion? Is there any resurrection in this post-Christian gospel, or is the end all cheerless, dark, and deadly, with Daniel dead and the priest and surviving actors worse off than before?

Arcand may not have made up his mind on this question. It is possible to argue that there is a life after Daniel's death in two senses.

1. The conclusion to Daniel's script was a message of hope. 'You must each find your own way of salvation. Self-forgetfulness and care for others is a simple, real, and present possibility.' And we do believe in the script's words because – for a brief moment at least – Daniel, Constance, Mireille, René and Martin really did love one another.

2. There is another, too obvious, resurrection. The dead Daniel provided three contributions to the new lives of others. His blood, type O, universal donor, was drawn for subsequent use. At the close of the film we see a heart and a cornea transplant – each from his body – succeeding. Daniel does live on.

Perhaps because the organ-transplant interpretation of the resurrection is so unconvincing, I am inclined to argue that 'Jesus of Montreal' ends in darkness, on Good Friday. Does Daniel live on, as they say at memorial services, in the lives of his friends? Does the moment of euphoria that the five actors experienced after the first performance really continue? It hardly seems so. Raymond, the priest, loses both his already slender self-respect and Constance. After Daniel's death, Constance, René and Martin are offered, by the same satanic lawyer that promised Montreal to Daniel, a memorial theatre in their friend's memory. But nothing that dreadful lawyer proposed should be construed as true resurrection. Mireille has been most profoundly changed by Daniel and the play, and she runs away when she hears the lawyer's plan. The last we see of her she is weeping, without Daniel, without hope for either life or work.

Isn't the hope of resurrection in 'Jesus of Montreal' illusory? Isn't this really a story about how Jesus is inserted into the life of Montreal, with Montreal winning, hands down?

The picture closes with two unforgettable images, neither of them types of resurrection. Mireille, in tears, looks out at the lights of the city that has destroyed her love and her hope. Finally, at the film's end, we move back to the subway station where Daniel had collapsed (what we called his third death). When the film's opening credits began we saw and heard a soprano and a mezzo singing a duet from Pergolesi's *Stabat Mater*, with the church's stained-glass window behind them. Now, at the end, we see the same singers, still singing Pergolesi, but now – banished from the church – singing in the subway station with an open cigar box for coins from the passers-by. Behind them is no longer stained glass but a large subway advertisement for a perfume called 'L'homme sauvage'. Hasn't the victory really gone to all those 'hommes sauvages' that killed Daniel: TV, businessmen who want to see a model's breasts, lawyers, broken priests? Jesus came to Montreal one day toward the end of the twentieth century, vividly, briefly. They killed him, and everyone was either unchanged or worse for his coming.

2. Beyond belief

Christian theology has always been most comfortable with the idea that there are only two intellectual spaces, belief and unbelief. It has always been at its best when it was either explicating the structure of belief or smoothing the way from unbelief to belief. But what does theology do and say if it should be the case that Christianity can no longer be construed as true in the traditional sense? What is to be said and done when Christianity continues to be important long after it has ceased to be true? Is there a third space between or beyond belief and unbelief? Bonhoeffer wanted to know how to speak of Christ in a world increasingly able to do without religion. My question is both similar and different: how does one speak about Jesus in and to a world that does not and need not believe in him?

I suspect I will never securely live in that new space, even if I should find it. I think I am both a believer and an unbeliever, and will always be both. Perhaps I may allow myself here a brief word of self-definition, as a kind of *caveat lector*. I can do this by reference to two unforgettable nineteenth-century passages.

Have you not heard of that madman who lit a lantern in the bright morning hours, ran to the market place, and cried incessantly, 'I seek God! I seek God!' As many of those who do not believe in God were standing around just then, he provoked much laughter. Why, did he get lost? said one. Did he lose his way like a child? said another. Or is he hiding? Is he afraid of us? Has he gone on a voyage? or emigrated? Thus they yelled and laughed. The madman jumped into their midst and pierced them with his glances.

'Whither is God?' he cried. 'I shall tell you. *We have killed him* – you and I. All of us are his murderers . . . How shall we, the murderers of all murderers, comfort ourselves? What was holiest and most powerful of all that the world has yet owned has bled to death under our knives. Who will wipe this blood off us? What water is there for us to clean ourselves? What festivals of atonement, what sacred games shall we have to invent? Is not the greatness of this deed too great for us? Must not we ourselves become gods simply to seem worthy of it? There has never been a greater deed; and whoever will be born after us – for the sake of this deed he will be part of a higher history than all history hitherto.'

Here the madman fell silent and looked again at his listeners; and they too were silent and stared at him in astonishment. At last he threw his lantern on the ground, and it broke and went out. 'I come too early,' he said then; 'my time has not come yet. This tremendous event is still on its way, still wandering – it has not yet reached the ears of man.'

Friedrich Nietzsche,
The Gay Science, no. 125 (1882)

'There's glory for you!'

'I don't know what you mean by "glory",' Alice said.

Humpty Dumpty smiled contemptuously. 'Of course you don't – till I tell you. I meant "there's a nice knock-down argument for you!" '

'But "glory" doesn't mean "a nice knock-down argument",' Alice objected.

'When *I* use a word,' Humpty Dumpty said, in rather a scornful tone, 'it means just what I choose it to mean – neither more nor less.'

'The question is,' said Alice, 'whether you can make words mean so many different things.'

'The question is,' said Humpty Dumpty, 'which is to be master – that's all.'

Lewis Carroll,
Through the Looking-Glass, ch. VI (1896)

Nietzsche's madman parable raises, directly and indirectly, most of the significant issues in the culture of the death of God which has been my resting-place for a good many years. The drama opens on a madman carrying a lamp in the morning. Already we are up to our necks in myth. The madman with secret wisdom suggests all those Synoptic demoniacs who see, when no one else can, that Jesus is the Son of God. The seeker with a lamp is a new Diogenes, looking here not for an honest man but an honest God. The lamp at midday further hints at darkness at noon, and that cross where Christians have traditionally found the most painful presence and absence of God.

The madman is a God-seeker, profoundly religious. There are unbelievers here, but he is not one of them. The villagers in the market place, hearing the madman's cries, are serenely comfortable in their unbelief, and find it amusing that anyone should be engaged in so outmoded a sport as God-seeking.

The madman confronts their secular security. We have all killed God, he cries; not just me in my seeking and you in your unbelief, but all of us together. Nietzsche is not proposing that God be killed; he is finding him dead in the hearts of his contemporaries.

Now there are two quite different responses that the nineteenth century makes to the great event of the death of God. One is horror, another is a sense of liberation. Ivan Karamazov speaks of the horror: 'if there is a God, then everything is permitted.' God is the foundation of our morality, and when he goes, the grounds for morality also go, and we are enveloped in chaos.

But if God makes us good in the nineteenth century, he also makes us evil. Nietzsche's Zarathustra declares: 'if there were a God, how could I stand not to be him?' God existing tempts those who believe in him to be like him, jealous, opposed to all who differ or dissent.

In other places, Nietzsche can speak of the cheerfulness and sense of liberation that the death of God can bring, but in this parable the experience is deeply serious, bringing terror and fear. The killers have wiped away the horizon, the boundary between heaven and earth. The universe itself is in disarray, with the earth moving erratically away from the sun into the cold darkness of empty space. The silence of the infinite spaces terrifies Nietzsche as profoundly as it had Pascal before him.

Furthermore, Nietzsche, trained in the Christian culture of Europe, raises some theological questions about the experience of the death of God. Without God, who will forgive our sins? Where is the atonement for the sin of murder? What sacred games, what sacraments, will give us a replacement for the forgiving grace that is lost? Suddenly, the madman's tone makes a strange and subtle shift. The killing, at first tragic, now becomes something else. He speaks of 'the greatness of the deed', having to become gods in order to seem worthy of it, moving as a result of that death to a 'higher history'.

Nietzsche does not answer explicitly all these questions posed by his parable. The remaining years of his rational life were devoted to that answer, and it is a simple one. In the time of the death of God, we are still sinners in need. The death of God has not led to the birth of human virtue. There must be forgiveness and atonement, and we are to do it ourselves. We must forgive one another, bear one another's suffering, grief, and pain, and find or create (to use language that Feuerbach and Marx had earlier used) in the human family what before we had found in the Holy Family.

Secular complacency cannot comprehend the religious passion of the madman, who concludes that he has not yet found his audience. He destroys his lantern and gives up his search. He has found neither God nor the understanding of his peers.

Of course we need the madman parable to understand the experience of the death of God, yesterday and today. But we also need that other sacred text from the last century, Alice's incomparable discussion with Humpty-Dumpty on the nature of language. Humpty defines 'glory' as 'a nice knock-down argument' and Alice complains that he cannot do that. Humpty insists that he can do with words whatever he wishes. It is a question of power.

The issue is one of the morality of language, the limits that can be imposed on the project of redefinition. Unless Christian theology is content to capitulate to the always powerful temptation to fall back to some past holiness of institution, book, or epoch, it must engage in the project of reinterpretation. The theological Humptys feel free, in the name of whatever virtue, of relevance, liberation, to turn the word *God* into a statement about hope or future or the power of love at the heart of reality. The Alices declare that you cannot make a word mean whatever you choose. You must respect the past of the word, the ways it has been used. If you cannot believe what the word has once meant, you may not make up new meanings for it; you must do without it or invent altogether new words that do not claim to be interpretations of the old. I have always been with Alice, proud of my humility before language, warning the revisionists and reinterpreters (like the feminist theologians?) of the danger lurking in their Humpty-like imperialism.

Radical theology, which is the world I happily inhabit, was (and is) 'an attempt conservative and an attempt religious', to use a phrase of Matthew Arnold, describing his own work of religious construction. It is both conservative and religious because it seeks to define the conditions under which Christianity might still be intellectually and morally possible. It was my undergraduate students in the late 1960s who reminded me how conservative I really was. They thought it amusing that someone would still be interested in defending a single religion, like Christianity. What they really asked of the professor of religion was not instruction on how one religion might be true, but how all of them might be useful. To both old atheists and new polytheists, radical theology will always seem odd and messy.

Is there something that is neither atheism nor faith, something between belief and unbelief? Atheism and unbelief are grounded in the absence of an experience of God; the theology of the death of God is grounded on an experience of an absence. For radical theology there is a hole where God used to be, and it is the work of that theology to explore that hole – within a Christian allegiance or, failing that, without it.

Death of God is, of course, a metaphor. It bears a close relation to other metaphors that have traditionally dealt with the coming and going of God. There is the eclipse of God; there is silence, disappearance, absence. In each of these usages, the negative experience is expected to come to an end. Eclipses are finished; from silence comes speech, from disappearance comes manifestation, absence becomes presence. Death of God is like all these metaphors, so beloved by the mystical tradition. It is just that, with death, the pendulum between having and not having swings much more slowly, in much wider arcs. It is not that language about the Christian God is deemed perpetually impossible. Resurrections can always follow deaths, at least in the realm of language. But the expectation of a return is faint, and not particularly longed for or desired.

What is there, we might ask, about the twentieth century that has made so plausible and so inevitable the rediscovery of this nineteenth-century metaphor of God's death? There are three points that have been significant for me.

1. Christianity, along with Judaism and Islam, was shaped in an agricultural climate, so that dependence on nature often was the natural basis of the religious impulse. Industrialization, and most especially modern technologies, have completely altered our relationship to nature. We have moved from dependence to control, and something has happened to our imagination and thus to our religion. Some years ago, one of my children needed to identify some constellations for a science assignment. One winter night we walked out into the back yard and managed to find what we were looking for. It was beautiful and clear, and we stood together for a moment, looking up. What would this eleven-year-old say? Would he be as moved by the starry skies above as his father? Instead, I heard him say: 'Which ones did we put up, Dad?' The

early years of the space programme had worked on his imagination more powerfully than on mine, and the 'heavens' were simply not the same for him as they were for me. There may still have been a real 'up', but it was not an 'up' of mystery and wonder, but an 'up' of destination and journey. Death of God is something that happens, perhaps quite gradually, as we begin fully to experience that impact of our technologies on our minds and imaginations.

2. The unique quality of the radical evil experienced by the twentieth century has fatally crippled much of the traditional religious language about the providence, sovereignty, Lordship of God. Providence in Christian, Jewish or Muslim forms requires the assurance that every moment on the horizontal continuum that comes to us comes not only from a prior set of historical causes but also from the hand of God. The Nazis' death camps have broken much of the religious language of the Western mono-theisms. The death camps have forced many to decide between two options: God is not behind such radical evil, therefore he cannot be what we have traditionally meant by God; or, God is behind everything, including the death camps, and therefore he is a killer. It is very hard to excise the language of Providence from the Christian understanding of God and to have anything recognizably Christian left. The journey from the death camps to the death of God is one many have taken, sometimes in sorrow, sometimes in relief.

3. More recently, a third piece of twentieth-century experience has emerged that has fed into the experience of the absence of God. I am speaking of the actual behaviour of religious people, the growing sense that religion, at least in its monotheistic forms, makes men and women evil more often than good. It is hardly necessary to go through the shameful list of monotheists killing monotheists today, Christians, Jews, Muslims. There is a kind of logic to monotheism that seems, in our day, to exacerbate the evil imagination. If I believe in one God, I believe in one truth, and I believe I possess that one truth. Saying 'yes' to God not only distinguishes me from those who say 'no' but involves my negating those nay-sayers. Those I negate I deny; I deny their right to deny my 'yes', and finally I deny their right to be. We are discovering afresh the wisdom of the Psalmist:

Do I not hate them that hate thee, O Lord
And do I not loathe them that rise up against thee?
I hate them with perfect hatred;
I count them my enemies

(Psalm 139.21–22).

To possess God is to possess the most powerful possible instrument of self-approval our times have devised, and the mirror of self-approval turns readily into a sword of judgment. The God of the Christian West is apparently transforming his advocates into dangerous and self-righteous sinners.

Some eloquent evidence for this twentieth-century perception comes from one of the greatest works of nineteenth-century America. Huck Finn is deeply uncertain if he should tell Miss Watson where her runaway slave Jim is located. His uncertainty is magically overcome when he realizes that the 'plain hand of Providence' requires that he turn Jim in. Everything he has learned in Sunday School points in that direction. He writes the letter of betrayal to Miss Watson, feels all clean and pure, and is able to pray. But then he thinks some more, thinks of his love of Jim and the laughter they have had together. He finally tears up the letter, says no to Providence, and declares, in one of the greatest sentences in American literature, 'All right, then, I'll go to hell.'

Christianity's most ruthless critics for the next decade will not be other ideologies or other religions, but those pointing to the dangers of sexism and antisemitism within its own borders. How will mainstream Christianity withstand the feminist critics? Is the gender of God negotiable? Is there a hospital, perhaps in Sweden, to which he may be sent? Is it enough to ordain the women, fix up the pronouns, get rid of all father- and brother-language? Or will the feminist sword prove to be a mortal one, suggesting that a degendered God may well have to give way to an absent one?

Antisemitism seems to be as adherent to Christian Scripture and tradition as sexism. How was it that the proper Jewish self-criticism of an Amos, an Isaiah, a Jesus, became the tortured Jewish self-hatred of a Paul? And what are we to make of the troubling questions raised by the Synoptics? Mark needs to assure imperial Rome in the middle of the first century, beginning to persecute, that the original Christian movement was of no political significance. It was not Rome that crucified, but the Jews. Thus, the bitter price of a sanitized non-political Jesus is a Jesus with no Jewish connections, a family and a set of disciples who misunderstand and reject; and a caricatured portrait of Phariseeism that has borne bitter fruit for nearly two millennia.

A significant methodological point must be raised by our reflection on these two themes. Charles Davis has put it well: 'the critique of Christian ideology exemplified in the critique of anti-Semitism and anti-feminism of the Bible . . . makes it impossible to use the historical criticism of the Bible theologically to establish norms of Christian belief and practice'.[5]

Once we allow – and we must surely do so – culture itself to criticize Scripture, we have given up a large part of our familiar theological territory. Scripture can no longer be said to possess a single, plain meaning. Not even Luther's topological simplification is sufficient. There is no return to security in Scripture. It is not, nor does it contain, the word of God. The Bible indeed; but neither Word nor God.

This is the autobiographical setting for this christological exploration. If Christianity has become intellectually and morally suspect – even to its advocates and friends – and belief in God either unnecessary or dangerous, how can Jesus of Nazareth – neither Lord nor Son – be re-inserted into our language and culture?

'Post-historical' and the christological consensus

It is time to turn to the adjective in my title. I really dislike almost all of the 'post'-words, and if it weren't for the fact that 'post-historical' gives me an excuse to use a nice post-Schweitzerian title for this book, I wouldn't bother with it.

I had better say what I don't mean by post-historical. I do not mean post-modernist. I'm too old to be a post-modernist, I suspect. Besides, modernism rescued me, as a teenager, from suburban boredom. The student movements in the late 1960s, which I deeply admired, were 'modernism in the streets', as Lionel Trilling remarked, and we can never – anywhere, Orient or Occident – have too many students in the street. (It is impossible to imagine a post-modernist student in the street.) Post-modernism didn't care

for some of modernism's provincialisms – its phallo- and Euro-
and logo-centrisms – but it has come up with its own set of near
fundamentalist certainties as silly as the older ones it rightly wants
to criticize. Post-modernism, in the United States at any rate, is
precisely the cultural response mandated by Reaganism and Thatcherism. In its view, there is no real world of politics or culture;
nothing but surfaces and texts and sound-bites. No quests for
certainty. Just irony, play, surface. Todd Gitlin's description is as
good as any.

> Post modernism is indifferent to consistency and continuity alto-
> gether. It self-consciously splices genres, attitudes, styles. It rel-
> ishes the blurring or juxtaposition of forms (fiction-non-fiction),
> stances (straight-ironic), moods (violent-comic), cultural levels
> (high-low). It disdains originality and fancies copies, repetition,
> the recombination of hand-me-down scraps. It neither embraces
> nor criticizes, but beholds the world blankly, with a knowingness
> that dissolves feeling and commitment into irony. It pulls the rug
> out from under itself, displaying an acute self-consciousness
> about the work's constructed nature. It takes pleasure in the play
> of surfaces and derides the search for depth as mere nostalgia
> for an unmoved mover.[6]

No unmoved mover, no gods, no prophetic longing for righteousness, no Jesus restlessly healing and teaching and running risks.
The passionless arrogance of the post-modernist style makes 'post-
modernist religion' oxymoronic. The post-modernists don't care
much for 'purpose' or 'meaning' or searches for them. That is why
they give us such large chunks of Nietzsche.

Behind my interest in a post-historical Jesus lies an allegiance to
a particular christological consensus, a belief about what can and
cannot be known about Jesus of Nazareth. It is *a* consensus, not
everyone's, but it shapes my understanding of the meaning of Jesus.
This consensus that I am both reporting and affirming is informed,
above all, by the conclusion to Albert Schweitzer's *The Quest of
the Historical Jesus* (1906, ET 1910), and also by the eloquent
Schweitzerian sentence of E. P. Sanders: 'The Gospels . . . were not
written to answer our questions . . .'[7]

This is what I think Schweitzer was saying at the close of his book (Chapter XX). The Jesus of history that the nineteenth century thought it had discovered was an illusion, a product not of objective scholarship, but of need.

> The Jesus of Nazareth who came forward publicly as the Messiah, who preached the ethic of the Kingdom of God, who founded the Kingdom of Heaven upon earth, and died to give His work its final consecration, never had any existence. He is a figure designed by rationalism, endowed with life by liberalism, and clothed by modern theology in an historical garb.[8]

But, Schweitzer insisted, our historical methods are not powerless. They have just been tendentiously employed. The Jesus of history *is* accessible to our research, and what we find is an enigma, a stranger, one who did not come to solve *our* problems. Historical investigation released Jesus from dogma, hoping he would thereby glide comfortably from the first to the twentieth century. He was released; he did visit us; and he returned at once to the apocalyptic-eschatological world of his own time. The historical movement that established his remoteness was a courageous one. But its strategies cannot solve the problem of the stranger that it defined. Eschatology cannot be separated from history, husk from kernel. Separated from eschatology, Jesus is a cipher. First-century eschatological world-denial simply cannot be blended with the world affirmation of our time.

Schweitzer's solution to his dilemma is a bold one. Even though Jesus is bound to the enigmatic first century, something can reach us from him. He puts that something in various ways, none of them historical, theological, or hermeneutic. Jesus can be for us 'a mighty spiritual force', 'spiritually arisen within men'. His very remoteness and irrelevance (determined by the eschatology) is still able to shape our lives. That irrelevant eschatology describes an authoritative ruler, one who is to be obeyed. It is possible for us to be ruled by the irrelevant Jesus our historical methods have discovered. Hence Schweitzer's lapidary conclusion, surely one of the great paragraphs of twentieth-century christological discourse.

> He comes to us as One unknown, without a name, as of old, by the lake-side, He came to those men who knew Him not. He

speaks to us the same word: 'Follow thou me!' and sets us to the tasks which He has to fulfil for our time. He commands. And to those who obey Him, whether they be wise or simple, He will reveal Himself in the toils, the conflicts, the sufferings which they shall pass through in His fellowship, and, as an ineffable mystery, they shall learn in their own experience who He is.[9]

Taking seriously yesterday's warning from Schweitzer (and today's warning from E. P. Sanders), I propose a consensus that will ultimately mandate my search for a post-historical Jesus.

1. Jesus is inaccessible by historical means. All we can know (or need to know) is that he has come. Faith arises elsewhere. This is Bultmann, following Kierkegaard. It is also Tillich, who, in his debate with C. H. Dodd, escaped what Dodd called the 'risk of historicity' by declaring that the only historical fact he needed was the portrait of Jesus presented by Mark. John Kent puts this sceptical position with clarity and conviction.

We can no longer be sure that we are in touch with the original meaning of the central stories of the Gospels. We can only tell the stories; we cannot really judge their effect. In fact, it is not just a question of whether we can 'understand' stories which are receding steadily into a lost world of the past, but whether we can go on believing – as we have to do if this is to be a case of revelation – that the stories are protean enough to communicate to twentieth-century readers lost in a maze which changes all the time, and in ever more terrifying ways.[10]

2. Or, following a two-step rather than one-step road to scepticism: we can know something about Jesus, but what we know is of little use to us in the late twentieth century (thus Schweitzer and Sanders).

3. Or, in an elegant blend of 1 and 2 above.

There is a good deal that we probably do know about Jesus; the trouble is that we can rarely, if ever, be sure precisely what it is.[11]

The post-historical Jesus is what remains after we have determined that some or all of the above three points are on target. If
history gives us a Jesus either invisible or irrelevant, what are we
to do? First of all, we gladly relinquish our anxiety about historicity, and begin to separate judgments of importance from judgments of historicity. This also means giving up trying to find, by
historical means, a Jesus who agrees with us. What else are we to
do? Turn from the elusive Jesus to God? From frying-pan to fire?
Or to unbelief?

We have been saying for years that the Gospels were never
designed to be read as history in the modern sense. But we have
rarely gone on to say what they are, apart from uttering such
magic words as 'gospel' or 'kerygma'. What my christological
consensus permits us to say is that the Gospels are fictions. We
must learn to give up our belief in a privileged position for the
canonical. If the Gospels themselves can be read as fictions, this
not only means a renewed importance for the apocryphal tradition,
it means also that contemporary fictions about Jesus take on new
importance and interest. By 'post-historical Jesus' I mean the Jesus
we can turn to after we have determined that the historical method
(and its cousin, theological interpretation based on that method)
has given us everything it is capable of giving.

In chapters V and VI of this book I will be examining the Jesus-
fictions presented to us by 'fictionists' and poets – those in the
twentieth-century (mostly in English, but not exclusively) – who
have written about Jesus in praise or blame, apart from the theologians and the New Testament historians: novelists, playwrights,
journalists, all kinds of amateurs – and poets proper.

I have tried to keep the literary Christ figures out of my essay,
and I have almost succeeded. I could not resist including Prince
Myshkin in my nineteenth-century chapter, and I have inserted one
modest group of Christ-figures into my fifth chapter: that odd
tradition in modern British drama in which a mysterious stranger
comes into a room and turns things upside down, usually for the
good of all.

My 'poets' usually make no claim to give us a Jesus as he really was.
What do they claim to offer? Are their fictions merely ideologies,

designed to confirm their belief or unbelief, as Schweitzer accused so many of the nineteenth century seekers for the Jesus of history?[12]

I do not wish to obliterate anyone – even theologians and historians – since I do not wish to obliterate myself. They will continue to do what they have to do. There are publishers longing for books, grants to win, tenure to be wrested from diabolical deans. Alongside, not instead of, the historians and the theologians, let the post-historical age begin by attending to the poets who, unlike the others, are persuaded that truth is more likely to be made than found. I am, of course, calling on the support of Richard Rorty in making this judgment.

> ... we should side with the Romantics and do our best to aestheticize society, to keep it safe for the poets in the hope that the poets may eventually make it safe for everybody else. 'Imagination,' in Dewey's words, 'is the chief instrument of the good ... art is more moral than moralities.'[13]

II

Jesus:
'These fragments I have shored against my ruins'[1]

So 'a cried out 'God, God, God!' three or four times. Now I, to comfort him, bid him 'a should not think of God: I hoped there was no need to trouble himself with any such thoughts yet.[2]

I am arguing that christology is not so much at a crossroads as at a dead end. If my formulation of the 'consensus' has anything to be said for it, it gives us a Jesus either unknowable or irrelevant. The historical-modernist era is at an end. Schweitzer, nearly a century ago, got many of the details wrong, but the heart of his argument was right. We have not transcended him.

My own conclusion is a simple one. The theologians and the historians can offer neither a convincing Jesus of history nor Christ of faith. The Gospels are not a mixture and interpretation that our wisdom can distinguish. They are, in fact, fictional or ideological portraits designed to meet need, to stimulate imagination, intelligence and action. It is time to turn from theological earnestness to the poet's play.

Before we turn to the fictionalized Jesuses of the nineteenth and twentieth centuries, I propose making two stops along the way. In my next chapter, I want to look at politics as a way round our theological and historical scepticism. Our need for political wisdom is desperate, and some believe that there is a politically relevant Jesus out there somewhere that will be of help. Several of those quests for a political Jesus in our time will be examined.

In this chapter, before I turn my back utterly on what might be called traditional christological reflection, I want to take note of the work of two contemporary Protestant theologians of great interest.

Both share something of my sense of christological crisis. Both know that there is no 'Jesus as he really was' that can be our ticket of admission into a post-historical Christian world. But both continue to do christology in something like the old sense in the face of their scepticism. If I were to believe in christology, I would follow their leads. They are raising quite traditional questions: is it morally and intellectually possible to 'be' a Christian today? With Christendom gone, can Christianity remain? If we really give up our arrogant claims to uniqueness and genuinely grant that there are other truths as good and as wise as our own, then does 'being a Christian' make any sense? As I read the work of Graham Shaw of London and Jens Glebe-Möller of Copenhagen, they would all answer such questions with a more assured 'yes' than I would. They are both incisive and loving inside critics of Christianity and are not looking, as I am, for some place beyond belief. Both have deeply serious questions about the idea of God. Both believe that somehow Jesus of Nazareth is a necessary and possible way of claiming a Christian identity.

1. Bonhoeffer revisited

Jesus in the time of the death of God. I don't suppose we could even raise such an odd question if Dietrich Bonhoeffer hadn't written a handful of pages from prison between 1943 and 1945. I propose, as an introduction to an examination of contemporary christologies, to revisit those letters and papers from that Berlin prison, and to see what christologies, what kind of Jesus, can be found there.[3]

During the first few months of Bonhoeffer's imprisonment, not surprisingly his writing about Jesus concerns only the suffering. There is no flavour of the triumphalist christology of the *Ethics* (1940–43). Prison had apparently sent him back to the pure *theologia crucis* of Luther, which was reflected twelve years before in the Berlin *Christology* lectures.[4]

If Jesus Christ is to be described as God, this godly essence, omnipotence, and omniscience may not be spoken of but rather the weak man among sinners, the crib and the cross.

Several months before he went to prison, at the beginning of 1943, Bonhoeffer was clearly thinking about how Jesus faced his own suffering. It is hard not to imagine that he is looking ahead to a similar future for himself. This sentence may be excessively Johannine for some tastes, but it is incomparable autobiography.

Christ kept himself from suffering till his hour had come, but when it did come he met it as a free man, seized it, and mastered it.[5]

Everything we know about the last two years of Bonhoeffer's life indicates that this is not only a description of the master, but of the disciple.

Some of Bonhoeffer's prose comments on Jesus and suffering could be a touch abstract: 'Socrates mastered the art of dying; Christ overcame death as "the last enemy" . . .' (240). It is the poetry that gives us the suffering-of-Jesus christology most vividly.

Lord Jesus Christ
You were poor
and in distress, a captive and forsaken as I am.
You know all man's troubles;
You abide with me when all men fail me;
You remember and seek me;
It is your will that I should know you and turn to you.
Lord, I hear your call and follow;
Help me (140).

And, of course, in the unforgettable central stanza of 'Christians and Pagans' we can discern a theological bridge between the auto-biographical Lutheranism of the early prison months and the later letters to Bethge on the sufferings of God.

Men go to God when he is sore bestead,
Find him poor and scorned, without shelter or bread,
Whelmed under weight of the wicked, the weak, the dead;

Christians stand by God in his hour of grieving (348–9).

In the earliest reflections on the need for a non-religious interpretation of Christianity, it is not clear whether Bonhoeffer includes himself as one of those moving toward a time of no religion at all. Sometimes he confesses an uneasiness with God-talk, sometimes he seems more worried about the godless world, out there, beyond him, not including him. We watch him weaving the early suffering-of-Jesus christology into the idea of a non-religious interpretation. 'How can Christ become the Lord of the religionless as well?' (280). When he comes to tie the early *theologia crucis* to the new religionless theme, there is no 'non-religious' Jesus at all; only the dying one on the cross.

> The Christian, unlike the devotees of the redemption myths, has no last line of escape available from earthly tasks and difficulties into the eternal, but like Christ himself ('My God, why hast thou forsaken me?'), he must drink the earthly cup to the dregs, and only in his doing so is the crucified and risen Lord with him, and he crucified and risen with Christ (337).

Here is no secular theology, no religionless christology. Here is a perfectly traditional protest against all false Christian otherworldliness grounded on a solid understanding of the passion of Jesus.

Bonhoeffer is more successful in relating Jesus to the non-religious interpretation when he confronts Jesus' life. One of the things he appears to mean by 'non-religious' (never sharply defined and therefore taken everywhere by the theologies of the 1960s) is simply 'not primarily concerned with the salvation of the soul and redemption from sin'. But Bonhoeffer doesn't 'interpret' the New Testament to get to this non-religious interpretation; he just declares that it has been there all along. It is exegesis, not a new New Testament theology confronting a godless world, that shapes Bonhoeffer's first perception of Jesus, interpreted non-religiously.

> It is true that Jesus cared about people on the fringe of human society, such as harlots and tax-collectors, but never about them alone, for he sought to care about man as such. Never did he question a man's health, vigour, or happiness, regarded in

themselves, or regard them as evil fruits; else why should he heal the sick and restore strength to the weak? Jesus claims for himself and the Kingdom of God the whole of human life in all its manifestations (341–2).

And when, in the important 16 July 1944 letter, he offers his most vivid portrait of the godless world mandating a non-religious interpretation, the godlessness turns out to be only apparent, willed or caused by God himself, and the 'non-religious' Jesus who alone can help us is – the man on the cross. The crucified redeemer is the answer to man's apparent ability to do without a redeemer. This magnificent letter, for all its talk about the godless world, still lives comfortably in the *theologia crucis* of the 1933 Berlin lectures. 'Religionlessness' is not some twentieth-century falling away from orthodoxy; it is what 'the Bible' has been saying all along. There is no real non-religious Jesus yet.

And we cannot be honest unless we recognize that we have to live in the world *etsi deus non daretur*. And this is just what we do recognize – before God! God himself compels us to recognize it. So our coming of age leads us to a true recognition of our situation before God. God would have us know that we must live as men who manage our lives without him. The God who is with us is the God who forsakes us (Mark 15.34). The God who lets us live in the world without the working hypothesis of God is the God before whom we stand continually. Before God and with God we live without God. God lets himself be pushed out of the world on to the cross. He is weak and powerless in the world, and that is precisely the way, the only way, in which he is with us and helps us. Matt. 8.17 makes it quite clear that Christ helps us, not by virtue of his omnipotence, but by virtue of his weakness and suffering.

Here is the decisive difference between Christianity and all religions. Man's religiosity makes him look in his distress to the power of God in the world: God is the *deus ex machina*. The Bible directs man to God's powerlessness and suffering: only the suffering God can help (360–1).

This remains the case in the following letter of 18 July 1944.

Man is summoned to share in God's sufferings at the hands of a godless world.

He must therefore really live in the godless world, without attempting to gloss over or explain its ungodliness in some religious way or other. He must live a 'secular' life, and thereby share in God's sufferings. He *may* live a 'secular' life (as one who has been freed from false religious obligations and inhibitions). To be a Christian does not mean to be religious in a particular way, to make something of oneself (a sinner, a penitent, or a saint) on the basis of some method or other, but to be a man – not a type of man, but the man that Christ creates in us. It is not the religious act that makes the Christian, but participation in the sufferings of God in the secular life (361).

What has caused the 'sufferings of God'? Why, the godless world has done so, just as the godless world was the origin of his own physical and spiritual suffering.[6] The secular life that the Christian must live is merely life in this world. It is not a non-religious life, nor is it a life without God. And it is a worldly life shaped by that most 'religious' of all Christian facts – the cross of Jesus.

When Bonhoeffer writes to Bethge after the failure of the 20 July attempt on Hitler's life, and in full awareness of the jeopardy in which his own life now stands, the traditional 'religious' language is not a reversion, not a contradiction to the demand for a non-religious interpretation. Non-religious interpretation is what the Bible has been recommending all along, and in this godless world non-religious interpretation seems to mean just holding fast to the Bible.

If we are to learn what God promises, and what he fulfils, we must persevere in quiet meditation on the life, sayings, deeds, sufferings, and death of Jesus. It is certain that we may always live close to God and in the light of his presence, and that such living is an entirely new life for us; that nothing is then impossible for us, because all things are possible with God; that no earthly power can touch us without his will, and that danger and distress can only drive us closer to him. It is certain that we can claim nothing for ourselves, and may yet pray for everything; it is certain that our joy is hidden in suffering, and our life in death;

it is certain that in all this we are in a fellowship that sustains us. In Jesus God has said Yes and Amen to it all, and that Yes and Amen is the firm ground on which we stand ... But the truth is that if this earth was good enough for the man Jesus Christ, if such a man as Jesus lived, then, and only then, has life a meaning for us.

If Jesus had not lived, then our life would be meaningless, in spite of all the other people whom we know and honour and love (391).

If Bonhoeffer's legacy were only the letters to Bethge, we would have been guilty of serious misinterpretation of his meaning to claim him as a significant source for the secular and radical Protestant theologies of the 1960s. The dark shadows of the letters – the godless world, living as if there were no God, the non-religious interpretation, participation in God's sufferings – would be only that, shadows. But at the same time as he was smuggling out those July and August letters to Bethge he was also drawing up an outline for a book. It is in this outline that Bonhoeffer goes beyond his inherited theology of the cross, beyond sharing in God's suffering, beyond that irritating habit of applying religious answers to non-religious questions. In this outline, Bonhoeffer comes very close to suggesting that Christians may have to do without God (not just learn to live as if there were no God when we know there really is), and that they will learn to do so because of their understanding of Jesus. Without the book outline, Bonhoeffer would not be a source for the movement I am studying in this chapter – the concentration on Jesus as a way of affirming a Christian allegiance when God has withdrawn.

There are some alluring fragmentary notes just prior to the outline (379–80).

live without God
But how, if Chri[stianity] were not a religion at all?
Worldly, non-religious interpretation of Christian concepts.

(and now, for the first time, we find a genuinely non-religious interpretation of Jesus)

Christianity arises from the enco[unter] with a particular man: Jesus.
(which is the same thing as)
Experience of transcendence. . . .
(and then, most significantly, that passage beloved of all the secular interpreters of the gospel)
Matt. 25.

Here is the decisive part of his outline for chapter two of the book the Nazis made sure we were never able to read.

Who is God? Not in the first place an abstract belief in God, in his omnipotence etc. That is not a genuine experience of God, but a partial extension of the world. Encounter with Jesus Christ. The experience that a transformation of all human life is given in the fact that 'Jesus is there only for others'. His 'being there for others' is the experience of transcendence. It is only this 'being there for others', maintained till death, that is the ground of his omnipotence, omniscience, and omnipresence. Faith is participation in this being of Jesus (incarnation, cross, and resurrection). Our relation to God is not a 'religious' relationship to the highest, most powerful, and best Being imaginable – that is not authentic transcendence – but our relation to God is a new life in 'existence for others', through participation in the being of Jesus. The transcendental is not infinite and unattainable tasks, but the neighbour who is within reach in any given situation. God in human form – not, as in oriental religions, in animal form, monstrous, chaotic, remote, and terrifying, nor in the conceptual forms of the absolute, metaphysical, infinite, etc., nor yet in the Greek divine-human form of 'man in himself', but 'the man for others', and therefore the Crucified, the man who lives out of the transcendent (381–2).

Here, I believe, is something new in the letters and papers. God is no longer the secure Lord in whose hands we are safe. He is either altogether absent, or has collapsed into a vague idea of transcendence. Jesus is the one to whom the Christian repairs when God has fled. And Jesus is both the crucified through whom our own suffering becomes bearable and the man at work in the world, healing, helping, teaching. The 'transcendent' is not the source of our love for neighbour. It *is* that love. God has been replaced by Jesus, his life and his death.

2. *Graham Shaw and the repudiation of God*

Karl Barth used to warn us that anyone who begins with Luther and the *communicatio idiomatum* (where the properties of the bread can be ascribed to the body, and vice versa) must inevitably end up with Ludwig Feuerbach (bread is only bread) and the disappearance of God. This is exactly what Graham Shaw is up to in his most recent book, *God in Our Hands*.[7] It is a brilliant attempt to Christianize Feuerbach: a passionate defence of the attributes – justice, mercy, love – and an equally passionate and almost explicit repudiation of God.

Shaw's repudiation of God is not based on the breakdown of the traditional proofs, or the perception of the human origin of religion, but – of all things – on exegesis. God is repudiated because he is a monster, and Shaw establishes this by a series of striking exegetical studies of those two Old Testament places where he properly believes the classical Christian God is born – Job and the Psalms. His point is quite simple: since the divine omniscience, divine Providence and divine creation cannot be sustained, the God (and this means the Christian God) behind these actions and attributes must likewise be dismissed.

Shaw begins his indictment of God, strangely enough, with a study of prayer. When Christians pray, he claims,

> we believe in the power which we attribute to God, because we hope to appropriate some of it to ourselves; it is that hope which leads us to assert or entertain the belief [in God] in the first place(19).

This is a moralist's indictment of the God to whom traditional Christian prayer is offered: because we are such as greedily seek both power for ourselves and control over others by means of this power, the God to whom such egotism is addressed must be relinquished. The modern atheist critics of religion are correct. We have come to 'the end of the God of power who promised privilege to his people'(20).

No special privilege should be asked for, therefore no God should be addressed. The God of power has been destroyed on the cross, that symbol of man's ruthless and destructive character. Thus, since it 'is from ourselves and each other that we seek deliverance, in prayer . . .'(21), the God of power must be replaced by his attributes, by the human virtues of compassion and peace. We are dangerous enough with our nuclear arsenals; we do not need the killer God to exacerbate our destructive inclinations, the evil imaginations of our political hearts.

This is Graham Shaw's elegant theological vision. The context is the contemporary nuclear crisis; the mentor appears to be Feuerbach, whom Shaw calls 'the most influential of all modern theologians' (38 – or if he *is* not, he should be). And exegesis is the weapon by which the God of power is dethroned. If the 'radical' theology of Glebe-Möller is political, that of Shaw is biblical. In his critical first three chapters, Shaw takes on omniscience, Providence, and creation in turn, and the Psalms provide his primary evidence. (An old friend of mine, who is a distinguished Old Testament scholar, years ago described the Psalms as accounts of man standing before God in unbelief. Not quite what Shaw does, but close. Shaw stands before God in anger, refusing to play servant to the master.)

The psalmists, Shaw writes, manifest an astounding self-righteousness as they look forward to the divine judgment without the slightest doubt of their own virtue. Neighbours are treated with suspicion; vindictiveness and anger are common traits of their language. Psalm 139 is, of course, the centrepiece of his argument.

> The omniscience of God is experienced at first as claustrophobic constraint. The soul is trapped in conditions curiously prophetic of the modern floodlit concentration camp. It is indeed in the total elimination of concealing darkness that the attitude of the psalmist is transformed. In one of those reversals with which the technique of brainwashing has made us so familiar, what he at first feared, he now affirms. The divine omniscience ceases to be a threat and becomes the object of wonder and praise (31).

Shaw's inference from his study of omniscience in Job and the Psalms is quite clear. God is in fact a subtle system of religious domination and control. To break from the tyranny of this God and of the religious leaders obedient to him, we must insist that the idea of God does not refer to anything that exists; it is nothing but a product of the human imagination, and an unhealthy imagination at that. This is the case with the biblical ideas of God, through the theories of the Schoolmen, down to our own time. The function of omniscience theories in any age has always been to facilitate and justify evasions of responsibility for our own actions. The more God is given the glory, the more convincingly we can wash our own hands.

> Harsh discrimination and savage penalties are not something for which the religious person has to accept any responsibility. The Jew refusing to countenance inter-marriage with Gentiles, the Muslim using punishments of amputation, Protestants stigmatizing Roman Catholics, the Roman Catholic demanding a Roman upbringing for the children of mixed marriages, are in the words with which Nazi Germans have made us so familiar, 'only obeying orders' – in their case, the orders not of men, but of God (51).

Believers in divine omniscience decline all responsibility, and attribute all to God. If God exists, avoidance of responsibility is not only permitted, it is required. So God must not exist, so that we may accept full responsibility for the damage we do in his name. We cannot be truly moral until God is dethroned.

Providence stands in the same witness box as omniscience. Biblical religion is, Shaw writes,

> primarily the rehearsal of threats and promises in the name of God, who has governed history in the past, and will do so in the future (54).

The function of affirmations about Providence is, he says, that of demanding submission and a privileged status in return for obedience. When we ask this God for immunity from affliction or personal vindication, we are hardly likely to grow in charity and compassion.

> When we no longer flatter ourselves in our prayer, we are free to discover the self-respect which needs no extraneous power to sustain it (89).

It is in his discussion of creation that Shaw comes to his decisive point about the biblical-Christian doctrine of God. To ascribe power to God is finally to seek power for oneself, often in a mood of extreme self-assertion. God, as creator, not only justifies an excessive self-assertion, not only promises rewards, not only sanctions a rigid system of religious control, but also provides a justification for religious obligation. If the earth in fact belongs to the Creator, then my small portion of it is not really mine, and I am therefore obliged to turn it over to the religious authorities when they ask for part of it.

A final example of Shaw's exegetical style lies in his comments on Psalm 95, in which God permits the singers of the song to exalt him at their neighbours' expense. The psalm begins with an affirmation of how God's power is validated by his power over the creation:

> the farthest places of the earth are in his hands;
> and the folds of the hills are his;
> the sea is his, he made it;
> the dry land fashioned by his hands is his (Ps. 95.3–5).

The human response to this display of power is predictable: it is utter self-abasement:

> Come! let us throw ourselves at his feet in homage,
> let us kneel before the Lord who made us (v. 6).

With such a proper response, we are bound to be rewarded by the divine protection and favour (95.7).

Shaw's conclusion from his studies of Job and the Psalms is clear. The God of the Bible and the Christian tradition was shaped in a cultural context that made it inevitably an ideology of domination and control. The precariously-placed people of God, surrounded by powerful and aggressive neighbours, needed a means (failing political or military strategies) of assuring themselves that the power of God might one day, somehow, be theirs. For the power of God

> is also the privilege of men, or more precisely the advantage of some men over others. Only in denying the existence of such a God and refusing the blandishments of such power can we be certain that our religion is not a form of disguised domination, encouraging human beings to seek privilege and shun solidarity. The God of power can only use the language of love as a rhetoric to silence dissent and conceal aggression. The radical denial of such a God is necessary if the language of love is ever to be credible on the lips of religious people (110).

This is the centre of the argument of this book, and it is both beautifully written and undeniably true.

This is not a rejection of just some forms of the doctrine of God, allowing others to pass. It is a moral repudiation of the Christian idea of God in all its forms. But if it is a moral repudiation, Shaw also claims that it is a Christian one. It is not modernity, or secularism, or Marxism that demands the rejection of all forms of domination and privilege, it is the crucified Jesus; the deliberate and willed vulnerability of the best of men destroyed by his fellows, killed by men in the name of God, killed indeed by the God of power himself. (Shaw does not cite, though he might well have, that lapidary sentence of Hegel: 'The death of Christ is, however, the death of this very death [i.e., the death of God], the negation of negation.')

> It is central to the argument of this book [Shaw writes] that the significance of Jesus is to be found in his confrontation with the religions of power, his repudiation of the means by which they were enforced, and his exposure of the violence and deceit which they harboured . . . Long before the criticism of modern atheists, Jesus in his life and death challenged the religions of power and the God to whom they appealed (169).

Even though Shaw rejects the Christian idea of God, he still finds it possible to use the word, but in what might be called a post-Christian sense. It no longer refers to what historical Christianity has meant by the word. He lives only in the imaginations of those who call upon his name. God is, or has become, his attributes, as Feuerbach argued more than a hundred years ago; in this case the attributes of peace, compassion, suffering love.

It is, I suppose, worth wondering whether Shaw's strategy of re-appropriation can plausibly follow his profound act of repudiation. Are there not some limits to this project of re-translation? Is it only to play it safe with the authorities that the word is maintained? Here I want once again to call in an undoubted authority to express my uneasiness with Shaw's imaginative God, rising from the grave of the Christian one (for the full context of the quotation see p. 10 above):

> 'The question is,' said Alice, 'whether you *can* make words mean so many different things.'
>
> 'The question is,' said Humpty Dumpty, 'which is to be master — that's all.'[8]

I am surprised that Shaw, with his powerful criticism of Christian faith as domination and privilege, should agree with Humpty Dumpty's use of the rhetoric of the God of power: the question is, who is in control? Why should the Christian God, effectively killed, be permitted to return with a brand new character, and an old name? Shaw's values – peace, compassion, sharing in the sufferings of this terrible century – these hardly need his imagined God to be validated. His mentor Feuerbach did not need to keep the old word; Shaw's case would lose nothing if he eliminated his new God, along with the old. All his convincing moral vision needs is the man of the cross, victim of corrupt political and religious power and model for our contemporary way of being in the world.

George McLeod used to say, back in the days when that kind of thing was said, that the chief contribution of Jesus to religion was that he did away with it. Graham Shaw takes one small step beyond that old world of the Barth-Bonhoeffer attacks on religion. The chief contribution of the life and death of Jesus is that they permit us to do without God, who has become too dangerous to be let out of doors.

We need to look more carefully at how Shaw expects Jesus of Nazareth both to replace the dangerous God and to provide warrant for remaining within some sort of Christian circle. There are two answers to this question, two parts of Jesus that Shaw depends on. There is first, as we have seen, the crucified man. This is the Jesus refusing all privilege, displaying his vulnerability, dying without serenity in the belief that his message was dying with him. The crucifixion enjoins Christians to repudiate all confidence in power, speaking as it does of the best of men killed by systems of religious and political power.

> In a world where every man is either a predator or a victim, only the man of God, sustained not by power but by goodness, can take the decision to be a victim (124).

The crucified man replaces the cruel God of privilege and power. He is also an invitation to live in the world in a certain way. Note that Shaw's Jesus is not at all a 'man for others'. He is a religious rebel, and he seems to own neither disciples nor constituency.

> Jesus conspicuously refused to submit. He does not humble himself before the High Priest, his insolent silence before Pilate defies the significance of that jurisdiction. He breaks the Sabbath, he associates with the renegade, he ignores the proscribed [sic] fasts. When he goes to the Temple it is to call in question its management. He is not therefore afraid either to draw attention to himself or to make a fuss. He is no example of self-effacing good manners. Equally he does not demand submission: in a way which has often embarrassed his followers his teaching is remarkably free of commands (132).

The crucified man is not the only Jesus-fragment Shaw finds to shore against the ruins. In his earlier book *The Cost of Authority*[9] he lays more stress on Jesus as forgiveness than on the crucified man victimized by power. Forgiveness is the one strand in the teaching of Jesus that Shaw believes can be rescued for our time. And with Jesus as forgiveness, Shaw sets Jesus in a social context that is missing for his analysis of Jesus' death. This is the Jesus of the Gospels as Shaw finds him.

> Jesus' life and teaching represent the initiative which brought a new freedom and peace into the world, an opportunity which is only available to us through the continuing mediation of other people. We have to be loved into loving, and our freedom is made possible by the trust of others.[10]

The narratives about Jesus are narratives about refusal of privilege, about forgiveness, freedom and reconciliation. Jesus *was* these values, so must be those who would follow him. In this following, the dangers of God can be overcome.

Graham Shaw is perfectly aware that a rigorously historical criticism cannot provide a solid basis for the claim that Jesus in fact embodied any of these values. He is inclined to agree with Protestant fundamentalism, with pre-Vatican II Catholicism, and a host of contemporary literary critics of the Bible, that historical criticism leaves everything in doubt and vitiates all of our christologies.[11] But Shaw is quite willing to do his post-historical reconstruction without needing to depend on the subtle calculus of probabilities that modern historical criticism leaves us with. He has no illusions about having discovered a 'real' or an 'historical' Jesus. I suspect he believes that such a discovery would be either impossible or worthless. The Jesus he attends to is on the surface of the text. It is the Jesus Mark presents to which Shaw calls our attention. God should probably not be talked about very much. Christianity is reeling from its inflated self-esteem. Shaw's Jesus, the Jesus there before us in the texts, is a fit replacement for the power-hungry God and an adequate entry visa into a renewed Christian tradition.

3. *'If God cannot do this, then it is time we got rid of Him'*

> But God – and I felt this even then, so long ago, on that tremendous floor, unwillingly – is white . . . It is not too much to say that whoever wishes to become a truly moral being . . . must

first divorce himself from all the prohibitions, crimes, and hypo-crisies of the Christian church. If the concept of God has any validity or any use, it can only be to make us larger, freer, and more loving. If God cannot do this, then it is time we got rid of Him.[12]

For nearly two hundred years, most Protestant theology has attempted to relate the Christian tradition to whatever was experi-enced as modern. Even Karl Barth, shattered by the apocalyptic experiences of the First World War, spent a long and distinguished career connecting an apocalyptic Europe to an apocalyptic gospel. My teachers after the more recent World War used to say, with splendid methodological insouciance, that the Christian must walk warily on the edge of the world balanced by the Bible in one hand, the daily paper in the other.

Jens Glebe-Möller, Professor of Dogmatics at the University of Copenhagen, accepts this modernist tradition, and in the first of his books to be translated, A Political Dogmatic,[13] he attempts to state what it might mean for the late twentieth century. He initially separates himself from both the existential and the political theologies. He finds Bultmann and Metz much too confident that the traditional theological categories are intact, needing only a modest translation into existential or political modes. If we are to take modernity seriously, many traditional terms of both liberalism and neo-orthodoxy cannot be re-interpreted; they must be set aside. Glebe-Möller sails into rocky and fascinating atheist waters.

He derives his sense of the modern from the social sciences, both the American and the German traditions. For example, he borrows Peter Berger's five-fold definition of modernity (without accepting Berger's own neo-conservative use of his analysis): abstraction, futurity, individuation, liberation and secularization. He takes for granted that the modern individual has an inalienable freedom to decide just how he or she is to live and how society's institutions are to be arranged.

It is in his discussion of Berger's fifth mark of modernity, secular-ization, that Glebe-Möller comes to the heart of his methodological argument. His analysis of the gulf between Christianity and mod-ernity is based on the study of societal types by the German social scientist Rainer Döbert. It is Döbert's contention that all religions are determined by the form of society in which they arose. For example, the religions of what Döbert calls the agrarian societies are Christianity, prophetic Yahwism, Buddhism, Islam and Zoroastrianism. There are common traits in all these agrarian religions: a radical dualism between this world and another world, the secular and the sacred, with the primary myths as myths of redemption from the former to the latter. When there is an idea of God in agrarian religion, it is a monotheistic and transcendent divinity offering himself for all to accept.

It is Glebe-Möller's claim that this combination of dualism and transcendence was valid in a society in which men and women were utterly dependent upon nature and attuned to its rhythms. But with the rise of industrial society in the late seventeenth century, a man's relation to the 'world' decisively changes. There is no longer any world beyond this one, and no longer any transcendent power in absolute control of human life. Glebe-Möller has no objection to the idea of transcendence. It is just that he sees no reason to attach it to the idea of God. It is not, in effect, an interesting theological term.

> To speak of transcendence within the conditions of modernity can only mean that human existence cannot be exhaustively explicated with reference to what can be immediately seen, touched, and manipulated . . . (38).

Modernity is born, in effect, in the transition from agricultural to industrial society. When that form of society dominates our lives, religion is intellectually possible only if it possesses certain features.

1. The person's autonomy is assumed.

2. Individuals are responsible for their choice of symbol systems, and demands for submission to revealed truth are impossible.

3. Because of the collapse of the sacred-secular dualism, religion must become political and this-worldly. In the New Testament, that significant document of an agrarian society, suffering could be tolerated, since in the world to come it will be abolished [true of John 9. 3, but surely not of the Synoptic healings]. When there is

no world to come, the sufferings of this world must be attended to here and now.

4. Without a world to come, there is no need for a God to punish the sinner and reward the righteous. The traditional personal God becomes a metaphor.

5. Finally, modernity will have many religions, each of which may in its own way be true. Claims to both universalism and superiority are ruled out.

Glebe-Möller knows perfectly well that in this pluralistic religious climate there must be degrees of usefulness and truth. To qualify his radical pluralism, he turns to a very interesting theory of language or speech which he calls the 'communicative ethic'. This is a central element in his portrait of modernity, and we should try to state what he means by it before we turn to his treatment of particular doctrines from the modernist perspective.

'Communicative ethic' is not a felicitous phrase in English, but all Glebe-Möller means by it is a particular way people are to speak to each other. Here are some of its marks.

1. In all true discourse, we are to acknowledge each other as having equal rights and an equal likelihood of having some truth. Each respects the other's norms, however strange and different.

2. Our actions must be such that communication can take place without oppression or domination.

3. The function of authentic moral discourse is to press toward the realization of specific goals or ideals; Glebe-Möller's fundamental goals are freedom, truth and justice.

4. In dominance-free speech, we must speak without fear of constraint. Each party has an equal opportunity to speak, and neither can be any danger to the other.

This discussion of what appropriate moral discourse is like defines the modern world in which we all live, a world in which autonomous individuals are free to speak without fear of domination. We can recall here Graham Shaw's rejection of the God of power; that God was properly rejected, we might note, because he failed Glebe-Möller's language test. Glebe-Möller defines precisely the nature of modernity. It is constituted by the unbearable, physically and psychically debilitating fact that we must always choose, always look to the future, always be alone, and not believe in anything (54).

Even with this fate, dominance-free discourse is essential, and our theological language is bound to reflect it. Glebe-Möller says he is not trying anxiously to adjust doctrine to modernity, but merely to insist that we cannot go behind modernity's back. All thought, including theological thought, is culture-bound. When traditional language and doctrines become incredible, Glebe-Möller has no interest in translating them, as do the liberal, existentialist and political theologies. What modernity makes impossible to believe one simply sets aside, without any sense of superiority.

In *A Political Dogmatic* Glebe-Möller deals with several traditional doctrines affected by his analysis of modernity and his theory of communication. I wish to call attention to what he says about God and about christology. He asks, in his chapter 'Thinking About God', whether we can claim any access to Jesus' own faith in God.

Can we in modernity imagine a God who will bring about his kingdom, and to whom we are to relate in an attitude of total obedience? Can we, in fact, contemplate a personified divine power at all? In my view the answer is no. The thought of a personified divine power necessarily involves heteronomy, and this is an idea that goes directly against the modern concept of human autonomy. A political dogmatic in the modern context must therefore be atheistic (102).

Some fragments of the old Yahwist portrait of God can be retained, somewhat selectively chosen and modernized. Glebe-Möller makes use of Norman Gottwald's analysis of the Old Testament God as the guarantor of the covenant, the opponent of political and economic imperialism, the one who would return the benefits of human productivity back to all the people. But this connection between Yahweh and the requirements of equality and justice does not mean that we can believe in the God of either Amos or Jesus. We cannot and must not; we cannot even believe in God as Abba, Father. We are no longer agrarians, and God is neither Father nor personal power. Glebe-Möller's rejection of the God of power is as decisive as, and more thorough than, that of Graham Shaw.

> Abandonment by God is for us not a consequence of having accepted the will of the Father, as it was for Jesus. It is simply ground zero, from which we are to start (104–5).

Glebe-Möller firmly repudiates all the attempts of contemporary revisionist theology to avoid the modern situation of abandonment by God by redefining God into what he calls a sexless neuter: as being, or the power to exist, or – we might add – the fact of love at the heart of reality, or that which calls us forward in hope, or the finite comrade evolving like ourselves, or the principle of liberation, or the nurturing mother. What takes the place of God in all such revisions may be true and important, but God they are not, for none of them can issue a normative claim.

If God is defined as the normative, as what must morally be the case, as that which stands behind and informs the moral passion of the Christian life, then neither the Christian God nor contemporary theology's re-translations will suffice. We must find the normative elsewhere, and Glebe-Möller finds it first in Jesus and then in an idea of human solidarity that reaches both before and after our own deaths; a solidarity especially with those who have gone innocently to their destruction. For modernity, Jesus' God is redefined as a set of moral demands to be affirmed by all who are willing to enter into that community defined by dominance-free communication. God has become translated, or better transformed, into a particular human community made up of equals trusting one another and attempting to bear one another's suffering. The redeemer God, the God of power, has disappeared, leaving redemption from oppression and sin as a human task for the Christian. There is a passage in Hemingway's *For Whom the Bell Tolls* that perfectly illustrates this human task. It is a conversation between Anselmo and Robert Jordan, who is the first to speak.

> 'Yet you have killed.'
> 'Yes. And will again. But if I live later, I will try to live in such a way, doing no harm to anyone, that it will be forgiven.'

'By whom?'

'Who knows? Since we do not have God here anymore, neither His Son nor the Holy Ghost, who forgives? I do not know.'

'You have not God anymore?'

'No. Man. Certainly not. If there were God, never would He have permitted what I have seen with my eyes. Let *them* [i.e., the Fascists] have God.'

'They claim Him.'

'Clearly I miss Him, having been brought up in religion. But now a man must be responsible for himself.'

'Then it is thyself who will forgive thee for killing.'

'I believe so,' Anselmo said.[14]

Death, in general, is not a special problem, but the modern Christian cares passionately about those who die before they need or want to. God, once again (Feuerbach once more), has become his attributes. The neutered God of the revisionists, from neo-orthodoxy down to the political and liberation theologies of our time, must be decisively rejected. If there is any point in talk about transcendence, anything still metaphorical about the abandoning God, it can only be

> a symbol for an existence that is beyond aggression, an existence of mutual and remembering solidarity. It expresses, in other words, the ideal of a life world built upon dominance-free communication (114).

His brief christology chapter is called 'Christology from Below', and what we find there does not come as a surprise. He had, after all, already referred to 'the necessity of an atheistic God-concept' (8) and to the fact that in the modern world God can only be, at most, a metaphor (42). He puts the dilemma of the Christian theologian as atheist very succinctly. What cannot be relinquished is the fact that 'the words and life-praxis of Jesus have had and continue to have decisive significance for human life' (86). Traditionally, of course, this has meant something further: that Jesus was the Christ, the Son of God who became flesh for the salvation of all. All of this christology 'from above', from the hymn of Philippians 2 and the prologue to John's Gospel down to contemporary liberalism, neo-orthodoxy and the liberation and political theologies, is quite appropriate to the agrarian society that was the context of Christianity's beginning. It will not do for ours. God descending from the heights to our lowliness makes some sense in a feudal society with its sharp distinction between higher and lower, but it is worthless in a democracy which has rendered all such hierarchies spurious.

So, Glebe-Möller begins his christology 'from below' with the image of Jesus in the New Testament, knowing full well how profoundly that 'image' has been mixed, from the New Testament on, with theological (and therefore incredible) interpretation. A few things about that image can be held on to. Jesus began his mission proclaiming the nearness of the kingdom of God and inviting his hearers to join in that proclamation in word and action. But a crisis occurred, and the mission changed its character. Instead of calling for discipleship, toward the end of his life, he began to prepare his followers for suffering. So, it is not power but suffering that overcomes sin. Jesus' 'life-praxis' ends with the anguish of the Gethsemane prayer and the sense of abandonment on the cross.

Glebe-Möller puts himself in something of a bind. He states that a theological interpretation of Jesus is false, and yet he also knows the folly of any appeal to an uninterpreted Jesus in the Gospels, while insisting that what cannot be affirmed must not be re-interpreted but abandoned. This is what his resulting christology from below looks like. Jesus is not himself the Son of God (that is, he cannot be so any longer for us), but he is in the process of becoming the Son by virtue of his faith in the Father. The disciples, then and now, are expected to follow that faith, so that 'Jesus' way to divinity involves also his contemporary and subsequent disciples' way to divinity' (90). (Emerson is reported to have responded to an orthodox critic who accused him of denying Jesus' divinity: 'By no means; I deny the divinity of no man!') Glebe-Möller cites a handful of New Testament passages that offer modest support for his low christology: Hebrews 12. 2 on Jesus as 'pioneer and perfecter of our faith'; and those Synoptic passages, rare as they are, on Jesus' own faith. He might also have cited the primitive adoptionist traditions in early Acts and Romans 1. 3–4. Glebe-Möller's christology, opposed to theological interpretation, uneasy with modernizing re-interpretation of traditional doctrines, has these distinctive emphases:

1. To the outsider and the broken, Jesus offers forgiveness, but to those who hold power, he demands that sin be given up.
2. Because the powerful do not readily relinquish their power (which is to say, their sin), only through suffering can the power of sin be broken.
3. The object of Jesus' faith is the Old Testament Yahweh, God of the prophets.
4. At the heart of this christology is a moral demand, an ethic, a way of life: 'to be a Christian also means to live morally' (95).

From this christology, discipleship follows. Jesus' way of being in the world, his moral demand and his participation in suffering, is to be that of his followers. This discipleship contains an emphasis on a set of universal moral principles, required of Christians, but not unique to them.

> . . . a prohibition against killing, a prohibition against maiming, a prohibition against lying, a prohibition against lack of respect for tradition, and a prohibition against causing pain (95).

The specific Christian element in the Christian life, reflecting what Glebe-Möller calls Jesus' own way to divinity, comes from his interpretation of the final weeks of Jesus' life. It is a readiness to take on suffering, one's own and that of others.

It will be observed that the role of God in this christological reconstruction is a touch equivocal. God is not wholly absent, for the Jesus to whom the modern Christian is obedient has his own moral way to divinity and his own confidence in the Father. Yet, it appears that God plays no role in Glebe-Möller's definition of Christian discipleship. It is not an obedience to God, as it was in the New Testament, but a moral and compassionate response to Jesus and his life-praxis. This is indeed a christology without God, even though Glebe-Möller struggles to hold on to some pieces of christology that traditionally have required the power of God to explain them. Here is his revealing confession of Jesus's resurrection.

> Every time the struggle against oppression is continued even
> though the battle, objectively speaking, is hopeless – every time
> one overcomes suffering in solidarity with others who suffer,
> despite all its intolerability – one experiences exactly what the
> disciples experienced after Jesus' resurrection. The theological
> task consists of recognizing the resurrected One in those who
> endure (101).

A touching and convincing affirmation, apart from the word
'exactly', which probably implies a little more than is warranted.
(However, Glebe-Möller informs me that this 'exactly' is a
mistranslation.) We can detect here some Bultmann as politicized
by Dorothee Sölle, and surely a dash of Albert Camus' sense of
solidarity with the victims, against the executioners and wielders
of power.

4. But is it really Jesus?

Graham Shaw and Jens Glebe-Möller embody, without consul-
tation, a new theological perspective for our day, a synthesis – I
have suggested – of the political and radical theologies of the
1960s. Their common vision is certainly worth setting alongside
the other religious ideologies now contending for our souls: the
liberation theologies, so impressive in action, so uninteresting as
theology, so sure of their correctness; or the post-modernists, brilliant, playful, indifferent to politics and ethics.

Both of these authors bear witness to the intellectual and moral
collapse of the classical Christian tradition. Their diagnoses of this
terminal illness vary. Shaw uses both psychological and exegetical
tools to define the biblical God (which he calls the God of power)
as the centre of a system of domination and control. The contemporary nuclear crisis is the context for his move from the old God
of power to the new God of peace (which is not God at all, for
religious language is imaginative not denotative). For Shaw, the
old God of power is destroyed on the cross, and our present faith
is in Jesus, but not Jesus' God.

Glebe-Möller makes use of the social sciences where Shaw uses
exegesis and psychological criticism. His rejection of the Christian

God is based on the fact of its origin in an agrarian society. With the advent of industrial society, that God has become unintelligible. The modernism that he refused to reject is primarily an affirmation of human autonomy and a consequent rejection of any ideology that requires assent to superior authority.

The Danish theologian's marks of our post-theistic consciousness are two: first, a new conception of language or discourse, a refusal of superiority, a language without domination or oppression. Second, a discipleship to Jesus, participation in his and in all human suffering.

Both of these theologians contrast a radical critique of contemporary Christianity with the abiding reality of Jesus of Nazareth. For both of them Jesus, and particularly the crucified Jesus, is the centre of their vision. Jesus, for Graham Shaw, is the crucified man repudiating power, refusing all privilege, killed by corrupt religious systems, forgiving his enemies. This Jesus can still be followed.

For Jens Glebe-Möller, Jesus is also the crucified one, forgiving to the outsider and the broken, judging the complacent and corrupt. Jesus' death on the cross gives comfort to all the oppressed, and Christians are defined as those who take on the suffering of others that the power of oppression and sin might be broken. Taking up the cross is a political act in the 'christology' of Glebe-Möller.

For both of these theologians, it is not the Jesus of the eschatological proclamation, and not the teacher, but the one who suffers, dies, and forgives at the hands of corrupt power that serves to bridge the otherwise unbridgeable gulf between the first century and ours.

III

How to Invent a Political Jesus

'The Gospels ... were not written to answer our questions.'[1] This is not only naughty, it is true, and it renders a great deal of traditional theology – especially christology – problematic. In the previous chapter, I looked at two impressive contemporary attempts to do christology without facing the implications of Sanders' scepticism. For Shaw and Glebe-Möller we do know enough about Jesus to be certain that his suffering, his love and his forgiveness are there, in history, to be followed. (Of course, that suffering, love and forgiveness can be 'followed' even if they are taken as fiction rather than history. But, only Graham Shaw seems tempted by that direction. Glebe-Möller seems to depend on a trustworthy historical core.)

In this chapter, I propose to look at a quite different attempt to do christology without succumbing to historical scepticism. If the old and the new searches for the historical Jesus are doomed, perhaps we can still pull off a successful search for a political Jesus. Perhaps historical scepticism can be exorcised if we can show that Jesus comes alive into our history as validation for our political hopes. Before putting ourselves wholly in the hands of the mad poets, their fictions and their ideologies; before succumbing to the desperate conclusion that every Jesus – from Mark until today – is both fiction and ideological construction, let us give ear to those who claim that a political Jesus can be both found and used. For this search there appear to be some initial requirements.

1. You should possess more confidence in the historical reliability of the New Testament text than you have any right to. Or, at least, you should have a theory that permits a ready distinction between interpretation and fact. This confidence that we really do know

what we know about Jesus will be found in nearly all of our christological politicizers.

2. You will probably be a man or woman of the left, looking for confirmation. The right seldom turns to Jesus for its politics, only to God and to original sin.

3. It will help if you have more than a touch of archaism – a belief that early in Christianity's development things began to go wrong, but that it is still possible to press behind all that distortion to something authentic and pure. Before Nicaea and Chalcedon Hellenized everything, or before the reactionary evangelists took over, or before all that inevitable myth obscured reality.

4. You must either ignore eschatology and find something non-eschatological in Jesus' message that you can use, or interpret Jesus' eschatological message as having radical political implications sufficient to frighten conservative Quisling Sadducees, threatened Pharisees and Roman politicians in love with domestic tranquillity. You must, or course, know what Jesus' eschatology really meant (see point 1 above).

5. Your views on the causes of Jesus' death will probably be determined by ideological, not historical methods. If you fancy a Jesus tilting towards Zealotism and thus truly guilty of sedition, you will blame the Romans for the crucifixion and find Jesus rightly accused. If you are suffering under an oppressive religious system of your own, you will need to find Jesus opposed by the Pharisees and priests and put to death mainly by them.

My distinguished seekers for a political Jesus all come from the same spiritual world – from that now outdated world of the Christian-Marxist dialogue. There is first the Uruguayan Juan Luis Segundo who emphasizes the parables as the focus of Jesus' attack on religion, and the Brazilian Leonardo Boff who finds the corruption of religion not in the teaching but in the death of Jesus at the hands of his own religious tradition. Milan Machoveč in his notable *A Marxist Looks at Jesus* offers an unbeliever's defence of Jesus, his message and – above all – his eschatology, directed towards his conventionally atheist Marxist colleagues. Finally, almost seriously, I will call attention to how a devout atheist – Pier Pasolini – can present a radically politicized Jesus in a film – *The*

Gospel According to St Matthew – without adding a single word
to the Matthaean text.

1. Two liberation christologies

The most impressive interpretation of Jesus that has emerged from
liberation theology is that of the Uruguayan Juan Luis Segundo in
his five-volume study *Jesus of Nazareth Yesterday and Today*. I
wish to examine the key second volume in this study, entitled *The
Historical Jesus of the Synoptics*.[2] Segundo begins by citing as
a kind of epigraph and introduction a concluding passage from
Leonardo Boff's study of the death of Jesus, *Passion of Christ,
Passion of the World*.[3] It will first be interesting to see how Boff
approaches the problem of the political Jesus before we turn to
the more traditional christology of Segundo.

Passion of Christ, Passion of the World is a very strange, very
powerful essay, or rather, tract. It is a piece of theological anti-
theology; it is self-defence and self-justification in the form of a
meditation on the passion. It is also a slightly poisoned joint of
meat thrown to a pack of mad Italian hounds.

Boff tries to pretend that his unconventional essay is really quite
traditional, and he is half right in this claim. He reminds us,
conventionally, that christologies today can begin either from
below with the humanity, or from above with the divinity. His
Franciscan tradition mandates, he tells us, the first approach. And
there can be no truer approach to Jesus' humanity than through
his suffering and death.

Boff's essay not only has a Franciscan origin, it has a purpose,
and that is action, praxis, discipleship. Boff states his purpose in
two elegant phrases. The essay attempts to be 'a help to those who,
in their pain, seek to confer a meaning on the painful passion of
this world' and it further attempts to 'awaken in us some unsuspec-
ted source of strength for resistance and resurrection' (xiii).

Beyond its origin and its practical purpose, Boff's essay implies
a particular pre-understanding, a certain perception of the world
that informs its every page. This pre-understanding is simply Boff's
experience in the world of oppression and the presence of liberation
movements that seek to alter and overcome that oppression. Boff

puts in end-of-century Latin American terms what Albert Camus said forty years before in a European context: that the world is divided between victims and executioners and one must stand with the first against the second.[4]

Boff means, of course, that the poor and powerless are at the mercy of the rich and powerful, and that the Christian must be with them in their struggle. But throughout this powerful essay there is a sub-text that suggests that the distinction between oppressors and oppressed is in part an ecclesiastical one and that Boff's own religious tradition, so assiduous in its attempts to silence him, is one of those oppressive systems that must be brought down. 'No authority,' he writes with an obvious Roman address on the mailing envelope, 'not even an ecclesiastical authority, that asserts itself independently of the community of the faithful, can lay claim to a share in Jesus' authority' (18). We are not surprised, therefore, to find Boff's exegetical scepticism deserting him when he comes to the cause of Jesus' death.

The Jews, corrupt religion alone, are the cause. Boff's quite valid need to assert himself against the idiots seeking to silence him leads him to far more historical certainty about the cause of the crucifixion than is warranted by the fragile and tendentious evidence.[5] A slight shadow of antisemitism thus falls across Boff's reading of the Passion story that is perhaps understandable, perhaps inadvertent, and deeply unfortunate.

Christology as encouragement of radical discipleship set in a context of the struggle against oppression: one would assume that Boff would turn to the 'political' Jesus of the Gospels to serve his needs. But this is just what we do not find. The way Boff faces the absence of a political message in the Gospels is the most fascinating thing about this fascinating book.

The central argument of Boff's christological essay, what I have called a passionate piece of theological anti-theology, can be set forth in three statements.

1. The Gospel records are so wrapped up in theological and interpretative garments that no Jesus as he really was, no historical Jesus, and – above all – no political Jesus, can be found there. This is Boff's note of Bultmannian pessimism.

2. Yet something very close to the contrary is also true. We do

know a great deal about the nature of Jesus' attack on religion, the implications of his proclamation of the kingdom and the narrative of the arrest, trial and death. Here is Boff's note of post-Bultmannian optimism.

3. There is no political Jesus in the New Testament. Yet what we do know, if not political in a straightforward sense, at least makes politics possible. Our own radical discipleship must make up for the deficiencies of the New Testament message, so that in effect *we* can become the political Jesus the New Testament denies us.

This is so odd and so interesting a way to the political Jesus that a modest expansion of Boff's three-fold scheme is in order.

1. Boff is, with at least a part of his mind – the academic-reflective part – fully aware that the Gospels do not have what he calls 'a liberative political interest'. Everything there is religious, transcendent, interpretation. There is no historical-political Jesus behind the Christ of faith, even for a man of the left. But the absence of a political interest in the Gospels is the premise, not the conclusion, and if the Christian thinker cannot find in the New Testament what he needs, he must bring it. Boff cannot find a political Jesus, so he must create one.

2. There are two ways to go about this act of creation. First, forget some of your initial exegetical scepticism. Boff does not actually reverse his field and find what he initially denies, but he comes very close to such an extraordinary self-contradiction. There are three elements in the life and work of Jesus that are not obscured by the early church's theological polemics and that can contribute to a portrait of a political Jesus that can be followed today.

(a) There is Jesus the religious revolutionary, victimized by a corrupt religious system, out to overturn it. Here Boff is obliged to accept the whole anti-Pharisee polemic of the Gospel record as a trustworthy guide to Jesus' own point of view. He has no sense of this material as reflective of first-century synagogue — church polemics. Jesus *had* to hate the Pharisees. One ugly sentence from Boff gives the game away: 'The Pharisees had a morbid conception of God' (13). Boff can forget his New Testament studies when it suits his purpose. Apart from the gratuitous antisemitism, which his view of Jesus as religious revolutionary really does not need, he can speak movingly of Jesus as the great secularizer of religion:

> 'Religion was no longer the way in which human beings expressed their openness to God. It had crystallized and stagnated in a world of its own, a world of rites and sacrifices. Jesus takes his place in the prophetical tradition when he says that love, justice, and mercy are more important than official worship (Mark 7. 6–8). The criteria of salvation are not to be sought in the sphere of cultic worship. They are found in the love of one's neighbour'(16).[6]

Boff has something here of Barth against religion, of Bonhoeffer's non-religious interpretation, even of Feuerbach. It is a wisdom we might deeply wish we could find in the New Testament. But for all of our desiring, it is not there.

(b) If we look at Jesus' eschatology correctly, we will find it can be relevant to our political needs. With one wise hand, Boff denies to the Gospels a political perspective, while with the other hand he finds in Jesus' proclamation of the kingdom a splendid left-liberal message. The translation goes like this. The kingdom is at hand; it demands a response. Jesus

> calls into question social, political, and religious interests (13),

and,

> awakens a sleeping hope of total liberation from everything that alienates men and women from their true identity (14).

How eschatology can deliver a biblical politics that exegesis cannot is perfectly shown in the following summary of an important part of Boff's christology.

> What the reign of God is in the concrete is revealed in his own praxis, in his 'pro-existence', his being-for-others, his free and liberated inauguration of a process of liberation that provokes

conflict with the social and personal rigidity of the historical agents of his time (53).[7]

Jesus, made invisible by the indelible 'religious and transcendental' interests of the Gospel writers, suddenly becomes visible (and available to our time and place): a thoughtful, psychologically secure left-liberal, unafraid of death – a role model for us all (males, at least)! Where does this suddenly relevant Jesus, this twentieth-century existentialist hero come from? The Gospels, or Leonardo Boff's (and all of our) needs? This is how Boff both does not find and finds a political Jesus in the Gospels.

(c) Boff can also find the Passion story, that most interpreted, most 'theological', portion of the Gospel record, further evidence for his twentieth-century political Jesus. What he finds in the death confirms what he has already found in Jesus as critic of religion and in the eschatological attacker of all systems (see [a] and [b] above). Politics comes out of the Passion in a series of gentle stages.

– The 'cleansing' of the Temple is about Jesus' own Messianic self-consciousness and was done in expectation of the immediate full arrival of the kingdom.

– The Gethsemane prayer is a creation of the early church (too intense a humanity in the Gethsemane Jesus, even for Boff?) and is part of the apocalyptic tribulation at the beginning of the new age.

– Jesus is condemned by the Sanhedrin for his liberal interpretation of the law: Sabbath, purity, etc. He himself made no political claims, but the Jews discerned in him a threat to their power, and they persuaded a timid Pilate what they knew to be false: that Jesus was guilty of sedition. The crucifixion was a judicial murder engineered almost entirely by the Jews.

This is, of course, far more than we can know about the records of the trial and death of Jesus. And if we do know anything, it is not what Boff is sure that we know. But this is not the point. Boff needs to find the Jews uniquely guilty because of his own unjust suffering at the hands of a later corrupt religious establishment.

3. Finally, there is another way in which Boff creates a political Jesus he cannot find in the Gospels. The Gospels can be liberated from their apolitical piety by what we do with them. In its present form the New Testament is not politically usable, but it can be

politicized. Not by modernizing exegesis (as Boff had already attempted), but by discipleship and obedience. In our obedience to the eschatological preacher of repentance, we can become what he was not. Just as Paul (or the author of Colossians) would add his sufferings to those of Christ, so Boff sees his political obedience as adding something to the eschatological Jesus.

Traditional christology is finally of no help,[8] but the political Jesus can be found in the world of our contemporary action.

In a striking passage at the close of his book, Boff spells out just what he means by discipleship. He defines it in unexpected homiletic-ecclesiastical, even Protestant, terms, as preaching the cross today:

1. We are to commit ourselves to the world of peace and community.

2. Suffering is to be expected as a result of this commitment: 'The martyr rips the mask from the face of the system' (131).

3. Taking up the cross means taking on a solidarity with all the world's suffering. 'There is a pain and a death at the hands of injustice that shreds the heart: the conclusion of the drama is foregone, and there is no escape' (131).

4. There is meaning beyond the sharing of suffering. Jesus has passed through this all, and forgiveness and trust are our ways out of despair. There is therefore a life out of death when we take up Jesus' cross.

Discipleship, preaching the cross, bearing the cross – this is how the Christian today makes visible the political Jesus that the New Testament hides from us.

The remarkable passage on preaching the cross at the close of Boff's book (130–2) is cited by Juan Luis Segundo at the beginning of *The Historical Jesus of the Synoptics* as an epigraph – indeed, he calls this passage a 'gospel'. The similarities and differences between Boff and Seguno will be interesting to observe.

The second volume of Juan Luis Segundo's five-volume christology is called *The Historical Jesus of the Synoptics*, and it is the place where he records his search for a political Jesus. It is a fascinating search: strange, angry, and – I think – unsuccessful. The book itself is a sandwich, but unlike most sandwiches the bread tastes better than the filling. The top slice of bread is Segundo's audience – those politically active atheists he tells us he is more comfortable with than most of his fellow Christians. Given this audience, we will not be surprised to find a non-religious interpretation of Jesus being attempted. The other slice of bread also recalls Bonhoeffer. This is Segundo (like Leonardo Boff) uneasy with theology and commending a radical discipleship willing to give its life to a cause greater than the individual. This suggests the early Bonhoeffer's lapidary sentence: 'When Jesus calls a man he bids him come and die.'

The mid-point between the atheist constituency and the call for discipleship, the sandwich-filler, is the struggle for a political Jesus itself in the New Testament if possible, without it if necessary. This struggle is shaped profoundly by Segundo's political loyalties and by his understandable anger at the bureaucrats of his own Roman Catholic tradition. Segundo tries to get Jesus on his side, and he believes he succeeds.

Traditional christology may be of use in a religious world, he argues. But ours is not such, and so Segundo offers what he calls an anti-christology, a call to action based on Jesus of Nazareth. It is Segundo's assurance that the Gospels do in fact contain a Jesus that can be put to work in twentieth-century politics that finally does him in and vitiates his book, so fascinating at the edges, so unconvincing and slovenly at the centre.

The historical Jesus that Segundo finds in the New Testament is, by definition, a political figure. He is political because he is engaged in one single task – the overturning of the religious establishment of his day. This overturning is the meaning of Jesus' procla-mation of the kingdom; it is the meaning of the parables. This overturning is all that he does. Since Jesus lived and died in the struggle against his own corrupt fellow-religionists, so must the rest of us.

So from the beginning Segundo needs for his own political exist-ence an anti-Pharisaic Jesus and the total responsibility of the Jews for the crucifixion. His sophisticated appreciation of historical criticism deserts him when he deals with Jesus and Judaism. Like Boff, he has no sense that the anti-Pharisee strand in the Gospels is a reflection of later first-century quarrels. He seems quite unaware of the scholarly tradition that for decades has shown that the New Testament portrait of Pharisaic life and thought has nothing to do with the first-century reality. Nor does he acknowledge that as the Gospel tradition evolves, from Mark to John, the guilt of the Jews increases and the guilt of the Romans declines. Now finding what you need to find in the New Testament is something Christians have done throughout most of their history. But it is intellectually and morally wrong to do so; Segundo is hardly alone, he is simply more open and obvious than most.[9]

Jesus must be allowed to live in his own century. Eschatology does not readily translate even into correct twentieth-century politics. The 'religious' and the 'political' are not the same. This is the most severe fault that lies at the heart of Segundo's anti-christology: the ease with which he finds New Testament answers to his own twentieth-century problems. Now the basis for this ease is his confidence – reflecting that post-Bultmannian optimism – that the historical method can deliver a great deal of trustworthy information about the real Jesus. But when we look at what he says we know, we cannot avoid listing Segundo among the most shameless modernizers of Jesus in our day. For example: Jesus was a 'witness to a more humane and liberated human life' (16), a phrase of unimpeachable meaninglessness or cant. As an eschatological prophet, Jesus – like the earlier prophets – both criticized and sought to overturn the religion of his day. His eschatological kingdom, while not explicitly directed against Roman occupation, was so subversive of Jewish religion that it was really a far greater political threat to Roman power than any Zealot could be. This is how he tries to convince us that Jesus' opposition to Judaism defined his political character.

> . . . if there is any datum implicit in all of the Gospels (including John's), it is that Jesus seriously threatened the foundations of the (theocratic) authority which was responsible for the marginalization of the poor in Israel, and which certainly was not the Roman Empire (64).

This political Jesus ('political' because anti-religious – the religious tradition being defined as that which kept the poor in their place!), strangely unthreatening to the Roman power, is pur-

chased at the price of an anti-Judaism, tending towards antisemitism, that cannot be justified on any historical basis at all. Segundo
shares with Boff such an intense, and understandable, desire to
fight his own religious establishment that he must, evidence aside,
have his Jesus against the Jews. This is the reason why liberation
theology has been so unsatisfactory on the matter of Jesus and
Judaism. In the struggle between evidence and need, evidence loses.

It is really very strange to find this hermeneutical naiveté in
Segundo, because his theoretical understanding of the hermeneutical problem of the New Testament is quite accurate. This is how
he sets up the problem.

1. If there is no historical Jesus accessible to us, standing beneath
and behind the several interpreted Christs of the New Testament,
then we are at the mercy of our own needs and desires as we
wander among the various Christs without a principle of selection.
2. But – if there were an historical Jesus behind the several
Christs of faith it would be without theological significance, bound
to the first century, unavailable to us today.

Segundo is properly uncomfortable with the various mediating
solutions to this problem common to the European theological
scene: 'we have a solid historical foundation on which to build'
(Dodd, Bornkamm); or 'both the Jesus of history and the Christ
of faith are needed, each to interpret the other' (Jeremias, Küng,
Pannenberg). He doesn't so much reject as ignore what is probably
the most convincing solution to this problem in the twentieth
century – that of Albert Schweitzer: 'we can know something of
the historical Jesus and what we know makes him irrelevant to
us'. But neither mediation nor tragedy are Segundo's way. He solves
the hermeneutical problem he has so well posed by simple denial.
It doesn't exist. It is really a trick played by all those corrupt
theologians who would beguile us from action and discipleship.
Now Segundo becomes predictably turgid when he proposes his
solution by denial, and I may have got him wrong. But this is what
he says.

I think that the only valid approach to Jesus of Nazareth is that
of the New Testament. It entails a process of successive readings

that start out from the concrete, historical interest he aroused in his own time and place and move on to the human problems of later times and our own present day. Those problems are bound up with *meaning-worlds that are radically akin to his* (by virtue of the values sought, not by virtue of confessional labels) and that are open, by existential logic, to the transcendent data brought by Jesus within his own historical coordinates (39, italics his).

I believe this is what this statement means. If we but look at that first-century teacher, ignore 'confessional labels' (whatever they might be – theologies, creeds, ideas, thinking?), and concentrate on 'values', we will see that the questions Jesus is prepared to answer are the very questions we wish to ask. There is no gulf between then and now after all. That gulf was invented by christology. There is nothing strange about the first-century otherworldly apocalypticism; there is a smooth path back to the past, paved by values and action, freed at last from the theologians. The political Jesus has been there from the beginning – only slightly concealed in the healer, the prophet of eschatological renewal, the critic of religious corruption, the proclaimer of the imminent kingdom of God. All we need to do is what bad preachers have always done: find a relevance even when it is not there, and pretend that our questions are really theirs.

Segundo's Jesus is political not because of secret Zealot sympathies, not because he was in any way guilty of what Roman crucified him for. He was political because he deliberately set out to overturn the religious establishment of his day.

. . . someone who is systematically destroying the *real* authority of the dominant group in a theocracy – even if, or rather precisely because, he is doing that in *religious* terms – becomes a fearful *political* adversary. Framed in the domestic context, the social structure, of Israel, Jesus is much more markedly *political* with his religious message than are the Zealots in their activity (94).[10]

Just as Segundo settles the hermeneutical problem by denying the gulf between the first and the twentieth century, so he defines his political Jesus by denying the difference between the political and the religious. Both mean 'that which refers to everything human'; each can mean the other. So 'everything said and done by Jesus of Nazareth had inherently political dimensions' (104), and 'we must first tear down the hermeneutic assumption that we must choose between the political and religious' (105). At last, a definition of the political: whatever Jesus did and said. The quest for the political Jesus is no quest at all; it is a trick of definition.

Even the Sermon on the Mount is political because it can be translated into political terms. Segundo can move from love to politics in a twinkling of an eye.

> When it comes to the Christian understanding of love, therefore, what valid reason do we have for excluding from consideration the field in which the most crucial decisions affecting love's exercise will be made? Would it not be much more logical to take Jesus' remarks, couched in apparently more interpersonal terms in line with his own era, and translate them into political terms? (83)

This manages to make Jesus political even when he is not.

The heart of Segundo's exegetical defence of his political (i.e. anti-Pharisaic) Jesus lies in the parables. For him, the parables of Jesus are not about a kingdom already inaugurated, or about the kingdom as a gift of grace apart from human action. They are witnesses to the evil of Jewish religion. In the parables Jesus makes

> attacks on the oppressive religious ideology of the Israelite majority and, for that very reason a revelation and defence of the God who has chosen sinners and the poor as the preferred recipients of the kingdom (120).

For the parables to be totally anti-Pharisaic, Segundo has to rely on Luke – the Prodigal Son and, above all, the Pharisee and the Publican. But Luke's anti-Phariseeism is notorious, and most would agree that the parable of the Pharisee and the Publican is a Lucan invention. How much of what has been written about the parables has to be ignored when Segundo writes that the parables are designed to set in motion a historical conflict, 'consciousness raising and dismantling the ideological mechanism of religio-political oppression' (149)!

Consciousness-raising, dismantling religious oppression, Jesus making irreversible a 'process of transformation that sooner or later will need *power* to displace *the powerful*' (182, italics his). Surely here is the desperation of Segundo's anti-christology? It seems as if he finally gives up his attempt to get the New Testament on his side. The relation of Jesus to our political needs is not settled by exegesis or christology; it is settled by a cry of longing: surely this splendid man will not turn us down! Once again, Segundo solves some of the trickiest problems of modern religious thought by a mixture of denial and hope.

At the close of the final volume of his christology,[11] Segundo suggests, with genuine passion, that a serious contemporary christology may finally require us to give our lives to a cause greater than ourselves. When all is said and done, 'giving our lives' *is* Segundo's Jesus; cause greater than self *is* God. Neither Segundo nor Boff can finally trust what their New Testament studies have delivered to them. They both end at the same point: 'the cost of discipleship' in place of a political Jesus that never finally convinces them. They would both agree with Boff's superb remark: 'The martyr rips the mask from the face of the system' (131). For both of them the contemporary man, willing to become a martyr, is all the political Jesus we need.

2. *Milan Machoveč,* A Marxist Looks at Jesus

A Marxist Looks at Jesus,[12] by the Czech philosopher Milan Machoveč, is a product of the European Christian-Marxist dialogues of the 1960s. I don't know how useful these dialogues were to the Marxists (as a result of them, Machoveč lost his teaching position and suffered, until quite recently, something like house arrest), but they were of great importance to both Protestant and Catholic theology, liberation theology being but one of the many spin-offs. This is one of the finest books on Jesus written anywhere in recent years, and on first reading it appears to be simply a securely unbelieving Marxist suggesting to his Marxist-atheist-materialist friends that their vulgar anti-Christian orthodoxy needs revision.

And the book is that, in part. Machoveč has many favourable things to say about Jesus, and Christians are always pleased with that. But there is a dark side to this book, an angry side that Machoveč does not conceal, and Christians will have a harder time enjoying that. This dark, almost despairing note does not come out often, but when it does it is unmistakable.

> Yet one can and must ask whether that message of the Prophet from Nazareth which he once delivered to his first disciples by the lakeside in Galilee and which then underwent a fantastic process of development in the work of philosophers and artists, in the efforts of pious and godless men alike, has not been so fruitless – in view of all the horror and inhumanity found precisely in the part of the world where it has been proclaimed for 2000 years – as to inspire despair (191).

This distinction between prophet from Nazareth and later development is familiar to students of liberal Protestantism: Jesus, usually ethical and non-eschatological, was fine, but Paul or Mark or Nicaea or acute Hellenization took over and spoiled things. Back, then, to Jesus, to the time before the rot set in. Now Machoveč has a version of this older interpretative scheme, but he makes his own use of it. He produces, I am convinced, the most persuasive political Jesus of our time.

Machoveč does not, like some earlier Marxist writers on Christianity, attempt to turn Jesus into a political revolutionary in order to overcome Marxist hostility. He quite correctly sees Jesus as probably choosing a middle way between Zealot activism and the Essene-apocalyptic sectarianism of John the Baptist: neither revolution nor withdrawal. Machoveč refused to create a political Jesus by selective exegesis; he seriously tries to look at the fullness of Jesus' message and to interpret all of it. (It is interesting to note, as an aside, that this Marxist makes no use of the Magnificat, Luke 1. 46–55!)

Machoveč's 'political Jesus', separated from later mythical and theological accretion, emerges from a subtle and convincing strategy of interpretation. We will see that what emerges is not, strictly speaking, a political Jesus at all, but a teacher and prophet whose message ought to be of great interest to anyone seeking to shape a coherent political vision for our time, more a Jesus important for politics than a political Jesus.

Machovec's hermeneutical style cannot be simply characterized. Marxist, existentialist, broadly ethical themes all play a part. If we keep in mind that his root question is not 'In what sense was Jesus of Nazareth a political figure?' but rather 'Why should a modern Marxist take Jesus seriously?', we will see what he is up to.

He reveals his hermeneutical strategy when he deals with Jesus' eschatology. Like Karl Barth, and practically no one else in the twentieth century, he is fascinated by the relevance of New Testament eschatology, and he is convinced that all Marxists should be the same. Like Harnack, Machovec rejects the church's early theologizing and tries to locate a trustworthy pre-theological truth. Unlike Harnack, Machovec's pre-theological truth is eschatological. Like Schweitzer, Machovec knows that Jesus is dominated by first-century apocalyptic thought, but unlike Schweitzer (who finds this a reason for Jesus' contemporary irrelevance), for Machovec it is just that eschatology that enables him to take Jesus seriously, as a Marxist. Like Bultmann, Machovec detects the mythologizing in the Gospel tradition; unlike Bultmann, Machovec would reject the myth, not interpret it. 'Early socialism,' he writes,

> had the concept of a totally different, incomparably 'other' future. It was thus 'radically eschatological' and much closer in mentality to some of the prophetic figures of the biblical tradition than anyone in the nineteenth century, Marxist or Christian, was prepared to admit (26).

What Machovec likes in the eschatology of the New Testament is the balanced emphasis on both present and future; the sense of urgency, of the radical claim the future kingdom makes upon the present. Precisely this eschatological tension – neither a complacent realized eschatology nor a fanatical other-worldly future kingdom – is the lesson that Jesus' *kerygma* can teach the Marxist, as he – in his own way – tries also to steer between complacency and fanaticism. Jesus announced a kingdom both arrived and arriving; Marxism holds to a socialism achieved yet deeply incomplete. It is the openness to the future, the urgency, the sense of not claiming completion in Jesus' eschatological preaching that Machoveč finds most useful for understanding the political life. It is eschatology that Marx can borrow from Jesus. And when the *parousia* does not arrive, the Marxist can learn from the early Christians as they struggled to deal with the time being. Never has first-century eschatology received such unusual good reviews. In a striking passage, Machoveč defines the lesson Marxists must learn from Jesus. To fault Machoveč as a bridge-builder, it is this passage that must be attacked.

> The imperfect, indeed painful present state of things will soon come to an end, and a wholly new order, a new era, a new Jerusalem will take its place. Here one must note that Jesus makes no fundamental distinction between 'this' world and the 'other' world (and this is true of the Old Testament also) and that therefore it is not stated whether the forthcoming catastrophe is an event of 'this' world or (Jesus himself would not countenance this 'or') the irruption of the 'other' world into the human situation. There are no barriers here between 'natural' and 'supernatural' powers. To construct them after the event means that one has imposed on Jesus the pattern of Greek thought, the categories of monism or dualism. This is precisely what is not true of Jesus. In his idea of the 'coming of the Kingdom of God' there were certainly elements which we today should describe as 'supernatural' or mythological or coming from another world. But because Jesus and his first disciples did not draw a line between this world and the 'other' world, the consequences of his reflections about the Kingdom of God concern this world, with its history, politics, social situations, and the real longings of real men for their earthly future (85).

Machoveč's hermeneutical strategy is not a single coherent theory but a set of presuppositions. In setting them down, we can summarize the argument up to this point.

1. Machoveč sees as the main function of his book the offering by a Marxist to other Marxists of a word of praise for the prophet from Nazareth. He divides the Gospel record sharply in two. On one side is what he generally calls mythology – the interpretative

theologizing of primitive Christianity that begins virtually with the beginning of the Christian movement – perhaps, Machoveč suggests, with Peter himself. Indeed, if Jesus did in fact identify himself with the coming Son of Man, then the unfortunate mythologizing begins with Jesus himself.

Machoveč is aware of the importance of myth, but he argues that early Christianity make the mistake of historicizing its myths, and thus departing from Jesus' own self-understanding as suffering Messiah. He knows how false myths can develop out of credible reality. Jesus proclaims that the kingdom is at hand, that a new humanity is within reach. Myth takes this truth (derived by Jesus from the first-century apocalyptic tradition) and falsifies it into the idea that the new man, the divine Son of Man, is coming, not metaphorically, but in time. Machoveč wants his myths as metaphors only, not as historic facts.

This is why he can both reject myth and affirm what he calls the real meaning of Jesus' eschatological message. Indeed, that 'real meaning' is at the centre of his political portrait of Jesus.

2. Since Machoveč rejects the traditional christological language that defines Jesus' uniqueness – Son of God, Son of Man, Lord, Christ – he turns to a tradition beloved by the older liberal exegetes and preachers – the unique and alluring personality of Jesus. I'm not sure myself just how far this attractive personality approach should be taken, if at all, but I suspect that Machoveč has taken it too far. We really do not know what he says we know: that Jesus had remarkable control over his nervous system (first century biofeedback?), a personal magnetism that drew others immediately to him.

Now he needs this language in order to talk about uniqueness, and the Gospels do suggest that there is something to it, but that 'powerful personality – immediately' strand is almost certainly part of the myth and as such it should be allowed to pass into the cloud of the unknowing along with the rest of the mythicizing.

There are two further principles that make up Machoveč's strategy of interpretation.

3. Machoveč is familiar enough with historical criticism to know that he cannot commend Jesus to his fellow Marxists by identifying

him with the Zealot movement. As a matter of fact, Jesus was in fact probably more genuinely threatening to Pilate than Machoveč allows.

4. He does not commend Jesus to his twentieth century by denying the first century, i.e. eschatology. As we have seen, eschatology is the key to Machoveč's praise.

We must watch how this strategy of interpretation works when applied to certain parts of Jesus' mission and message. Even though we have seen that Machoveč rejects the New Testament's mythical and theological interpretations, he is still interested in finding a plausible psychological truth behind the legends and tales. He is not interested, for example, in the historical problems associated with John the Baptist, but he does talk about the importance, in the life of a gifted young man, of an older mentor who can serve as a guide to self-enlightenment. The voice from heaven, whether it 'happened' or not, is a poetic way of describing a decisive career choice, while the retreat into the wilderness is the moratorium all sensitive young people require. (One can almost discern a copy of Erik Erikson's *Childhood and Society* at Machoveč's elbow as he probes the truth of the early days of Jesus' ministry.)

Machoveč doesn't care for the idea of the Fatherhood of God, particularly in its Johannine form, where he rightly suspects that Jesus' identity with the Father implies a child-like dependency required of the believer. (Which means that Machoveč probably wouldn't care for God's Motherhood either.) Yet he characteristically finds some truth in the idea of the Christian as child, for all his dislike of infantile dependence on authority. Putting forth the child as an example of both how the kingdom is to be presented and also how it is to be welcomed by the true disciple (cf. Mark 9. 37; 10. 14) is, he argues, an important moment in the history of culture, a civilizing moment that led inevitably to the taking seriously of the child as child. Perhaps Machoveč's praise of Jesus on the child is not unrelated to Marx's similar praise.

Machoveč on Jesus' ethics is particularly interesting. He knows (as the liberation theologians do not, or do not care to, know) that the Gospels' anti-Phariseeism is a product of late first-century Jewish-Christian polemics, but he still insists on holding on to the wisdom of Jesus' opposition to what he calls 'Phariseeism'. This turns out to be defined as self-righteous complacency and the destructive cult of dead heroes. So 'Phariseeism' as 'Stalinism' becomes the clue to a unique Marxist approval of this strand in Jesus' teaching.

Nor should Marxists ignore, Machoveč insists, what Jesus meant by discipleship and taking up the cross. Notice how this very carefully written piece of political demythologizing works.

> His own [i.e. the Marxist's] experience of life now teaches him that there are many situations in which he must suffer injustice rather than contribute to it. In this way he stands on the threshold where the deepest mystery of the New Testament appears no longer as mythology [note once again how myth is the enemy that drags Christianity into the darkness!] but as a profound and highly relevant truth. An atheist who takes his life and his work for his beloved movement really, 'deadly', seriously cannot be undermined by any cynicism or by opportunist considerations and can recognize that Jesus' victory was one of the greatest moments in the history of mankind and humanity, as Peter discovered – even though there was no apocalyptic miracle on Calvary, no *deus ex machina*, only a tormented dying on the cross – and that Jesus is still the victor.

He concludes his interpretation of taking up the cross by putting a challenge not to Marxists but to Christians.

> I do not say that the majority of Marxists have put this experience so clearly into words. I can only bear witness that hundreds of thousands of them are on the threshold of this knowledge. It depends partly on Christians whether they go any further (34).

It will come as no surprise that Machoveč has a keen eye for the centrality of *praxis* in the ethic of Jesus. The miracle tradition reminds him (whatever one may make of the question of historicity) that Jesus' message is more than word or idea, it is action in relief of mental and physical suffering. He is well aware of the close identification of faith and action in various parts of the gospel tradition. Disciples are known, even defined, by their fruits (Matt. 7. 16); crying 'Lord, Lord' is not enough, unless the disciple is willing to obey and to act (Luke 6. 46, and, of course, the great [Matthaean] parable of the last judgment, 25. 31–46).

Finally, Machoveč faces that element in Jesus' teaching apparently most opposed to the Marxist tradition in which revolutionary violence is not eschewed: pacifism, non-resistance to evil, love of enemies. He knows that force is inherent in the political enterprise, and he is well aware that if the Sermon on the Mount were literally followed, there would be no politics at all. So instead of seeing Jesus' radicalization of the law as a guide to repentance, in order that man may live by grace; instead of paradoxical discourses on the relevance of an impossible ethical ideal and of course instead of the purchase of purity by a Tolstoyan world-rejection, Jesus' pacifist ethic is a heuristic device. The critique of violence is a reminder that some uses of force can be self-destructive and uncontrollable; that alternatives to violence must always be rigorously pursued in the political world.

Machoveč is aware that there are times when Jesus himself did not forbid the use of force, and insisted always on uncompromising resistance to evil. Here is how he applies the ethic of non-resistance to the revolutionary's world in which resistance is essential. A brave, even if unsuccessful, bridge between the two worlds:

> The principles of pacificism and forgiveness of the enemy cannot, of course, be applied to every possible situation in human life; but in general the task of the man who is gripped by the ideal of a renewed future [note how this formulation encompasses both obedience to Jesus' eschatological ethic and a genuinely Marxist perspective] is that he should always and in all circumstances look for better moral means than the other, including his enemy, is now using . . . Then pacificism appears neither as flight nor as capitulation but as a form of total responsibility for others, including enemies (109).

A final comment on Machoveč's Jesus. Unlike Leonardo Boff, he makes surprisingly little use of the Passion story in his Marxist reading of the Gospels, This was, of course, because Jesus' 'political' significance derived from his eschatological preaching and not from any supposed anti-Roman activism. So Machoveč makes no use of the attack on the Temple. It was not an attempt to take it over or to overthrow the high priest. Indeed, what it was Machovec does not say, and in this reticence he is probably correct. In any case, the 'cleansing' was not the cause of the arrest; the Temple debates were.

So Machovec, rather strangely, wishes to maintain the historicity of the Sanhedrin trial. The religious authorities were afraid of public unrest that might be caused by Jesus' eschatological teaching, and they were uneasy with the messianic claim. So they were right to submit him to the ecclesiastical hearing. Both Roman and Jew bear responsibility for Jesus' death, even though Rome's responsibility is doubtless underplayed in all the Gospels.

The under-use of the Passion story is consistent with Machovec's approach to the problem of the political Jesus. Jesus can be politically significant (to present-day Marxists, for example), not because of his seditious behaviour or teaching, but because of his eschatological message. That message invites us to live in an imperfect world, pressing toward a real future good, invulnerable both to complacency (the kingdom is fully present so there is nothing more to do) and despair (nothing new has happened in Jesus, the future alone redeems). Without Segundo's tendentious identification of the 'religious' and the 'political', Machovec can agree that Jesus' 'religion' is the significant political factor in his teaching. The reason for his death was his 'religious' teaching about himself and the public disorder that that teaching either was creating or was expected to create, giving cause for apprehension to Jewish and Roman authorities alike. Machovec's Jesus – both the message and the death – was political because he was eschatological.

3. 'The Gospel According to St Matthew' – the camera produces a political Jesus

The title of Milan Machovec's book *A Marxist Looks at Jesus* could describe Pier Paolo Pasolini's 1964 film, 'The Gospel According to St Matthew'. Pasolini was a devoted Communist and a devoted ex-Catholic who objected to the use of the 'St' in the title. The film was dedicated to John XXIII.

It is a strange reading of the Gospel, shot in a wild and sandy part of southern Italy. There is no visual charm, no beauty, not even much narrative continuity. It is really a documentary: a series of set pieces, vignettes, filmed pericopes, with even less coherence than the Gospel whose words it uses.

The music is beautiful, and often carelessly selected. The opening moments of the birth scene give us passages from Bach's *Passions*, and as we catch our first glimpse of the child, we hear Odetta singing 'Sometimes I Feel Like a Motherless Child'. That really would be a miracle.

The film as biblical interpretation gets it force from Pasolini's decision to use untrained actors for the leading roles (except for the voice of Jesus, which is clearly professional). This decision does not really make for greater realism in the portrait of Jesus. The young man (a Spanish student visiting Rome) chosen for the role has a sad, expressionless face. It rarely smiles; it can't handle anger against enemies or anguish at Gethsemane. It makes for an iconic, almost puppet Jesus.

Yet Pasolini does manage to move his iconic young non-actor and to move the cameras about him in such a way that the solemn icon becomes a restless revolutionary, an activist moving swiftly across the screen, rarely facing even the disciples, uncomfortable in personal relationships, unable to love, to care, to attend to human suffering and need.

Icon as revolutionary. This is apparently Pasolini's way of merging the two streams that have shaped his reading of the Gospel: Marxism and Catholicism. His Jesus has all the docetism of popular Catholic piety and, at the same time, a driving passion to attack the Jewish establishment at whatever cost to himself.

There isn't much eschatology in Pasolini's Jesus; not even much teaching in parables. No reconciliation; only a longing for and creation of conflict. Most of the teaching takes place in bitter weather – lightning, wind, and rain. The director's central text is clearly Matthew 10.34–39: not peace but a sword, against the family, taking up the cross.

In spite of the look of restless activism, this Jesus is no political revolutionary. Roman occupation is hardly present, and at the trial it is almost impossible to find Pilate. All the enemies are Jewish, and Jesus is an enemy of the Jews. Pasolini's Jesus is murdered by the Jews.

There is one moment of passion from this wooden Jesus. It is not at Gethsemane – that is rather bland. Nor is it on the cross. The real 'passion' takes place in Pasolini's filming of a series of indictments of the Pharisees: 'Woe to you, scribes and Pharisees, hypocrites'. This rhythmic phrase, repeated again and again, builds to a feverish climax until we become utterly convinced that this young intense religious revolutionary has consented – even chosen – to die at the hands of his fellow-Jews. If Marx insisted that the beginning of all criticism is criticism of religion, Pasolini's Jesus is a moody, unattractive Marxist Jesus, criticizing religion.

There is no popular following. The disciples are worthless. Jesus, from the baptism on, is alone. The crowds watching the crucifixion provide some emotional intensity that the portrayal of Jesus lacks. There is no suffering on the cross, no darkness at noon, no tearing of the Temple curtain, no mocking by soldiers or crowds, no centurion's faith. Just Jesus and the evil Jews getting their way. Even the risen Lord, proclaiming the commission to baptize, is sorrowful, isolated from the disciples, passionless.

There is probably not much political Jesus in Matthew's text, or in the traditions lying behind it. But Pasolini, without needing to alter or supplement the biblical language, uses the witchcraft of the camera to show us a revolutionary, even though the enemy is Jewish. He politicizes Jesus for the reason that all the twentieth-century seekers for a political Jesus do it – because he needs to.

The twentieth century's search for a political Jesus, for a Jesus, that is, to validate an already determined political stand, has turned out to be as fruitless as the older (and newer) search for the historical Jesus. We just don't know enough to extract a politics from him, just as we don't know enough to get a self-understanding or a christology. Some of our political christologies have given the Jesus of history a political consciousness and have drawn their present politics from the Jesus so defined. Others, admitting Jesus' apparent indifference to the political realm, have found in his eschatology, or attack on religion, or radical forgiveness, enough to build a present politics upon.

Christians, as always, will require of themselves both a radical discipleship to Jesus (whatever that might mean) and a political self-consciousness. But the two will apparently not stay connected. The politics of Christians will inevitably be secular. This means that just as our theological needs cannot lead us to a Jesus as he really was, no more can our political needs. There is no Jesus as he really was. What we find, wherever we look, is always fiction, and usually ideology.

IV

Four Nineteenth-Century Studies

If the great movement of historical criticism has delivered to us a Jesus either inaccessible or irrelevant; if, as E. P. Sanders has persuasively argued, the one thing we do know for sure is that Jesus did not come to solve our problems – then it follows that theologians, however resourceful, cannot use Jesus to define their Christian existence after God has withdrawn, and it also follows that nothing significant about Jesus can be discovered from those who seek to use Jesus to validate their own politics. If all is fiction and ideology in the face of our historical scepticism, then we ought to look more favourably – in our own post-historical time – upon those who have written about Jesus knowing they were doing fiction. What have the 'poets' said, and why?

My 'poets' will turn out to be practically anyone not doing history or theology: poets proper; novelists best-selling and otherwise, good and bad; imaginative biographers, playwrights, journalists. But before entering our own century, I wish to stop briefly in the nineteenth and look at four very great writers who struggled, in quite different ways, with the problem of Jesus: Fyodor Dostoevsky, Leo Tolstoy, Harriet Beecher Stowe and Emily Dickinson. We may move more comfortably into our own time when we see what these four have tried to do.

First of all, what they did and what they thought they did may not have been the same thing. Dostoevsky, in his portrait of Prince Myshkin, was struggling for his own understanding of Jesus, for a faith, as he put it, that could rescue him from his crucible of doubt. Whether or not he thought he was portraying the actual Jesus of the New Testament, we do not know, though Berdyaev thought he thought he was. But Myshkin was a Jesus answering his deepest needs, not solving an historical puzzle.

Incidentally, Dostoevsky is the only author I am studying whose Jesus is mediated solely through a fictional character. I have deliberately stayed away from the 'Christ-figures' of twentieth-century fiction, mainly because of the making of these there is no end, and never will be. Dostoevsky's poetic christology is so powerful that it is an exception that may be allowed.

Tolstoy's religious conversion was triggered by his discovery of what he took to be the true Jesus of the New Testament (and by the parallel discovery of his own admirable obedience to that Jesus). He was wrong about his historical claim, but that Jesus he invented (not found) so genuinely met his needs and so radically changed his life that his Jesus serves as a perfect example of the fictional-ideological figure that the great poets are capable of offering us.

Harriet Beecher Stowe neatly combines the approaches of the two Russian novelists. She gives us a Jesus as she believes him to have truly been in her life of Jesus (Tolstoy) and she invents a fictional equivalent of that later portrait in her masterpiece (Dostoevsky). Her struggle for a credible Jesus had two parts: it was first an attempt to find a form of Protestantism that was as unlike as possible the rigid Calvinism of her father; it was also an attempt to find a Jesus who could bear the burden of her own passionate opposition to slavery.

Emily Dickinson is a perfect example of what I mean by 'poet'. She has no historical agenda, makes no attempt to discover Jesus as he truly was, offers no Jesus in fictional form. Her poetry, as I read it, is a sustained cry of anger against Jesus and the religion he brought into being. Here is the post-historical poet at work before her time: giving us the Jesus she hated and, towards the end of her life, a Jesus that might be possible not to hate.

We should attend to our authors' fictions and their distinctive ideologies, so that we may have the best possible guides when we come to fashion our own.

1. *Prince Myshkin as Jesus: 'Hints, half-uttered words, silences and riddles'*

> Like Dostoevsky posing as a sort of Jesus, but most truthfully revealing himself all the while as a little horror.[1]

The Idiot was written in 1867–68 in Genoa, Vevey, Milan, and Florence, 'in cold flats, poverty, sickness, personal tragedy, home-sickness, despair and in hope' . . . 'between fits of gambling and fits of epilepsy'.[2] The notebooks give us a little help in making the connection between Myshkin and Jesus. In the early drafts of the novel, the Prince is both evil and good, and only gradually does the character evolve towards a more unambiguous purity and virtue.

At some point in the midst of his writing and rewriting, Dostoev-sky expresses in his letters the desire to portray a really good man, even a perfect man. To his friend Makov:

> I have long been haunted by a certain idea, but I was afraid of making a novel out of it, because the idea is very difficult and I am not ready for it . . . This idea is – *to create a wholly beautiful character.*

He writes a little later to his niece that the

> main idea of the novel is to present a positively beautiful human being . . . There is only one positively beautiful character in the world . . . Christ.

First, a mixture of good and evil; then good, beautiful Christ. Three separate and identical entries in the notebooks encourage an identi-fication of Myshkin with Jesus: 'N.B. Prince Christ' (without punctuation).

There is some irony here. Dostoevsky apparently believed that the morally ambiguous Prince of the early drafts had been tran-scended, as the character of the Prince drew closer to Jesus in action, word and suffering. But the awkward fact is that the Prince does not cease being evil as he becomes more and more like Jesus;

it is just that his evil is inadvertent and unintended, not overt. Dostoevsky's Myshkin is indeed Jesus, but he is also a destroyer.

Dostoevsky's portrait of Prince Myshkin as Jesus can best be traced by attention to three key scenes or moments in the novel. The first is the story the Prince tells about his friendship with Marie (I.6). This is one of the author's most heartfelt pieces of writing, and it provides an insight into Myshkin's view of himself, how he sees himself as a child, at home only with other children: Myshkin as a genuine innocent.

The second key scene is Ippolyt's 'confession' (III.5–7). Ippolyt is a young man deeply troubled by Myshkin's virtue. To him, the Prince is a pious, gentle 'idiot', and he is indeed called this by many of the characters in the story; an idiot out of place and lost in the real world, which is a world of radical evil ruled by the spider God. If the Marie story gives us Myshkin on himself (child), Ippolyt's statement represents much of what others take the Prince to be (idiot).

The final key to my christological meditation on *The Idiot* is not a scene at all, but a description of a print of a painting that hangs in a drawing-room at Rogozhin's. It is the 'Dead Christ' by Hans Holbein the Younger, which Dostoevsky actually saw in 1867 in Basel while he was at work on the novel.[3]

This painting shimmers through the entire novel, casting its tragic shadow over the Prince's impotent and dangerous innocence. If this good man so long ago was so brutally killed, the author seems to suggest, how can it surprise us that innocence ever after will both destroy and be destroyed? The 'Dead Christ' adds a final dimension to the child and the idiot; the Marie story, the Ippolyt confession, and the painting make up the substance of our christological reading of Prince Myshkin.

I

Mrs Yepanchin once called the Prince an idiot and a fool 'who doesn't know the way of the world and has no place in it' (IV.5). Idiot, fool, simpleton – such descriptions come both from others and occasionally even from the Prince himself. 'Yes,' he said, 'I am an idiot, a real idiot,' and when we first meet him returning from Switzerland he acknowledges that he has not been fully cured.

Actually, Dostoevsky is imprecise on the matter of the Prince's diagnosis. At times, the problem appears to be neurological (epilepsy) and at other times – or in addition? – the author clearly has a psychological disorder in mind. 'I have,' Myshkin says,

> no sense of proportion, my words don't express my ideas, and that's degrading to – to my ideas. And that's why I have no right to – besides, I'm so morbidly sensitive – I mean I – I'm sure that in this house no one would want to hurt my feelings and that I'm loved here more than I deserve, but I know (oh, I know very well) that after twenty years of illness there must be some trace of it left, so that people can't help laughing at me – sometimes – isn't that so? (III.2).

In spite of his fairly lucid medical self-understanding, Myshkin sees himself primarily as a child, not as an idiot or an epileptic, and it is this childlikeness that becomes central to Dostoevsky's final vision of the Prince as Russian Jesus. Myshkin tells the story of Marie to the Yepanchin sisters who have asked him if he has ever been in love. No, he says, but I have been happy. He describes his friendship with a group of children in the Swiss village where he was being treated, and how the village schoolmaster was jealous of the children's affection for him. Marie was a twenty-year-old tubercular who did menial work in the village. She was raped and taken away from the village. She later returned, taciturn and covered with sores. Everyone, even the children, rejected her. Everyone but the Prince, who befriended her and finally turned the village children into her friends as well. Marie finally died, and the schoolmaster and the village pastor continued to persecute Myshkin because of his friendship with the children and their devotion to the memory of Marie. His own doctor told Myshkin that he was a 'complete child'. As a result of this experience with Marie, the Prince tells the sisters, he decided thereafter always to be frank and courteous with everyone. How can I truly be the idiot people take me for, he asks, when I know I am intelligent?

In narrating the effect of Marie on his life, Myshkin says that he has become a little child, that – in effect – he has achieved a kind of cure by choosing to be a child. 'Compassion – the whole of Christianity' and 'Meekness is the most powerful force that

exists in the world': two significant entries from the *Idiot* notebooks. Myshkin's becoming Jesus is prepared for by his becoming
a child. 'Whoever receives one such child in my name, receives me'
(Mark 9.37). Child and Jesus are identical, interchangeable. And,
'whoever does not receive the kingdom of God like a child shall
not enter it' (Mark 10.15). Myshkin receives the eschatological
kingdom like a child. Myshkin cannot become Jesus until he first
becomes a child.

But there is something strange about this child on the way to
becoming Jesus. Myshkin recounts the whole touching Marie story
to explain why he has never loved and cannot love. In the Prince
and in the Jesus Dostoevsky is fashioning in the form of the
Prince, there is only compassion, only pity; no love. *Agape*, if you
will, without either *eros* or *philia*. The weakness of Myshkin's
innocence, indeed the key to its destructiveness, may well lie in his
stated inability to love, and in the inherent destructiveness of pity.
Myshkin's childlike *agape* or pity or compassion or inability to
love will finally lead to the destruction of Nastasya, Aglaya, Rogozhin and, of course, himself.

Before we examine how Dostoevsky turns the Prince into Jesus,
something must be said about what might be called the Prince's
own 'religion'. What, if anything, does he believe? There are two
interesting notebook entries on this subject: 'He is a Christian yet
at the same time he does not believe', and 'perhaps I don't understand Christ in the least, or anything else'. Myshkin is asked about
his belief in God, and he does not answer. He speaks to Rogozhin
somewhat incoherently about true religion. He talks about
thoughtful atheists and about buying a worthless cross from a
beggar.

It appears that his own 'religious experience' is distinctly mystical, and related to his epilepsy (II.5). Here is an extraordinary
account of what might be called a secular or natural mysticism,
one that one can easily imagine William James copying into his
notebook.

He was thinking, incidentally, that there was a moment or two
in his epileptic condition almost before the fit itself (if it occurred
during his waking hours) when suddenly amid the sadness, spiritual darkness and depression, his brain seemed to catch fire at

brief moments, and with an extraordinary momentum his vital forces were strained to the utmost all at once. His sensation of being alive and his awareness increased tenfold at those moments which flashed by like lightning. His mind and heart were flooded by a dazzling light. All his agitation, all his doubts and worries, seemed composed in a twinkling, culminating in a great calm, full of serene and harmonious joy and hope, full of understanding and the knowledge of the final cause.

I believe this analysis is an important part of Dostoevsky's portrait of the Prince. No past, no future, only an eternal now. This is characteristic of both the child and the Jesus of the Sermon on the Mount. Myshkin had already spoken of his fascination with the idea of freedom from anxiety about time when he told (I.5) the Yepanchin sisters of an acquaintance who had come within twenty minutes of being executed for a political crime. The prisoner afterwards spoke of the moments before the expected end as giving birth to a desire to 'turn every minute into an age' and 'to count every minute separately and waste none'. But, after the reprieve, he admitted that he forgot that insight. Myshkin confesses to the sisters his conviction that it is indeed possible to live by the prisoner's wisdom, without anxiety, taking no thought for the morrow. Indeed, Myshkin does so live, to his distress and the distress of others.

2

Dostoevsky uses several strategies to persuade the reader to see Myshkin as Jesus. He gives to the Prince certain virtues we associate with the Christian tradition. He always listens with rapt attention to whomever is addressing him; he is incapable of discerning hostility or derision directed against him. Himself having no enemies, he cannot imagine that anyone would see him as one.

The author also ascribes to Myshkin several mildly supernatural traits. He can read character from a face: he infers Nastasya's madness from her picture. Dostoevsky darkly refers to the 'forebodings and the outrageous whispered suggestions of his [i.e. Myshkin's] demon'.

Myshkin can even occasionally mimic the proclamation of Jesus.

But what an unusual eschatological prophet of the kingdom of God he is! After an uncharacteristic (for Myshkin, that is, not for Dostoevsky) attack on Roman Catholicism as a scourge worse than atheism, and after an unlovely interpretation of socialism as Catholicism's child (IV.7), Myshkin strangely predicts the resurrection of a new Russian Jesus who will transform the Russian people into a 'mighty, truthful, wise, and gentle giant'. Just after this prediction, Myshkin loses physical control, weaves erratically about the room, and accidentally breaks a costly vase. He then turns, half out of control, to those in the Yepanchin drawing-room and proclaims to them his own vision of the coming eschatological kingdom.

> You're not offended because I'm telling you to your face that you are absurd, are you? Now I'm no longer afraid for you: you're not angry with a boy like me for saying such things to you, are you? Of course not! Oh, you will be able to forget and forgive those who have offended you and those who have done nothing to offend you. For it is more difficult to forgive those who have done nothing to offend you just because they have *not* offended you and because your complaint is, therefore, without foundation: that's what I expected of men of a high order of intelligence, that's what I was so anxious to tell them as I came here, and I'm afraid did not know how to . . . I am saying this to save you all, so as to prevent our class from vanishing for nothing into utter darkness, without realizing anything, abusing everything and losing everything. Why should we vanish and give up our position to others, when we might remain in the front rank and be the leaders of men? Let us stay in the front rank and be leaders. Let us be servants in order to be leaders.[4]

The most powerful portrait of Myshkin as a flawed Jesus comes at the close of Ippolyt's 'confession' (III.5–6). Suddenly the rambling and incoherent essay that Ippolyt is reading aloud turns into a bitterly angry attack on the gentle Christian world of the Prince. The form of the attack is really an alternate christology to the Prince's inept innocence. The 'Jesus' Ippolyt pits against Myshkin is the 'Dead Christ' of the Holbein painting, a print of which hangs in Rogozhin's drawing-room. This is an utterly dead Jesus, emaciated, rigid, flesh already swollen and beginning to decompose, solidly in the late-mediaeval tradition of meditations on the Passion. Here is Ippolyt's description of the picture.

The picture depicted Christ, who has just been taken from the cross. I believe that painters are usually in the habit of depicting Christ, whether on the cross or taken from the cross, as still retaining a shade of extraordinary beauty on his face; that beauty they strive to preserve even in his moments of greatest agony. In Rogozhin's picture there was no trace of beauty. It was a faithful representation of the dead body of a man who has undergone unbearable torments before the crucifixion, been wounded, tortured, beaten by the guards, beaten by the people, when he carried the cross and fell under its weight, and, at last, has suffered the agony of crucifixion, lasting for six hours (according to my calculation, at least). It is true, it is the face of a man who has only *just* been taken from the cross – that is, still retaining a great deal of warmth and life; rigor mortis had not yet set in, so that there is still a look of suffering on the face of the dead man, as though he were still feeling it (that has been well caught by the artist); on the other hand, the face has not been spared in the least; it is nature itself, and, indeed, any man's corpse would look like that after such suffering . . .

   Looking at that picture, you get the impression of nature as some enormous, implacable, and dumb beast, or, to put it more correctly, much more correctly, though it may seem strange, as some huge engine of the latest design, which has senselessly seized, cut to pieces, and swallowed up – impassively and unfeelingly – a great and priceless Being, a Being worth the whole of nature and all its laws, worth the entire earth, which was perhaps created solely for the coming of that Being! The picture seems to give expression to the idea of a dark, insolent, and senselessly eternal power to which everything is subordinated, and this idea is suggested to you unconsciously.

Dostoevsky uses Ippolyt on Holbein to cast a tragic shadow over Myshkin's inadequate *agape*. Holbein's is a world Myshkin leaves out, that evil world where innocence does not redeem but destroys and is destroyed. In Holbein's world, Ippolyt insists, God is in control and He is evil. A world in which God is a poisonous spider.

> But at times I did imagine that I saw, in a sort of strange and impossible form, that infinite power, that dark, deaf-and-dumb creature. I remember that someone seemed to lead me by the hand, with a lighted candle, and show me some huge and horrible tarantula, assuring me that that was the dark, deaf-and-dumb, and all-powerful creature, and laughing at my indignation.[5]

Anticipating the tormented confession of Ivan Karamazov, Ippolyt contrasts his own religious world, with its utterly dead Jesus, with the religious world of Myshkin, even though later Myshkin seems to accept the truth of the young man's confession.

> Religion! I admit the existence of eternal life, and maybe I always have admitted it. Granted that consciousness, kindled by the will of a higher power, has turned around upon the world and said: 'I am!', and granted that it has suddenly been ordered by this higher power to destroy itself because it is for some reason necessary – no explanation is vouchsafed for it – granted all that, I admit it all, but the old, old question still remains: what has my humility to do with it? Can't I simply be devoured without being expected to praise that which has devoured me? Will somebody up there really be offended because I refuse to wait another fortnight? . . .

Dostoevsky's Jesus is both Ippolyt and Myshkin together. Or, in other words, Ippolyt on Holbein reminds us that there is dreadful evil lurking in the Jesus that Myshkin represents. Without Ippolyt, we could not understand the role of Myshkin in the novel's tragic finale.

3

The dying Ippolyt is not the only character in *The Idiot* who perceives the evil lurking in Myshkin's christological goodness, but he does indeed see it with brutal clarity. Nature, that ironic jade, he says,

> is responsible for the fact that the only being that is recognized on earth as the acme of perfection – it is she who is responsible for the fact that, having shown him to men, she made him say things which have caused so much blood to be shed that if it had been shed all at once, men would have drowned in it for certain! (II.10).

Jesus brought disorder and violence into the world by means of his innocence. Ippolyt turns on Myshkin as the embodiment of that evil.

> I hate you more than anyone and more than anything in the world – you jesuitical, treacly soul, you damned idiot, you philanthropic millionaire, you! I understood and hated you long ago, when I first heard of you; I hated you with all the hatred of my heart (II.10).

Aglaya, while acknowledging that no one is worth Myshkin's little finger (II.2), can still call him a ridiculous man worthy only of derision. What constitutes the Prince's threat to Aglaya? All he can give her, once again, is *agape* – no *eros*, no *philia*. I'd like you to be awfully happy, he cries. But no one can stand such virtue. Real men and women want to be loved, not redeemed.

Dostoevsky has presented in Myshkin not only a Jesus too innocent to perceive his own evil, but a profound attack on the very idea of *agape* or sacrificial love as available to the real world. It is finally Myshkin's beautiful redemptive love for the beautiful and tormented wanton Nastasya that destroys her, Rogozhin, and Myshkin himself.

There is, of course, a biblical element in Myshkin's offer of a redemptive marriage to the mad Nastasya. It is Hosea's symbolic marriage to Gomer, designed both to redeem her and to stand for the possibility of Israel's redemption. It is Jesus' openness in the New Testament to the outcast, the whore, the mad ones at the edge of life. Myshkin's offer to the suffering Nastasya, a woman whose madness he has always discerned, is Luke 7.36–50; it is Mark

14.3–9, and, above all, it is John 7.53–8.11. In the new eschatological age inaugurated by Myshkin the lost woman will be sought out and welcomed, like the lost coin, the lost sheep, the lost son.

Nastasya cannot finally abide such an offer: pity, no real love. She calls the Prince, erroneously but understandably, 'the first human being I've seen', and she is irresistibly driven from the oppressiveness of Myshkin's unselfish pity to the candid evil – matching her own, offering no redemption but only *eros* – of Rogozhin.

In *The Idiot* – Myshkin plus Ippolyt's critique – we have Dostoevsky's truest, most tormented and complex interpretation of Jesus, far richer than that concealed in the character of Alyosha or than the silent listener to the Grand Inquisitor's monologue in his final novel. His Myshkin-Jesus made a profound impression wherever he went, leaving permanent traces. And most of those traces were destructive. In his offer of redemptive love to Nastasya, he drove her straight to the destructive passion of Rogozhin, who ultimately murdered her. His decision to redeem Nastasya by marriage humiliated Aglaya and drove her into the arms of a corrupt Polish count, turning her child-like faith into a decadent and evil romanticism.

We can never forget those haunting words that Dostoevsky wrote on his return from the four years of forced labour in Siberia.

> At times God sends me moments of peace; on these occasions, I love and feel that I am loved; it was in one such moment that I composed for myself a credo in which all is clear and sacred. This credo is very simple. This is it: I believe that there is nothing on earth more beautiful, more profound, more appealing, more virile, or more perfect than Christ; and I say to myself, with jealous love, that greater than he does not and cannot exist. More than this: should anyone prove to me that Christ is beyond the range of truth, and that all this not to be found in him. I would prefer to retain Christ than to retain the truth.[6]

In *The Idiot* the Prince is Jesus inserted into the real world of men and women. This is a Jesus so good, so decent, so destructive in his innocence. This is a Jesus whose very presence embodies a moral demand too burdensome to bear. This is a Jesus whose *agape* is not only irrelevant to the world, but who actually makes the world worse. This is a Jesus destroying the real world, and destroyed by it.

The final scene in the novel is a dreadful Pietà beyond sadness. It evokes sheer terror, undermining every foundation. Nastasya is lying on the bed, murdered by Rogozhin. Rogozhin is feverish, in and out of consciousness, screaming and rambling incoherently. Myshkin, stroking the murderer's brow in a sacrament of immoral forgiveness, is driven permanently back into his old madness. Nastasya has not been redeemed from her suicidal depression; the power of Rogozhin's evil has not been broken. This idiot, this mad, decent, innocent man came into the world to help, and it didn't work. Is this still the Jesus Dosteovsky would prefer to the truth, or has he given us the tragic truth that must replace his Jesus?

2. Tolstoy: Jesus as law

Dostoevsky sought Jesus in his fiction: in Alyosha, in 'The Grand Inquisitor', and, most successfully, in *The Idiot*. Tolstoy fled fiction in order to find Jesus. He found him, or found that he already knew him, and he turned out to look very much like the Count himself.

There are two stages in Tolstoy's 'conversion', his painful journey from the world (and from fiction) to Jesus. The first is the conversion from the world, and it is recorded in *A Confession* (1879). Here he does not quite arrive at Jesus, but he does achieve a generalized faith, a faith in the child-like, Levin-like faith of the peasant. But this archaism doesn't stand before his ruthless self-criticism. The final stage of the conversion (recorded most vividly in *What I Believe*, also called *My Religion*, 1884) brings us Tolstoy's formidable law-giver Jesus. The Old Testament background is wiped out; there is no passion story, no kingdom, no parables, no eschatology, no grace, no forgiveness for the broken and lost, no father rushing down the road to embrace the prodigal. Tolstoy's Jesus is pure law, pure Matthew 5–7. All you need to do is put away sensuality and hypocrisy and the law can be obeyed. Tolstoy obeyed; everybody can and should. To Luther, the law was a cruel mirror showing us our sin. To Tolstoy it was a clear pane of glass through which one could see a powerful bearded face. It is Jesus; no, it is Tolstoy. Both right.

Tolstoy, it was said, could not love others and was himself very difficult to love. His self-love was formidable, and that may explain why there is no grace or forgiveness in his Jesus. He didn't need it. He was afraid that grace would make him dependent and keep him from the strenuous moral action obedience to the law required.

The gulf between *Anna Karenina* (1873–78) and *A Confession* is not as great as Tolstoy imagined. Even though he repudiated *Anna* as an abomination, it contains the seeds of his two-stage conversion. It is not the gospel, but it is invaluable *preparatio evangelica*. Indeed, there are some things in *Anna Karenina* that contain a better *evangelium* than any of his later non-fiction religious writing.

At the heart of Tolstoy's way to Jesus is his decisive repudiation of any Protestantizing emphasis on faith and rejection of works. It is Karenin's Jesus that Tolstoy rejects. Karenin finally refuses Anna's request for a divorce on religious grounds, insisting that she must be made to pay for her crime of adultery. It is Karenin's pietistic religion that makes Anna's suicide inevitable. Karenin's Jesus believes that evil must be resisted: Tolstoy's rejects all such resistance.

There is another Jesus in *Anna Karenina* besides that of Karenin. It is a Jesus I would prefer to both Karenin's and Tolstoy's, but it may well be that my preference is as vivid a reflection of my needs as their preferences are of theirs. I am speaking of the Jesus of radical forgiveness, touchingly expressed in words of Dolly to Anna.

'I don't think anything,' she said, 'but I've always loved you, and if you love anyone you love them as they are, not as you want them to be.'

Then there is that fascinating discussion in the studio of the artist Mikhailov about his painting of Jesus before Pilate. Anna sees in Jesus' face a compassion for his accuser, a forgiveness. Tolstoy's law-giver could never love as profoundly as Dolly or forgive as gently as the figure on the painting.

Levin is, of course, Tolstoy on the way to Jesus. He does find something at the end of the novel. It is not Jesus, or even religion. He faces his own despair and fear of death, and moves from an idealized vision of marriage and family to a wise understanding of human love. Like Tolstoy himself, Levin solves his problem of love by a reflection on work, which alone overcomes life's meaninglessness. Levin is most at peace when he gives himself unself-consciously to the work of mowing the hay. Despair is cured by work, not faith, and Levin's decency is basically secular.

There is a strange imprecision in Tolstoy's narrative of Levin's final steps towards self-acceptance. It is described from the outside, imposed on the reader; designed to coerce, not to convince or clarify (I am speaking of Part 8, Chapters viii-xiii). Levin's despair is apparently based on his belief that all systems of human thought affirm that death is the end of all. Levin was certain that this belief was a cruel mockery from which he needed to be freed.

He takes his fear-of-death existentialist despair (unhealed by both marriage and fatherhood) into the fields. He talks to a peasant who casually remarks

> 'Just so – people are different; one man lives just for his own needs . . . but Uncle Fokanich is an honest old man. He lives for his soul, he remembers God.'

The peasant's words dazzle Levin with their light. His search had come to an end. Don't live for your own needs, live for God. I didn't find this out, Levin says, I've known it all along. It is clear and simple and everybody knows it. And we cannot know it by reason.

> I've discovered nothing. I've simply learned what I knew already. I've understood the force that gave me life not in the past alone, but is giving me life at this very moment. I've liberated myself from deception [How Tolstoyan is this imperial 'I'!]; I've learned to know my Master.

He finally decides that faith has probably happened to him, but his enthusiastic definition of his new life makes that faith seem equivalent to deliberate self-deception, believing what you know not to be the case. Levin looks up to the sky.

Don't I know that to be infinite space, and not a rounded vault?
But no matter how I screw up my eyes and strain my eyesight I
cannot help seeing it as rounded and limited, and in spite of my
knowledge of its being infinite space I'm undoubtedly right in
seeing it as a firm blue vault . . .

Levin's new 'faith' does not merely go beyond the evidence of sense
and reason, it goes against them. Small wonder that when Tolstoy
comes to *A Confession* he will briefly admit his temptation to
follow the peasant's simple faith (i.e. Levin) – and go beyond it.
Anna Karenina is serious preparation, but it is not yet Tolstoy's
gospel.

A Confession is not a record of Tolstoy's journey to Jesus. It is
a record of his decisive rejection of the world and of his indecisive
discovery of something like religion. As *Anna* prepared the way
for *A Confession* (no to the world), *A Confession* prepared the
way for *What I Believe* (yes to Jesus).

Confession begins with Tolstoy's teenage repudiation of his
inherited Orthodox tradition and speaks – almost as unconvinc-
ingly as Augustine – of his terrible youthful sins: killing in war,
gambling, 'lying, thieving, promiscuity of all kinds, drunkenness,
violence, murder . . . there was not a crime I did not commit . . .'
(ch. 2).

How splendid to be so corrupt, and how proud he must have
been of his corruption! He later came to believe that artists like
himself had the power to teach truth to the world. All in all, he
assured us, as a young man he behaved like a madman, and like
all madmen he believed that everyone was mad but himself.

Two events broke into this life of sensuality and self-righteousness. A beloved brother died a slow and painful death, and he
witnessed a public execution in Paris. These, plus his marriage, put
a stop to his old corrupt life, but nothing emerged to take its place.
He describes his sense of despair, his fear of death. It is not clear
whether suicide was ever an option; on the same page in Chapter
4 he can say both that he did not want to kill himself and that the
thought of suicide came to him naturally. Suicide, in any case, will
become an important part of his defense of religious faith.

In Chapter 5 he stops pretending to be Augustine and starts
pretending to be Faust. He searches through 'all branches of know-

ledge' (must have taken him a couple of weeks, at least) and finds – of course – nothing. 'I learnt,' he writes, 'everything that knowledge has to answer to the question of life.' All worthless. Humbly, as is his wont, Tolstoy doesn't blame himself for his failure; he blames 'knowledge' and its pretentiousness.

His next move is an interesting one. He decides to establish truth the way political parties do today – he uses the techniques of a pollster. 'Look at all those simple uneducated peasants. They have true faith; why don't I?' The answer is easy: there are two kinds of knowledge, rational and irrational. The first kind Tolstoy looked for, the second kind the peasants had by nature. If they can live so naturally with faith, he asks, why can't I? Tolstoy in this way does not so much 'discover' faith – under some pear tree in a Milanese garden – he concludes that he has had it all along. (Is it that he is too proud to admit that there is anything out there to be discovered that he doesn't already know?) The 'proof' for faith – if his inept argument can be so dignified – lies in his refusal to take his own life. Since I did not kill myself when I was in despair, I must have 'had' faith all along. This is the only sense I can make out of his climactic passage (ch. 9).

> Faith is a knowledge of the meaning of human life, the conse-quence of which is that man does not kill himself but lives.

Everyone who lives therefore has faith?

> Faith is the force of life. If a man lives, then he must believe in something. If he did not believe that there was something he must live for he would not live. If he does not see and comprehend the illusion of the finite . . .

Levin, we may recall, preferred the senses' illusion that the sky is rounded and finite to the truth about infinite space. Tolstoy had studied all knowledge, and had convinced himself that the finite was the realm of illusion.

> . . . he will believe in the finite. If he does understand that illusion of the finite . . .

The illusion defined as the belief that human knowledge has some-thing important to say about the meaning of life . . .

> . . . he is bound to believe in the infinite. Without faith it is impossible to live.

Or, whoever has not already committed suicide – which means most of us – has faith already.

Later (in ch. 12) this argument from the absence of suicide becomes a fully-fledged argument for the existence of God.

> . . . I should have killed myself long ago, were it not for a dim hope of finding Him.

But he really didn't find; he 'found' that he had already found.

> I live truly only when I am conscious of Him and seek Him. What then is it you are seeking? a voice exclaimed inside me. There He is! He, without whom it is impossible to live. To know God and to live are one and the same thing. God is life.

Or, to sum up: the fact of not being dead proves the existence of God. (Is this what Anselm really meant?)

But whose faith and in what kind of God? Not the faith of the Orthodox Church. The church is too busy blessing wars to be taken seriously. Should he then not follow the joyous faith of the peasants? They indeed know something important: that thought gets nowhere and that life alone counts, 'the conviction that know-ledge of the truth can only be found in life . . .' (ch. 12).

But Tolstoy, even at his most careless and sentimental, cannot stay content with a numerical solution to these deep problems (there are more simple believers than cynical unbelievers, therefore God exists). So *A Confession* ends on a note of great certainty about the conversion from the world, and deep uncertainty about the conversion to – faith, God, religion, whatever. Both traditional Orthodoxy and the simple faith of the peasant are imperfect and incomplete.

Confession closes with this dilemma. Tolstoy's Jesus will solve it. In *What I Believe* Tolstoy will become the founder of a new

religion, just as he had dreamed in 1855. It will be neither Orthodoxy nor peasant piety. It may not even be Christianity, but it will
be Tolstoy, and it will be Jesus. (There may finally be no difference
between the two, since both imperiously lay down the law from a
position of absolute certainty.)

Although Tolstoy spoke of his discovery of Jesus' law as taking
place suddenly (in 1879), there is an 1855 diary entry from the
time of his military service that suggests that a longing for a new,
non-dogmatic Jesus was present well before Tolstoy 'found' him.
Indeed, in this perhaps too-revealing extract, Tolstoy comes forward not as an ordinary religious enquirer, like the rest of us
mortals, but as founder of a new religion, of a new and improved
Jesus. This undercurrent of identity between Jesus and the Count
is a theme in many of the later religious writings. He writes in this
diary extract of

> ... a stupendous idea, to the realization of which I feel capable
> of dedicating my whole life. The idea is the founding of a new
> religion corresponding to the present development of mankind:
> the religion of Christ purged of dogmas and mysticism – a
> practical religion not promising future bliss but giving bliss on
> earth.

There was nothing particularly original about this proposal in
nineteenth-century Europe: both Protestant liberalism and Catholic
modernists were working along these lines, but none of them ever
saw themselves as 'founders' of a new religion.

The new religion of *What I Believe* was a religion of Jesus laying
down the law: Jesus proposed the new law to the disciples on the
Mount; Tolstoy proposed his discovery of the true meaning of that
law to his disciples in the world. Same task, differing only in time
and place. Maxim Gorki once observed that when Tolstoy spoke
or wrote of Jesus there was 'no enthusiasm, no feeling in his words,
and no spark of real fire'.[7] No surprise really, since this Jesus
redeemed or saved no one. He was the law-giver whose laws,
Tolstoy assures us, he is the first correctly to understand.

> ... it was long before I could accustom myself to the strange

idea that after Christ's law had been professed by millions of people for 1800 years, and after thousands of men had devoted their lives to the study of that law, it had now been my fate to rediscover it as a novelty (*What I Believe*, V).

We will meet this note of Christian humility again and again as Tolstoy describes his Jesus.

Tolstoy's Jesus gives commandments that are in accord with man's nature and reason. He is divine only in the sense that he is the one (before Tolstoy?) who perfectly performed God's will. Everybody's New Testament opens at a different place when he or she stands it on its spine and lets it fall open naturally. Tolstoy's opens at Matthew 5, and that is all the Jesus he needs or wants. His bitter struggle with despair, with the fear of death, with the church – all these came suddenly to an end when he discovered that the words of Jesus in Matthew 5 were meant to be taken literally, without any ecclesiastical addition or interpretation. Indeed, Tolstoy tells us he is not interpreting Jesus' words at all, just 'describing' what (he has determined) they really mean in all their simplicity.

Jesus' new law abolished the law of Moses; it replaces everything the church has since taught in its christologies and doctrines of the Trinity. The six 'you have heard that it was said...' sayings of Matthew 5.21–48 are reduced to five basic commandments.

1. Live at peace with all men; anger is never justified.
2. Sexual relations are never to be taken as amusement; a husband must have but one wife, a wife one husband.
3. Never take an oath anywhere, about anything.
4. The fourth commandment is the key to Tolstoy's reading of Jesus' full meaning. This is the commandment that originally abolished his despair, that changed his life. 'You have heard that it was said, an eye for an eye and a tooth for a tooth. But I say to you, resist not him that is evil' (Matthew 5.38–39). Or, in his formulation: 'Never resist the evildoer by force, do not meet violence with violence. If they beat you, endure it; if they take your possessions, yield them up; if they compel you to work, work; and if they wish to take from you what you consider to be yours, give it up' (ch. VI).

5. The fifth commandment on love for enemies Tolstoy 'interpreted' as a refusal to distinguish between one's own nation and another's, and as a repudiation of all forms of warfare.

Ten years after *What I Believe* Tolstoy offered his most concise summary of his five commandments, moving slightly away from the language of Matthew 5.

> Share all that you have with others, do not heap up riches, do not steal, do not cause suffering, do not kill, do not unto others what you would not they should do unto you, all that has been said not eighteen hundred, but five thousand years ago, and there could be no doubt of the truth of this law if it were not for hypocrisy.
>
> (*The Kingdom of God is Within You*, XII). [8]

In *What I Believe* Tolstoy has fulfilled the hope of the 1855 diary entry: he has so astutely perceived the true meaning of Jesus' words (indeed he is the only one to get them exactly right) that he may truly be said to be a founder of a new religion. His further claim not to be an 'interpreter', but just a humble revealer of the text's plain sense (wilfully obscured by evil ecclesiastics from the beginning) can be tested by his comments on what he calls the fifth commandment, Matthew 5. 43–48. His rejection of interpretation deserts him here, and he consequently makes some interesting points. He rightly notes that this is one place in Matthew 5 where the old law cited by Jesus cannot be found in the Old Testament. The Old Testament nowhere recommends the hatred of enemies. So, Tolstoy concludes, Jesus must not have defined 'enemy' as 'personal foe'. Jesus never would have told us to love our personal enemies – that is an impossibility, and Jesus would never recommend an impossibility! So, using two hermeneutical devices, 'enemy' may be redefined so that Jesus' command can be turned into a possible one. Therefore, since

1. Jesus would never have proposed a moral impossibility – love of personal foes –

2. And, the Old Testament never says one may hate one's enemies,

Tolstoy is able to rescue Jesus from embarrassment by claiming that 'the dictionaries and concordances of the Bible' permit him to redefine 'enemy' as non-Jew and 'neighbour' as Jew. Thus, in one stroke, Jesus' citation of the Old Testament is vindicated, for hostility to the non-Jew is permitted by the Old Testament, and Jesus' 'law' is miraculously changed from impossible to possible. Love for enemies becomes a protest against nationalism, a commandment not to make distinctions between one's own and other nations.

This illuminating and outrageous piece of interpretation from this foe of all interpretation and believer that the meaning of Jesus' words is simple and rational, waiting only for Tolstoyan wisdom to make it all clear – this is an important key to his ultimate picture of Jesus. The law of Jesus must be rendered possible to follow. Tolstoy's very survival – spiritual and intellectual – seems to hang upon his conviction that he, and perhaps even he alone, has discovered the true sense of Jesus' words: that they are words that must be obeyed, and that are easy for all to obey. Hence Tolstoy had to turn 'love of enemies' into something he believed he could manage, something that he was already managing – especially if, as has been suggested, the enemy to be loved was first of all his own disapproving and harassed wife.

Given the ease with which the commandments can be obeyed, it is no surprise to discover that there is no sense of sin in Tolstoy, no element of forgiveness or grace in his Jesus. There can be no forgiveness if there is nothing to forgive. After all, Tolstoy insists again and again that resistance to Jesus comes not from his own sinful nature, but from the stupidity and hypocrisy of everyone else, especially from blind ecclesiastics and theologians who are incapable of seeing what is simple to everyone else: that Jesus meant what he said and that he meant us to obey and fulfil.

It is not only the sense of his own sinlessness that gives us this cold Jesus without grace, it is Tolstoy's association of sin with church dogma. He delights, like some liberal Protestant, in pillorying dogma. 'Only Russian Orthodoxy believes in original sin; I may not and do not.' For him to call upon grace from Jesus would be to rely on something external.

There are three final points to be made about Tolstoy's 'discovery' (which was not a discovery) of Jesus in 1879.

1. When all become as obedient to Jesus' law as Tolstoy himself, there will come a realm of this-worldly peace. Tolstoy on Jesus is, finally, a this-worldly utopian, a believer in a fully realized eschatology, not brought by Jesus' proclamation but by obedience to the law. He hints at this this-worldly vision in one of his most splendid summary passages on Jesus.

> Christ says: Do not be angry, do not consider any one your inferior – to do so is stupid. If you get angry and insult people it will be the worse for you. Christ also says: Do not run after women, but unite with one woman and live with her – it will be better for you so. He also says: Do not promise anything to any one, or else they will oblige you to do stupid and evil actions. He also says: Do not return evil for evil, or the evil will return to you yet more bitterly than before ... He also says: Do not consider men foreign to you merely because they live in another country and speak another language. If you consider them as enemies, and they consider you such, it will be worse for you. So do not commit all these stupidities, and it will be better for you (*What I Believe*, X).

2. Tolstoy is quite realistic about his utopian promise of earthly bliss. It will come only when all men achieve the level of obedience he knows and recommends as easy. What then is his this-worldly promise for the time between the times: between his full obedience now and the full obedience of all? There is an attractive candour to Tolstoy's answer. The true Tolstoyan Christian (apparently the only true kind) communicates the power of his obedience to Jesus by his suffering. He teaches in this interim not by words but by acts, and mainly by acts of suffering, a suffering imposed by the non-obedient upon the obedient. I cannot read this statement in any other way.

> Violence, imprisonment, or execution, to which a Christian is subjected in consequence of this, affords him the possibility of witnessing, not in words, but in deeds. Every violence by war, robbery, or execution, is not a result of the irrational forces of nature, but is perpetrated by erring people, deprived of know-ledge of the truth. And, therefore, the greater the evil these

people do to a Christian, the further they are from the truth, the more unfortunate are they, and the more do they need a knowledge of the truth. But a Christian cannot impart to men that knowledge otherwise than by refraining from the error in which those dwell who do him evil, and by returning good for evil. And that alone is the whole business of a Christian's life, and its whole meaning, which death cannot destroy (*What I Believe*, XII).

This idea of teaching by martyrdom is both honest and deeply unexpected. Tolstoy, steadfastly refusing to believe in Jesus' redemptive death, comes perilously close to a belief in the redemptive quality of the individual Christians' inevitable deaths at the hands of an unbelieving, or at least non-Tolstoyan, world.

3. Finally, it is important to remember that Jesus' ethic of non-resistance is not a quietistic withdrawal from the world; it is a head-on, radical attack on the whole modern world of civilization, culture and art. Tolstoy's Jesus requires that the existing order be violated, repudiated, utterly disobeyed. He sees with perfect clarity the meaning of his rejection of military service, of the legal system, of taxes for weapons.

At the end, Tolstoy becomes as radical and consistent a critic of culture as any subsequent revolutionary theorist. Even Lenin gave him his reluctant admiration.[9] Tolstoy differed from the Marxists (and from the Old Testament prophets he so resembled stylistically) by his disbelief in any kind of institutional improvement, whether gradual or sudden. He was a prophet disbelieving in change, an apocalypticist who didn't believe that God could do what man could not. At the heart of his vision of a full obedience to his lawgiver Jesus was a kind of communitarian, anarchic, anti-institutional vision of men and women living together in peace without sin (like himself) and therefore without those socializing institutions that are required because of sin (cf. 'man's capacity for injustice makes democracy necessary'). The Jesus of Leo Tolstoy is surely one of the most complex and fascinating fictional portraits that Tolstoy the novelist ever fashioned.

3. The christologies of Harriet Beecher Stowe[10]

Before we attend to the striking christologies woven into the fabric
of *Uncle Tom's Cabin* (1850–1), we must jump ahead a generation
to examine Mrs Stowe's life of Jesus, *Footsteps of the Master*
(1877). It is a sentimental, almost unreadable book, beginning as
a rather fanciful biography of Jesus and then declining into a series
of vapid homilies with such titles as 'The Friendship of Jesus', 'The
Attractiveness of Jesus', 'The Tolerance . . .', 'The Silence . . .',
'The Prayers . . .', and so on.

In spite of (or because of) her father's Calvinism, Mrs Stowe's
Jesus in this late book is a clear victory of sentiment over scripture.
The portrait is very Johannine, very docetic; Jesus is personally
present in all of the Old Testament theophanies, and when he
finally arrives for a longer visit to our first century he comes only
as a 'sympathetic foreigner'.

But her Jesus is not always this phantom. For all of his spooky
unreality, he is also, and pre-eminently, the one who bears our
suffering and sin.

> He was always, from the foundation of the world, the devoted
> sacrifice: bearing on his heart the sinning, suffering, wandering
> race of man, afflicted in their afflictions, bearing their griefs and
> carrying their sorrows, the friend of the Jew and the Gentile, the
> seeker for the outcast, the guide of the wanderer, the defender
> of the helpless, the consoler of the desolate, the self-devoted
> offering to and for the sins of the world (I).

It is this ghostly stranger that is also the sin-bearer, the one whom
we must imitate in the inevitable sorrows of our earthly life.

Yet Mrs Stowe keeps taking away what she gives, and so sometimes the redeemer of our domestic distresses doesn't really mean
it at all, so imperfect is his humanity and compassion.

> For, of Christ as he was during the three years of his public life,
> it could not be said that he was in all respects in our situation
> or experiencing our trials. He had unlimited supernatural power;
> he could heal the sick, raise the dead, hush the stormy waters,
> summon at his will legions of angels. A being of such power

could not be said to understand exactly the feelings of our limitations and weaknesses. But those years of power were only three in the life of our Lord; for thirty years he chose to live the life of an obscure human being (VII).

This might be called a theory of the atonement as sentimental compassion, with a Jesus healing not our sin so much as our nuisances and minor middle-class irritations. This non-atoning atonement becomes particularly clear when she comes to the actual death on the cross, which she virtually ignores apart for some perfunctory remarks on the last words.

The most interesting contribution of *Footsteps* to a christological reading of Mrs Stowe's masterpiece comes, unexpectedly, in her passionate embrace of the virgin birth of Jesus. By the time she finishes brooding over this joyful mystery, Jesus is not only scarcely human, he is scarcely male.

He had no mortal father. All that was human in him was her nature; it was the union of the divine nature with the nature of a pure woman. Hence there was in Jesus more of the pure feminine element than in any other man. It was the feminine element exalted and taken in union with divinity (IV).

This sex-change, or degendering, is so astonishing that it should probably be sheepishly ignored by contemporary feminist theologians. Jesus not only had no father; he himself was really a mother.

His mode was more that of a mother than a father. He strove to infuse Himself into them [i.e. the disciples] by an embracing, tender, brooding love; ardent, self-forgetful, delicate, refined (XII).

Thus, when we come to Uncle Tom as Mrs Stowe's most vivid fictional portrait of Jesus the redeemer, we will understand why Tom is so dreadfully passive, so piously willing to forgive even the unrepentant, so sexless. James Baldwin has some silly things to say about *Uncle Tom's Cabin* (partly because he seems to confuse the actual novel with the melodramatic theatrical versions current in the late nineteenth century), but he is right about Tom.

> Tom, therefore, her only black man, has been robbed of his humanity and divested of his sex.[11]

Baldwin misses the theological point that Tom (and in general all of Mrs Stowe's blacks) must become feminized if he is to function as redeemer. He is not feminine because he is black, but because he is Jesus. For Mrs Stowe, all redeemers must be passive, suffering, accepting, forgiving. That is what blacks do, what Tom does, what Jesus did and does. There are therefore three christological paths through the forest of *Uncle Tom's Cabin* – Tom himself, the black, and Jesus – and they are finally interchangeable and identical. To become Mrs Stowe's Jesus, black Uncle Tom must become black Aunt Tom.

I

The black feminine Jesus of Harriet Beecher Stowe is not a product of a mid-life theological crisis. It was not something she happened upon as she made her journey from daddy's Calvinism to Episcopal Arminianism. She had always known well the Puritan tradition, and she had always known that it was not for her. It was too scholarly for one thing, but most of all she never could experience a deep enough sense of sin or a vivid enough experience of salvation to gain admission to her father's house. The gentle Jesus was always there to rescue her from Calvin's holy God, and *Uncle Tom's Cabin* is as important as an example of evangelical-romantic christology as it is as a novel about slavery. I suspect it is more successful as the former than as the latter.

A brother's suicide in 1843 and a son's death from cholera in 1847 deepened her identification with the suffering Jesus, who was obliged, in effect, to become a woman in order to meet the spiritual needs of this gifted, troubled and passionate woman. Before she decided to write about the suffering of slavery, she was already a deeply anguished woman prepared to understand the anguish of others.

The Fugitive Slave Bill of 1850 was the trigger for the book.

Northerners suddenly became responsible for slaves escaped from the South; indeed, the bill – originally a response to southern interests – transformed slavery into a northern problem and moved the nation considerably closer to civil conflict. Mrs Stowe received a letter from her sister-in-law pleading with her to present to the whole nation the curse of slavery. She read the letter to her children, crumpled it up, and declared, 'I will if I live.'

Uncle Tom's Cabin, then, is both about slavery and about redemption. It speaks both of a nation's need and an author's. American historians today remain uncertain whether *Uncle Tom's Cabin* is part of American history or American literature: bad literature, good history, it has been suggested. I am interested in another geological fault in the novel, and a more interesting one. *Uncle Tom's Cabin* is a novel about slavery (and thus is both literature and history) and it is also an important document in the history of nineteenth-century American Protestantism. It is literature and history – *and* theology. Everything Mrs Stowe wrote, and *Uncle Tom's Cabin* above all, was about the crisis in Calvinist theology. She took from her father's Calvinism the certainty that all problems are religious, but she is deeply troubled by her own inability to discover any basis for a Calvinist-Christian critique of slavery. This is why readers of the novel are surprised to discover that the novel is not an indictment against the South drawn up by a sensitive New England conscience. God wrote the book, not I, she always said, and her 'visions' must be granted her. She meant it, and it was true; God guided Mrs Stowe in her masterpiece as surely as he guided Eliza in her miraculous flight across the Ohio River on her way to freedom. But this was not Calvin's God; not the father's Father. The God of Eliza and Mrs Stowe, the God that successfully helped the author banish Calvin's God from her sky, was not God at all. It was Jesus, a figure with infinite capacity for love. Stowe's God, Eliza's maternal love – these are really Jesus. Jesus *is* maternal love for Harriet Beecher Stowe, and this is the key to her theological critique of slavery. Calvin's God demands only obedience, and Mrs Stowe is uneasy with both white and black Protestantism's application of that obedience to the evil of slavery. White Christians (except, in her novel, Mrs Shelby and the Quakers) defend slavery on Calvinist grounds, and black Christians are too acquiescent, too ready to fall back on the duty of obedience to the master. Indeed, Uncle Tom is an Uncle Tom largely because he is a Christian.

Mrs Stowe may say she loves the Sermon on the Mount and call it 'the most disturbing and revolutionary document in the world', but her theological criticism of slavery is neither from the Sermon nor from the Calvinist God of obedience. Slavery is evil because of her identification of Jesus with maternal love. Slavery is evil because it destroys the black family. Only from the ironic secularist Augustine St Clare do we hear the traditional abolitionist attack on slavery.

> Whatever is too hard, too dirty, too disagreeable, for me, I may set Quashy to doing. Because I don't like work, Quashy shall work. Because the sun burns me, Quashy shall stay in the sun. Quashy shall earn the money, and I will spend it. Quashy shall lie down in every puddle, that I may walk over dry-shod. Quashy shall do my will, and not his, all the days of his mortal life, and have such chance of getting to heaven, at last, as I find convenient. This I take to be about what slavery is. I defy anybody on earth to read our slave-code, as it stands in our law-books, and make anything else of it. Talk of the abuses of slavery! Humbug! The thing itself is the essence of all abuse! (XI).

Mrs Stowe of course agrees with this abolitionist critique, but her real passion is directed toward that attack on slavery based on her post-Calvinist Jesus, the maternal lover.

The problem of *Uncle Tom's Cabin*, then, is that it attempts to criticize Calvinism and slavery at the same time, and that it is better at the first than at the second. Some of Stowe's blacks and some of her whites accept slavery because they are Christians, and Mrs Stowe is clearly uneasy that she cannot find a convincing Christian critique in either form of Protestantism. She would surely agree with St Clare's cry 'the country is almost ruined with pious white people' (XIV). So what she cannot find in white or black Protestantism, she must create herself. Hence *Uncle Tom's Cabin*: Jesus equals Uncle Tom equals maternal love. Uncle Tom as Aunt Tom; Jesus as woman.

Both the power and the weakness of *Uncle Tom's Cabin* spring from Mrs Stowe's attempt to indict both Calvinism and slavery at the same time. Her dual task leads her to some interesting positions. Her specifically religious ideas (for the most part, her means of escape from the faith of her father) are placed on the lips of blacks. Thus we get redemption as maternal love which is Jesus which is Uncle Tom. This radically forgiving Jesus does indeed constitute her escape from Calvinism (no mean task, when we think of the tormented escape-attempts of Hawthorne, Melville, Dickinson), but this theologically successful Jesus is a failure as a social critic. About all he enables her to say against slavery is that it is bad for the family. This is true enough, but inadequate as social criticism. Mrs Stowe's religious truth is black, but her best social truth is white; her most trenchant criticism of slavery comes from whites: the Quakers in Ohio, Mrs Shelby and, of course, St Clare.

It appears that Mrs Stowe is aware of the inability of her post-Calvinist-feminine-Uncle-Tom-christology to show up slavery as the radical evil she knows it to be. This awareness leads to two quite different comments on slavery: one secular and this-worldly, one other-worldly and eschatological. Mrs Stowe did not believe that the United States could solve the problem within its own boundaries. Her only genuine this-worldly hope became the return to Africa. Was it not the Christian quietism, the Uncle Tom christo-logy, that ruled out the possibility of slavery's abolition in her own land? Africa alone, she declared, can heal the terrible wounds that slavery has brought to black men and women. Africa alone can provide a physical setting for the bringing together of the families that slavery has sundered. (Of course, Abraham Lincoln was tempted by this solution, as was – and is – Stokely Carmichael today.) Only in Africa, Mrs Stowe writes, will blacks recover their full humanity 'in their gentleness, their lowly docility of heart, their aptitude to repose on a superior mind and rest on a higher power, their childlike simplicity of affection, and facility of forgive-ness' (XVI).[12]

But Africa and the feminine christology is not quite everything in Mrs Stowe's collection of weapons against slavery. There is an aggressive Christian answer to slavery after all, beyond the pro-posal for a return to Africa. And, surprisingly enough, it is a christological answer placed on the lips of two of her central white characters: Eva and her father Augustus St Clare. This christolog-ical answer has nothing to do with the historical (and distressingly gentle) Jesus. It is eschatological. During the first coming, Jesus may have been the perfect mother, accepting, loving, forgiving. But when he comes again – that will all be changed. Mrs Stowe's secret (and repressed) christology is really apocalypticism. Eva spoke of her love of the Book of Revelation because it told of 'a wonderous something yet to come' (XXII).

Shortly before his death, St Clare plays and sings portions of the Mozart *Requiem*, particularly the '*Dies irae*' and the '*Recordare*'. He is overwhelmed by the power of both music and words. Even given his deep distrust of the Christian church, he can say as he looks toward his own death:

What a sublime conception is that of a last judgment. . . . a righting of all the wrongs of ages! . . . a solving of all moral problems, by an unanswerable wisdom! (XXVIII).

Dissatisfied with her rather bland criticism of slavery as family-destroying, Mrs Stowe turned to apocalypticism and found that Jesus coming again might right the wrongs that he was powerless to do anything about on his first coming. Is she not saying something like this: 'Slaves, because you are Christians, you cannot do anything about slavery now. Maybe Africa will help. But in any case, stick with Jesus and he will teach you to bear all and forgive all. When he comes again, all will be well.'

Usually christological this-worldliness is activist, world-changing, while other-worldliness is acquiescent. Mrs Stowe reverses this convention, and her reversal becomes the orthodoxy of black Protestantism for the next hundred years. She either created or discovered the theological secret of the spiritual:

When I get to Heaven
Gonna put on my shoes,
And walk all over God's Heaven . . .

I have no shoes on earth to put on, and I will not try to find any. On earth, there are places I cannot walk. But in Heaven (i.e. when Jesus comes and turns the earth into a Heaven) I will have both shoes and the ability to walk wherever I choose. Not really until Dr King did this orthodoxy find a worthy and qualified theological adversary. Until Dr King, Uncle Tom as Jesus was in control. One of the wisest outsiders ever to write about America, D. H. Lawrence, made this significant point.

> Justice is a great and manly thing.
> Saviourism is a despicable thing.[13]

2

We must now clarify the fascinating strands of the triple christology that Mrs Stowe weaves into her masterpiece. Both the structural weakness and the emotional power of *Uncle Tom's Cabin*, I am arguing, derive from the fact that the author is trying to draw a bead on two enemies at the same time: Calvinism and slavery. When she concentrates on one, the other eludes her. In her flight from nineteenth-century Calvinism, with its holy God and demand for a specific conversion experience, she concluded that loving Jesus, studying his earthly life and doing good was all that salvation required. The submissive black and the caring mother are models of the truly saved. But the passive black and the woman, so full of noble feeling, so ready to forgive even the oppressor, leave the evil world unchanged. That is why the sweet Jesus must come again to turn history upside down. Mrs Stowe turned to apocalyptic because she was convinced that white Christian Anglo-Saxons are doomed. They have broken the covenant with God and are fit only for the *dies irae*.

Mrs Stowe's alternative to Calvinism was a mixture of evangelical Protestantism and the romantic movement: heart over head, the winsome personality of Jesus, the idealization of the woman, the family as a means of grace. This emotional amalgam could find no way, short of the last judgment, to abolish slavery. It valued forgiveness and humility too much for that. It did provide one thing: a unique if incomplete criticism of slavery as a violation of the redemptive family, countenancing sexual relations between slave women and their masters. Her gentle Jesus could define the evil in slavery, but it could not abolish it. If Mrs Stowe was an abolitionist (and the character of St Clare suggests a genuine sympathy for the movement) she was one on secular, not theological grounds.

The poignant fact about the christology of evangelical romanticism when applied to slavery was that both Jesus and the black male must be degendered, even castrated, in order to fulfil their redemptive roles. If only a mother's love can save, and if the black is the supreme example of *imitatio Christi*, then both the black man and Jesus must approach the status of woman if they are to become Christ.[14]

If redemption means feminizing the black, it also means feminizing Jesus. There is little masculinity in Mrs Stowe's Jesus. We have already noted her celebration of the Virgin Birth which produced a child without male cooperation. Conception without a penis produces a redeemer similarly deprived. He was, quite literally, a mother's boy with an intuitive understanding of the woman that no other male, conceived in the traditional way, could claim. And not only did he understand women better than any, women understood him better than men. 'We can see no image,' Mrs Stowe writes in *Footsteps*, 'by which to represent the Master but one of those loving, saintly mothers, who in leading along their little flock, follow nearest in the footsteps of Jesus.'

It is finally in black, sexless, loving Uncle Tom himself that the fragments of Mrs Stowe's christological passion settle into a pattern. The most important thing to say about Uncle Tom is that he *is* Mrs Stowe's Jesus.

Tom teaches others about Jesus and ultimately becomes the One he teaches about. We first come upon him, weak and passive as he will always be, bursting into tears when he hears he is to be sold by the Shelbys. Mrs Shelby unsuccessfully tries to dissuade her husband from making the sale by observing, quite correctly, that Tom would readily lay down his life for his master.

Just before he is sold to Legree, he tries to counsel his fellow-slave Lucy, just before her suicide. He told her of 'a heart of love in the skies, of a pitying Jesus, and an eternal home' (XII). But neither God's nor Tom's heart helped Lucy very much and she took her own life to avoid being sold once more. But the author comes to Tom's defence; his preaching is not as irrelevant as Lucy's suicide makes it seem.

Not one throb of anguish, nor one tear of the oppressed, is
forgotten by the Man of Sorrows, the Lord of Glory. In his
patient, generous bosom he bears the anguish of a world . . .
[and then, as if herself uneasy with Tom's ineptness, she adds:]
the year of the redeemed *shall* come.

In this world of slavery there is only suffering and death. Tom
preaches the same truth to old Prue, just before *her* suicide. It is
almost the case that Mrs Stowe detects the seeds of suicidal
depression in Tom's pessimistic gospel of the irredeemable world.
Why not hasten – like Paul – to the next world as soon as possible?

Tom's christological *kerygma* is all forgiveness: no judgment, no
demand for repentance. He forgives his first master for selling him
and he even (as we shall see) forgives the unrepentant cruelty of
Legree. Tom, we are told, loved John's other-worldly gospel best
of all, with its portrait of the Father's house. He read his Bible
frequently, and very slowly. Mrs Stowe makes this point in a lovely
sentence:

Fortunate for him was it that the book he was intent on was
one which slow reading cannot injure . . . (XIV).

During his teaching of little Eva just before her death, Tom
shifts from proclaimed to proclaimer; from teaching about Jesus
to becoming him. He tells Eva of 'the image of One who loved the
little child', and Eva, fixing on her beloved Tom's words, replied:
'if my dying could stop all this misery I *would die* for them,
Tom, if I could . . .' (XXIV). But even if Eva's death was redemptive,
and Tom's more so,[15] neither had the slightest impact on 'all this
misery'. Tom as Jesus bore suffering, but he did not overcome it.
Tom as Jesus may have made a Christian or two, but he did not
(and could not) free a single slave.

Under the irrational cruelty of his master, Legree, Tom's faith
gets its final test. He has his Gethsemane, his cry of dereliction.
Shut up in a dark room, afraid that God had abandoned him, he
is rescued from despair by a vision of the crucified Jesus, crowned
with thorns, 'buffeted and bleeding'. Tom, in the darkness, goes
beyond faith in the crucified or obedience to him. He *becomes* the
suffering and dying Lord.

The transformation of Uncle Tom into Jesus is completed in the final months of his tormented life under Legree. He had come through his despair, and he gave himself to the welfare of his fellow slaves. The vision of the crucified determined everything he did. Tom became the One he spoke of.

Tom's whole soul overflowed with compassion and sympathy for the poor wretches by whom he was surrounded. To him it seemed as if his life sorrows were now over, and as if, out of that strange treasury of peace and joy, with which he had been endowed from above, he longed to pour out something for the relief of their woes. It is true, opportunities were scanty; but, on the way to the fields, and back again, and during the hours of labour, chances fell in his way of extending a helping hand to the weary, the disheartened and discouraged.

Tom refuses to tell Legree what he knows about the escape of the slaves Cassie and Emmeline. This stubbornness infuriates Legree, who beats Tom unmercifully. Tom asks his abuser to repent; he refuses and continues to beat him. Tom knows he cannot save himself, but he offers – from his cross – a forgiveness Legree neither asked for nor merited.

'Ye poor miserable crittur!, there an't no more you can do! I forgive ye, with all my soul!' (XL).

The death of Tom becomes a Calvary in one more sense. He has forgiven his murderer, but there remain the two thieves. Sambo and Quimbo were slaves that all along had been willing instruments of Legree's cruelty toward Tom. The sight of the dying Tom got to them, and – repenting for what they had done – they tried to offer some relief to the dying Tom. Tom's death doesn't take place until the repentant slaves are saved.

'Oh, Tom!' said Quimbo, 'we's been awful wicked to ye!'
'I forgive ye, with all my heart!' said Tom, faintly.
'Oh, Tom! do tell us who is *Jesus*, anyhow?' said Sambo, – 'Jesus, that's been a standin' by you so, all this night? – Who is he?'

The word roused the failing, fainting spirit. He poured forth a few energetic sentences of that Wondrous One, – his life, his death, his everlasting presence, and power to save.

They wept, – both the two savage men.

'Why didn't I never hear this before?' said Sambo; 'but I do believe! – I can't help it! Lord Jesus, have mercy on us!'

'Poor critturs!' said Tom, 'I'd be willin' to bar all I have, if it'll only bring ye to Christ! O Lord! give me these two more souls, I pray!'

That prayer was answered (XL).

And then Tom gave up the ghost.

Mrs Stowe both affirms and denies this crucified Jesus: weak enough for compassion and for salvation, but too weak for liberation.

4. *Emily Dickinson: 'If Jesus was sincere'*

The poets vary in their forms of theological guidance. Dostoevsky and Mrs Stowe each fashioned a fictional character to stand for the Jesus in whom they sought to believe. Emily Dickinson's (1830–1886) way is a little different. In her poetry she does two things: she portrays the Jesus she rejected and, beyond that, the one she could not reject.[16]

I will first rehearse the story of Emily Dickinson's attitude to her inherited Christian tradition and to the God of that tradition. Then we will be prepared to see if the Jesus she fled to – escaping the evil God – provided a stable form for her theological self-definition.

Sometime around her twenty-first birthday, and well before she seriously began to write poetry, Emily Dickinson decided not to give herself to the Jesus defined by the evangelical Protestant tradition of Amherst, Massachusetts. She did not cease to 'be' a Christian, but she did reject Amherst Protestantism and most of the current alternatives to it: the sentimental piety of Mrs Stowe, or the more serious anti-Puritan worlds of Unitarianism and transcendentalism. She wrote to a friend in 1852:

Christ is calling everyone here, all my companions have

answered, even my darling Vinnie believes she loves, and trusts him, and I am standing alone in rebellion, and growing very careless (I, 94).

All she had done was to refuse faith as her culture defined it: going to a church meeting and giving your reason away, is how she might have put it. Why did this gentle young woman need to make so radical a break with her family and her world? Did she feel that accepting the family's faith would please them too much? Was she incapable of 'giving' herself to any man?

There clearly was something frightening to her about the very idea of self-loss. This comes out vividly in a poem from around 1861.

> The Drop, that wrestles in the sea –
> Forgets her own locality –
> As I – toward Thee –
>
> She knows herself an incense small –
> Yet *small* – she sighs – if *All* – is *All* –
> How *larger* – be?
>
> The Ocean – smiles – at her Conceit –
> But *she*, forgetting Amphitrite –
> Pleads – 'Me?'

(no. 284)

Christian mystics have often used the figure of the drop of wine falling into the wine-glass and losing its separate identity. Here the poet is the drop, refusing to lose herself in the All/Ocean. Instead of humility before this All, she argues with him: 'If you are really All, you certainly have no need to capture an insignificant little self like mine.' God smiles at the impudence, and the poet concludes with an act of self-affirmation – 'Me'. 'Look at me; I'll never lose myself in such as You.'

I

Emily Dickinson, rejecting faith, refuses to fall into Jesus' arms. She did not reject God; she simply decided he was not to be trusted.

> I know that He exists.
> Somewhere – in Silence –
> He has hid his rare life
> From our gross eyes.
>
> 'Tis an instant's play.
> 'Tis a fond Ambush –
> Just to make Bliss
> Earn her own surprise!

(no. 338).

He *is* there, after all, teasing us with unfunny hide-and-seek games.

Emily Dickinson's decision not to submit to the evangelical Jesus began her life-long battle with the despised Puritan God she never wholly escaped. I wonder if these lines are about that evil God lurking in the dark.

> Parting is all we know of heaven
> And all we need of hell

(no. 1732).

We know him only when he goes away, and that parting, however inevitable, is like damnation. Emily Dickinson's unique pious godlessness comes out movingly in one of those extraordinary loveletters known as the 'Master letters' (we do not know who the Master was, nor even if the letters were sent):

One drop more from the gash that stains your Daisy's bosom – then would you believe? Thomas' faith in Anatomy, was stronger than his faith in faith. God made me – [Sir] Master – I didn't be – myself. I dont know how it was done. He built the heart in me – Bye and bye it outgrew me – and like the little mother – with the big child – I got tired holding him. I heard of a thing called 'Redemption' – which rested men and woman. You

remember I asked you for it – you gave me something else. I
forgot the Redemption [in the Redeemed – I didn't tell you for
a long time, but I knew you had altered me – I] and was tired –
no more – [so dear did this stranger become that were it, or my
breath – the Alternative – I had tossed the fellow away with a
smile] (II. 373–4. The words in brackets were crossed out in the
original draft).

The poet admires Thomas' doubt, and then offers a characteristic
piece of theological irony, blending rebellion and faith. God made
me, she admits, but the 'me' he made grew so independent that it
was able to do without the Maker. She thought she wanted redemption, but what she really wanted was love.

God is the angel with whom the poet-Jacob wrestles. But, unlike
Genesis 32, in her version the poet wins.

> A little East of Jordan,
> Evangelists record,
> A gymnast and an Angel
> Did wrestle long and hard –
>
> Till morning touching mountain –
> And Jacob, waxing strong,
> The Angel begged permission
> To Breakfast – to return –
>
> Not so, said cunning Jacob!
> 'I will not let thee go
> Except thou bless me' – Stranger!
> The which acceded to –
>
> Light swung the silver fleeces
> 'Peniel' Hills beyond,
> And the bewildered Gymnast
> Found he had worsted God!

(no. 59).

Emily Dickinson can be a playful critic of God's traditional attri-

butes. Of course He is a jealous God, because He knows we would
rather play with our friends than with Him.

> God is indeed a jealous God –
> He cannot bear to see
> That we had rather not with Him
> But with each other play

(no. 1719).

There are two themes, two theological subjects, that Emily Dickinson concentrates upon in her project of redefining transcendence:
creation and eschatology. In 'Two swimmers wrestled on the
spar –' the poet splits herself in two: one self looks happily to
land, earth, this world; the other raises her hands and eyes
to heaven, looks upon death, and dies.

> Two swimmers wrestled on the spar –
> Until the morning sun –
> When One – turned smiling to the land –
> Oh God! the Other One!
>
> The stray ships – passing –
> Spied a face –
> Upon the waters borne –
> With eyes in death – still begging raised –
> And hands – beseeching – thrown!

(no. 201).

That the creator is both playful and cruel is the theme of one of
Emily Dickinson's darkest religious lyrics.

> It's easy to invent a Life –
> God does it – every Day –
> Creation – but the Gambol
> Of His Authority –
>
> It's easy to efface it –
> The thrifty Deity
> Could scarce afford Eternity
> To Spontaneity –

The Perished Patterns murmur –
But His Perturbless Plan
Proceed – inserting Here – a Sun –
There – leaving out a Man –

(no. 724).

It's as easy to destroy as to create; God does both readily. Those whom He destroys may complain, but He doesn't listen. He simply goes about, undisturbed, creating a solar system and destroying a human being. *C'est son métier.*

In another lyric, God is portrayed as the petulant destroyer of a bird, and apparently the bird stands both for ordinary human suffering and the crucified Jesus.

His Bill is clasped – his Eye forsook –
His Feathers wilted low –
The Claws that clung, like lifeless Gloves
Indifferent hanging now –
The Joy that in his happy Throat
Was waiting to be poured
Gored through and through with Death, to be
Assassin of a Bird
Resembles to my outraged mind
The firing in Heaven,
On Angels – squandering for you
Their Miracles of Tune –

(no. 1102).

For God to kill a human, or his Son, is like killing the angels beside his throne, singing 'Holy, Holy, Holy'.

Emily Dickinson's second divine indictment concerns eschatology: the promise of heaven and the hope of immortality. God's false promises for the future define him as a liar and a cheat. We are arrogant fools indeed, to need such hope: 'a conceited thing indeed, this promised Resurrection' (II, 328). Sometimes she simply affirms that death cannot be transcended: 'All but Death, can be Adjusted – . . . Death – unto itself – Exception – /Is exempt from Change . . .' (no. 749).

In other moods she portrays the Christian hope as a terrible, almost mystical, sense of nothingness in which we, like the bird, are swallowed up and lost for ever in some remote sky. Just as the travelling circus folds up and disappears overnight, so it is with us.

> I've known a Heaven, like a Tent –
> To wrap its shining Yards –
> Pluck up its stakes, and disappear –
> Without the sound of Boards
> Or Rip of Nail – Or Carpenter –
> But just the miles of Stare
> That signalize a Show's Retreat –
> In North America – . . .
>
> Dissolved as utterly –
> As Bird's far Navigation
> Discloses just a Hue –
> A plash of Ours, a Gaity –
> Then swallowed up, of View

(no. 243).

The ascending bird may look like a resurrection, but it isn't.

Sometimes there is no heaven, sometimes heaven swallows us up, and sometimes heaven is there but it turns out to be more like hell than heaven is supposed to be. (Surely the reflection of William Blake is intended here.)

> Far from Love the Heavenly Father
> Leads the Chosen Child,
> Oftener through Realm of Briar
> Than the Meadow mild.
>
> Oftener by the Claw of Dragon
> Than the Hand of Friend
> Guides the Little One predestined
> To the Native Land

(no. 1021).

Like the Puritan she never ceased to be, Emily Dickinson loved to present her attack on God's delight in killing and maiming in exegetical form. Here is her nasty little sermon on Abraham and Isaac. (Not even a whiff of a defence of the teleological suspension of the ethical here!)

Abraham to kill him
Was distinctly told –
Isaac was an urchin –
Abraham was old –

Not a hesitation –
Abraham complied –
Flattered by Obeisance
Tyranny demurred –

Isaac to his children
Lived to tell the tale –
Moral – with a Mastiff
Manners may prevail

(no. 1317).

God, the wild dog, flattered by Abraham's instant obedience, decided for once not to kill. This was not the case with the Wild Dog on the first Good Friday on a hill outside Jerusalem.

Split the Lark – and you'll find the Music –
Bulb after Bulb, in Silver rolled –
Scantily dealt to the Summer Morning
Saved for your Ear when Lutes be old.

Loose the Flood – you shall find it patent –
Gush after Gush, reserved for you –
Scarlet Experiment! Sceptic Thomas!
Now, do you doubt that your Bird was true?

(no. 861).

God had to cut Jesus open and watch his blood pour out before He could prove Himself to be God, and before Jesus could prove to Thomas that he was indeed the wounded Son of the killer.

Why is it that we so often want our greatest rebels to achieve serenity at the close of their troubled lives? Is it our compassion for their torment or is it a deep-seated uneasiness with rebellion itself? Melville was supposed to have offered a 'testament of acceptance' with *Billy Budd*, while Shakespeare's final romances and Beethoven's last quartets are said to be victorious affirmations after artistic lives of nay-saying. Emily Dickinson has suffered the same interpretative fate. Does she finally overcome her life-long rebellion against God? The answer, I think, is a very faint 'maybe'.

In a letter written to a friend just three years before her death in 1886, Emily Dickinson still sounds like her marvellous rebellious self.

> You are like God. We pray to Him, and He answers 'No'. Then we pray to Him to rescind the no, and He don't answer at all, yet 'Seek and ye shall find' is the 'boon of faith' (III, 780).

One thing she could not tolerate from either Jesus or God was a broken promise. 'You told me that if I sought I would find, but I didn't.'

The sufficiency of earth is the subject of a late (1877) lyric:

> The fact that Earth is Heaven –
> Whether Heaven is Heaven or not
> If not an Affidavit
> Of that specific Spot
> Not only must confirm us
> That is [i.e. the Christian heaven] is not for us
> But that it would affront us
> To dwell in such a place –

> (no. 1408).

Yet – there are two haunting short poems from her final years that hint that some of Emily Dickinson's terrible theological wrath may have been burned away.

How brittle are the Piers
On which our Faith doth tread –
No Bridge below doth totter so –
Yet none hath such a Crowd.

It is as old as God –
Indeed – 'twas built by him –
He sent his Son to test the Plank,
And he pronounced it firm.

(no. 1433).

Is some sort of faith possible, after all, however brittle and old? How exquisite is this mixture of fear and longing:

We shun it ere it comes,
Afraid of Joy,
Then sue it to delay
And lest it fly,
Beguile it more and more –
May not this be
Old Suitor Heaven
Like our dismay at thee?

(no. 1580).

After all, flight was one of the ways Emily Dickinson affirmed what was of greatest importance to her. In her later years she fled even from her closest friends. Perhaps flight from God was her special form of witness. 'To escape enchantment' [i.e. bondage, and thus to become truly free], she wrote, 'one must always flee' (II, 454).

3

End-of-life acceptance or not, it would be much too simple to argue that Emily Dickinson fled from the Puritan God she hated into the welcoming arms of Jesus. Her whole religious programme – life-long or nearly so – of rebellion began with a refusal to go to church and give herself to Jesus. Is her Jesus, then, the same enemy as her God? They do often seem to be interchangeable terms.

(Could anyone but Emily Dickinson illustrate the doctrine of the Incarnation by 'The Courtship of Miles Standish' – Standish = God, Alden = Jesus?)

> God is a distant – stately Lover –
> Woos, as He states us – by His Son –
> Verily, a Vicarious Courtship –
> 'Miles', and 'Priscilla', were such an One –
>
> But, lest the Soul – like fair 'Priscilla'
> Choose the Envoy – and spurn the Groom –
> Vouches, with hyperbolic archness –
> 'Miles' and 'John Alden' were Synonym –

(no. 357).

Before we try to discover from the poetry something about the Jesus that Emily Dickinson may have both distrusted and trusted, I wish to call to mind an argument in John Cody's careful and affectionate psychoanalytical study of the poet. I am persuaded that he is fully justified in detecting psychological reasons for her refusal to give herself to Jesus. He has argued that Emily Dickinson could not become the kind of Christian Amherst expected because it would please her parents too much, and because – primarily – it would mean giving herself to a man (Jesus) which was out of the question. What lies behind Cody's conjectures?

He finds substantial evidence that Emily Dickinson was deprived of that magic period of intimacy between mother and infant and that, therefore, she never learned that basic trust in parents that is a condition of normal adulthood. Her mother couldn't give her love, and her father wouldn't – he was too busy. Cut off from a mother's love, she was from the start an emotionally starved child ravenous for affection that never came.

> In the case of a girl in Emily Dickinson's circumstances, in which the mother model cuts a ludicrously inferior figure in relation to the father, real acceptance of a feminine identity may never come about.[17]

With a rejecting and rejected mother, Emily Dickinson tried to disown her own femininity, lest she come to resemble such an unloving mother. It is difficult for a woman who cannot feel she is a woman to give herself to a man.

The poet's view of heterosexuality was partly shaped by her father, who dominated and humiliated all the women in his family. Fearing femininity, heterosexuality and marriage, Emily Dickinson's attitude to men was a combination of envy and hatred: envy because of their social freedoms that she lacked; hatred because they were beginning to take away her girl friends with whom alone she was fully at ease.

But she not only feared her father, she greatly overestimated him, and thus made it impossible for any other male to compete. This strange father-daughter bond meant that she could love only father-images, with all the anxiety that was likely to entail. To fear, over-value and identify with the father thus severely defeminized this affection-starved daughter.

What she needed, of course, was human love of a warm and maternal kind. A gentle man might have been able to offer that, but he could never survive a comparison to the aggressive father. Uncertain of her own attractiveness, fearful of heterosexuality, Emily Dickinson needed what was impossible for her to get. Flight was her response, since her personality ruled out heterosexual love, and her culture banned the homosexual option.

Emily Dickinson's poetry is sublimated rage – grounded in a feeling of being cheated by mother, fate, friends, God, and – finally – Jesus, whom she had so stubbornly refused to embrace when she was twenty-one. Will the poetry concerning Jesus reveal the same pattern of rage and flight, the same irony, anger and despair that we found when God was the subject? In one important sense, the answer is an unambiguous 'yes'. Emily Dickinson is a good Chalcedonian christologically, convinced of both the full humanity and the full divinity of Jesus. After all, weren't Jesus and God synonyms, just as Miles Standish and John Alden were? 'Synonym' is Emily Dickinson's translation for *homoousios to patri*. Let's try this conclusion (and then see if the poetry will confirm it): in so far as Jesus is fully divine, synonym of God the Father, he is to be as radically rejected and pilloried as God Himself ever was. In so far as Jesus promises a divine redemption he is a false promiser, not in the least sincere, and redemption must be sought from other sources.

But – and here I think we will find that Emily Dickinson's theological anger is not absolute – in so far as Jesus is also fully human, there may be something positive that can be said of him. Not much; but something. This does not mean that Emily Dickinson found faith or God or peace at the end of her pilgrimage, but I do think she found a Jesus that was not quite the intrusive busybody she rejected somewhere around 1850.

Jesus the divine redeemer is rejected. His resurrection is nothing but timidity and flight (see the strange and almost wilful reading of Jesus' resurrection in no. 225). The crucifixion, on its divine side, is part of the phony redemption game and a symbol of utter meaninglessness. But as a human story of a suffering man, it enriches our life. Maybe the human Jesus is a voyeur and a promise-breaker, but there are some important poems (nos. 964, 190, 461, 449, 362) in which Emily Dickinson sees herself as forming a simple friendship with Jesus the man, a friendship that bears some resemblance to the idea of mystical union. If I had to define the place where Emily Dickinson finally may have made some sort of peace with her Christian tradition, the word 'mysticism', even Jesus-mysticism, would be the closest I could come.

Let us see what the evidence for this summary conclusion looks like. We don't need more evidence for her rage against the divine redeemer, but it will be interesting to see how redemption is still needed even when God and Jesus are denied as sources for it. In a striking letter to her friend Susan Gilbert (who later married her brother), Emily Dickinson makes it quite clear that she is willing to live without Jesus, in a world of only human love. She even imagines that she may not make it through the final judgment because of this preference for human over divine love.

Sue – I have lived by this [i.e. I have lived by my human love for you, though I fear I may be losing it]. It is the lingering of the Heaven I once dreamed [human love, being loved, is my substitute for God and otherworldly love], and though if this is taken, I shall remain alone, and though in that last day, the Jesus Christ you love [note her bitterness and jealousy over Sue's conversion] remark he does not know me – there is a darker spirit [in half-confessing her allegiance to the Devil, is she just teasing her devout friend and does she somehow mean it?] will not disown its' child (I, 305–6).

Some years later, when Sue's son dies, Emily Dickinson blames Jesus directly: 'Ineffable Avarice of Jesus, who reminds a perhaps encroaching Father, "and all these are mine" ' (III, 823).[18]

Just because the redeemer cannot be trusted, it doesn't follow that we do not need something like redemption. The fear of death, for example. Even if we cannot take Jesus' resurrection as a promise of victory over death, we are not without resources. The poet herself can do what Jesus is powerless to do – she can turn our faces so powerfully toward our own deaths that our fear is annihilated by her intuition and wisdom.

'Tis so appalling – it exhilarates –
So over Horror, it half Captivates –
The Soul stares after it, secure –
A Sepulchre, fears frost, no more –

To scan a Ghost, is faint –
But grappling, conquers it –
How easy, Torment, now –
Suspense kept sawing so –

The Trust, is Bald, and Cold –
But that will hold –
If any are not sure –
We show them – prayer –
But we, who know,

Stop hoping, now –

Looking at Death, is Dying –
Just let go the Breath –
And not the pillow at your Cheek
So Slumbereth –

Others, Can wrestle –

Your's, is done –
And so of Woe, bleak dreaded – come,
It sets the Fright at liberty –
And Terror's free –
Gay, Ghastly, Holiday!

(no. 281).

In one of Emily Dickinson's great love poems, human love is described as a replacement for Jesus, putting whatever he may have to offer in the shadows. My love for you, she writes, banishes Jesus.

Nor could I rise – with You –
Because Your Face
Would put out Jesus' –
That New Grace

Glow plain – and foreign
On my homesick Eye –
Except that You than He
Shone closer by –

(no. 640, stanzas 6–7).

Emily Dickinson can forget her rage over the Redeemer and see something in Jesus' divinity she can make use of. In the Incarnation, God stooped so low, entered so fully into human flesh, that Jesus became weak like the rest of us. And the poet, in her compassion, helped him in his lowliness. It is as if she is saying: 'If God became truly like us in the Incarnation of the Son, He needs all the help he can get.'

I rose – because He sank –
I thought it would be opposite –
But when his power dropped –
My Soul grew straight.

I cheered my fainting Prince –
I sang firm – even – Chants –
I helped his Film – with Hymn –

And when the Dews drew off
That held his Forehead stiff –
I met him –
Balm to Balm –

I told him Best – must pass
Through this low Arch of Flesh –
No Casque so brave
It spurn the Grave –

I told him Worlds I knew
Where Emperors grew –
Who recollected us
If we were true –

And so with Thews of Hymn –
And Sinew from within –
And ways I knew not that I knew – till then –
I lifted Him –

(no. 616).

If the crucifixion is that point in the drama of redemption where
Jesus' divinity and humanity uniquely intersect, we might expect
some ambivalence from Emily Dickinson about the cross, and that
is just what we do find. The crucifixion is for her, first of all, an
example of the bloodthirsty cruelty of God. We have already seen
in 'Split the Lark' (no. 861) how God rips Jesus' body open to
prove his own divinity. The cross was always a horror to Emily
Dickinson, a gift of the bloody God, the place where Jesus nearly
lost his faith.

That after Horror – that 'twas *us* –
That passed the mouldering Pier –
Just as the Granite Crumb let go –
Our Savior, by a Hair –

A second more, had dropped too deep
For Fisherman to plumb –

The very profile of the Thought
Puts Recollection numb –

The possibility – to pass
Without a Moment's Bell –
Into Conjecture's presence –
Is like a Face of Steel –
That suddenly looks into our's
With a metallic grin –
The Cordiality of Death –
Who drills his Welcome in –

(no. 286).

Cynthia Wolff catches the poem's passion perfectly:

> We have been abandoned by the Father . . . we have been
> exposed to a 'Horror', the bestial blood-lust of a God who
> required the execution of His own blameless Son. We have wit-
> nessed the unspeakable appetite of God the Father . . . We are
> that '*after Horror*'.[19]

The poet's anger over the cross takes a less violent form in a
very late (1884) poem in which Jesus – still on the cross – is
portrayed as auctioning off souls to the highest bidder. The crucifixion as an evangelical Sotheby's.

The Auctioneer of Parting
His 'Going, going, gone'
Shouts even from the Crucifix,
And brings his Hammer down –
He only sells the Wilderness,
The prices of Despair
Range from a single human Heart
To Two – not any more –

(no. 1612).

If 'Four Trees' is about Calvary, it articulates a mood different
from the anger we have so far observed. Here the cross is blank
despair, meaninglessness. The poem has the feel of the opening
scene of *Waiting for Godot*.

Four Trees – upon a solitary Acre –

Why four: Jesus', the two thieves', and – ours?

    Without Design
    Or Order, or Apparent Action –
    Maintain –

The Sun – upon a Morning meets them –

Sometime between nine and twelve, before the darkness at noon.

    The Wind –
    No nearer Neighbor – have they –
    But God –

    The Acre gives them – Place
    They – Him – Attention of Passer By –

'And those who passed by derided him . . .' (Mark 15. 29).

    Of Shadow, or of Squirrel, haply –
    Or Boy –

    What Deed is Theirs unto the General Nature –
    What Plan
    They severally – retard – or further –
    Unknown –   (no. 742).

Yet Emily Dickinson's cross (like the divinity of Jesus itself, of which it is the supreme definition) is more than despair, more than anger, more than the auctioneer's platform. It is also the place where a suffering man hangs. And we, who are also suffering, need that man.

When Jesus tells us about his Father, we distrust him. When he shows us his Home, we turn away, but when he confides to us that he is 'acquainted with Grief', we listen, for that also is an Acquaintance of our own. (III, 837).

I find this hopeful cross in a single poem, the elegantly yearning no. 225.

> Jesus! thy Crucifix
> Enable thee to guess
> The smaller size!
>
> Jesus! thy second face
> Mind thee in Paradise
> Of ours!

'Jesus,' I think she is saying, 'may the form of your death help you understand our deaths, when they arrive. May your "second face" – the face of acceptance, beyond the first face of dereliction – remind us of what might lie beyond despair, beyond anger.'

4

When Emily Dickinson turns to the human Jesus – to the teacher, to the proclaimer of the kingdom of God – she suffers from a curious literalness. Her human Jesus is everything the Gospels say he is; she has no interest in history, context, or interpretation. Her human Jesus is the Jesus of the biblical literalist, and she doesn't trust him at all. He never speaks to her, or answers her: 'I have a King, who does not speak – ' (no. 103). Jesus' main offence, it appears, is that he does not answer her prayers.

> Of course – I prayed –
> And did God care?
> He cared as much as on the Air
> A Bird – had stamped her foot –
> And cried 'Give Me' –
> My Reason – Life –
> I had not had – but for Yourself –
> 'Twere better Charity
>
> To leave me in the Atom's Tomb –
> Merry and Nought, and gay, and numb –
> Than this smart Misery.   (no. 376).

There is a childish petulance to this scolding of Jesus for not granting the poet all she has asked for. No one gets that, not even (especially not) the saints. What is it that she wanted and did not get? We can guess: love, friends, faith, heaven – the presence of God. If earthquake and hurricane damage come from you, Jesus, surely you could spare a moment for little me!

The most striking indictment Emily Dickinson makes of the human Jesus is insincerity. Jesus is a breaker of promises, a liar and a dissembler. Much of this accusation derives from her literalness. She has no sense of the parabolic style, of the kingdom of God as the overturning of normal expectation. In a letter (III, 751) she writes: 'No verse in the Bible has frightened me so much from a Child as "from him that hath not, shall be taken even that he hath".' Now this is to take Jesus' message seriously, but does she have to be so simplistic, so literal? It is strange indeed to see a poet reading the parable in Matthew 25. 14–30 in so unpoetic a way.

Her final indictment of Jesus' eschatology is comic, and intended to be so. She seems to be saying something like this: 'Let me make Jesus' basic message about the kingdom of God as absurd as possible by translating it into Daddy's capitalist language. Then no one can take it seriously.'

> You're right – 'the way is narrow' –
> And 'difficult the Gate' –
> And 'few there be' – Correct again –
> That 'enter in – thereat' –
>
> 'Tis Costly – So are *purples*!
> 'Tis just the price of *Breath* –
> With but the 'Discount' of the *Grave* –
> Termed by the *Brokers* – '*Death*'!
>
> And after *that* – there's Heaven –
> The *Good* Man's '*Dividend*' –
> And *Bad* Men – 'go to Jail' –
> I guess –   (no. 234).

Jesus is not only an insincere promise-breaker, he is much worse. He is intrusive, voyeur, violent, a bridegroom who rapes and does not woo the bride-soul. Even before he gets to the bedroom, this Jesus is a peeping Tom.

> Just so – Jesus – raps –   [Revelation 3. 20]
> He – doesn't weary –
> Last – at the Knocker –
> And first – at the Bell.
> Then – on divinist tiptoe – standing –
> Might He but spy the lady's soul –
> When He – retires –
> Chilled – or weary –
> It will be ample time for – me –
> Patient – upon the steps – *until* then –
> Heart! I am knocking – low at thee
>
> (no. 317).

Emily Dickinson's Jesus-bridegroom has more in mind than the pleasures of the eye. He 'takes' the soul, and surely with less than her consent.

> She lay as if at play
> Her life had leaped away –
> Intending to return –
> But not so soon –
>
> Her merry Arms, half dropt –
> As if for lull of sport –
> An instant had forgot –
> The Trick to start –
>
> Her dancing Eyes – ajar –
> As if their Owner were
> Still sparkling through
> For fun – at you –
>
> Her Morning at the door –
> Devising, I am sure –
> To force her sleep –
> So light – so deep   (no. 369).

The theme of forgiveness unexpectedly enters one of the Jesus-rapist poems. Here the poet tries to resist Jesus' aggression. She seems to succeed spiritually while being overpowered physically. While Jesus attacks, she asks him for forgiveness, and the request is ignored. Spiritual strength and physical weakness. The poet wins; the seducer is successful and is rewarded with the poet's contempt.

> He strained my faith –
> Did he find it supple?
> Shook my strong trust –
> Did it then – yield?
>
> Hurled my belief –
> But – did he shatter – it?
> Racked – with suspense –
> Not a nerve failed!
>
> Wrung me – with Anguish –
> But I never doubted him –
> 'Tho' for what wrong
> He did never say –
>
> Stabbed – while I sued
> His sweet forgiveness –
> Jesus – it's your little 'John'!
> Don't you know – me?

(no. 497).

In another forgiveness lyric, there is no sign of the seducer-Jesus. The poet, after she finally understands whom she is addressing, treats Jesus this time as a friend, an equal. There is no proud refusal of his forgiveness, but a simple pattern or repentance and forgiveness, asked for and quietly received.

> 'Unto Me? I do not know you –
> Where may be your House?'
>
> 'I am Jesus – Late of Judea –
> Now – of Paradise – '

Wagons – have you – to convey me?
This is far from Thence –

'Arms of Mine – sufficient Phaeton –
Trust Omnipotence – '

I am spotted – 'I am Pardon – '
I am small – 'The Least
Is esteemed in Heaven the Chiefest –
Occupy my House – '

(no. 964).

5

I wish to bring this study of Emily Dickinson's Jesus to a close by looking at three poems where Jesus is not the enemy but the friend. Her ambivalence about both the human and the divine Jesus has been there, wherever we have turned. Her rage against God turned into rage against the divinity of Jesus, but there was that divine humiliation in the Incarnation she could not reject. We observed her portrait of the crucifixion as a piece of divine blood-thirstiness, yet on that bloody cross was more than a vicious God; there was a suffering man about to die who could help us in our own suffering and dying. The human Jesus was a promise-breaker, a liar, and an intruder. Yet this deceiver has a gracious side, and Emily Dickinson is nowhere more moving when she speaks simply about the Jesus she does not reject. Here is a dialogue taking place in heaven (too free of anger for earth?).

I died for Beauty – but was scarce
Adjusted in the Tomb
When One who died for Truth, was lain
In an adjoining Room –

He questioned softly 'Why I failed?'
'For Beauty,' I replied –
'And I – for Truth – Themself are One –
We Brethren, are,' He said –

> And so, as kinsmen, met a Night –
> We talked between the Rooms –
> Until the Moss had reached our lips –
> And covered up – our names –   (no. 449).

This seems to be a joyous meeting, until we come to the last two lines with their vision of obliteration in which the union of the poet and Jesus, achieved for a brief moment, passes into nothingness.

Oddly enough, the two most powerful expressions of the poet's positive relation to Jesus are set forth in the same erotic language with which she had so passionately proclaimed her resistance and rejection. Here is a lyric of pure bridegroom-mysticism. Violence and hatred have disappeared, and all is peace. This 'journey' will remind the reader of St John of the Cross's 'On a Dark Night', though here the roles are reversed: in John's poem Jesus waits in bed for the soul's ascent. Here the poet waits while the Saviour approaches, and the maid becomes the wife.

> A Wife – at Daybreak I shall be –
> Sunrises – Hast thou a Flag for me?
> At Midnight, I am but a Maid,
> How short it takes to make a Bride –
> Then – Midnight, I have passed from thee
> Unto the East, and Victory –
>
> Midnight – Good Night! I hear them call,
> The Angels bustle in the Hall –
> Softly my Future climbs the Stair,
> I fumble at my Childhood's prayer
> So soon to be a Child no more –
> Eternity, I'm coming – Sir,
> Saviour – I've seen the face before!   (no. 461).

Shall we bring Emily Dickinson and Jesus together at the close of her life? Did the young woman's rejection of Jesus in 1850 turn into something like faith? Does she finally find a Jesus to be trusted amidst all the Christian wreckage? Does the furious Puritan finally become a mystic, united with Jesus as comrade and friend? Perhaps, and as 'most of us are half in love with this girl' anyhow, we wish her all the relief she deserves from her torments.

But I don't think things are quite that simple. True, she clearly both hated and loved Jesus, and in this mixture of hatred and love her final, serious Christian commitment rested. Beyond God the enemy was Jesus the enemy – and friend. His presence was always both destructive and healing. Perhaps, when all is said and done, Jesus served Emily Dickinson best when he was absent. My favourite of her poems is the one I wish to conclude with. I think it is about the poet and Jesus. I know it is passionate, sexual, and very sad. The Jesus she finally learned to love – must leave her.

> He was weak, and I was strong – then –
> So He let me lead him in –
> I was weak, and He was strong then –
> So I let him lead me – Home.
>
> 'Twasn't far – the door was near –
> 'Twasn't dark – for He went – too –
> 'Twasn't loud, for He said nought –
> That was all I cared to know.
>
> Day knocked – and we must part –
> Neither – was strongest –
> He strove – and I strove – too –
> We didn't do it – tho'!   (no. 190).

After the death of God, there remains some kind of gentle and suffering Jesus who does not participate in the cruelty of God. But he is not present; he is absent, inaccessible.[20] After all,

> Parting is all we know of heaven,
> And all we need of hell.

The perfect, definitive Dickinsonian christological confession.

V

Novelists, Journalists, Playwrights and Others

But I'd go further and ask an even more provocative question:
What was the true nature of Christ's words? Were they the
beginning of an era of salvation and among the most powerful
cultural impulses in the history of the world – or were they
the spiritual source of the crusades, inquisitions, the cultural
extermination of the American Indians, and, later, the entire
expansion of the white race that was fraught with so many
contradictions and had so many tragic consequences, including
the fact that most of the human world has been consigned to
that wretched category known as the 'Third World'? I still tend
to think that His words belonged to the former category, but at
the same time I cannot ignore the mountain of books which
demonstrate that, even in its purest and earliest form, there was
something unconsciously encoded in Christianity which, when
combined with a thousand other circumstances, including the
relative permanence of human nature, could in some way pave
the way spiritually, even for the sort of horrors I mentioned.

(Václav Havel, 'A Word About Words', in *Open Letters*, New York
1991, 382).

I have already said that I am using 'poet' in a very broad sense
here, to cover almost anyone writing fictions (including fictionalized lives) about Jesus, even when they may not be fully aware
that they are doing fiction: poets proper, novelists both popular
and distinguished, imaginative biographers, journalists, advertising
men, and even Protestant professors and Islamic physicians using

the fictional mode. All of my prose fictions lie somewhere along the line between 'novel' and 'life of Jesus': some are purely novels, many are mixtures of both.

And the motives of my poets? (I can't remember whether I'm allowed to ask about authors' motives today). They vary as widely as the forms. For example:

– writing a best seller, with the hope that there is a solid market out there in popular piety ready to receive it: Lloyd Douglas (novel); Emil Ludwig, Fulton Oursler, Jim Bishop (lives, more or less); Sholem Asch (mixture of novel and life).

– defending an assured orthodoxy or belief system: Dorothy Sayers and Elizabeth Goudge (Anglicanism); Shusaku Endo and François Mauriac (very Catholic lives); Gerd Theissen (twentieth-century Protestantism); M. Kamel Hussein (Sunni Muslim); Joseph Girzone (devout Roman Catholic self-criticism).

– defending a heterodoxy: D. H. Lawrence and Nikos Kazantzakis, who adopt some of the conventions of the apocryphal gospel: What if Jesus didn't really die on the cross, or, What kind of sex-life might Jesus have enjoyed?

– just having fun (often including tweaking the noses of the pious): Robert Graves, Anthony Burgess, Romulus Linney, Gore Vidal.

– defending American capitalism: Bruce Barton; or socialism: Upton Sinclair.

– simple literary delight: George Moore, and Per Lagerkvist, who both use the device of the minor New Testament character as narrator; and the poets proper, whose work seems to me more purely literary (and playful) than theological or interpretative.

– or finally, I wonder about a motive that interests me: the use of a fictional form not to express but to discover an attitude to Jesus of Nazareth; fiction as the author's self-discovery.

Some questions will be popping up along the way. Why shouldn't we read all of the writings about Jesus, from the Gospels to Anthony Burgess, as fictions? Or, why is the result so depressingly bad when a great novelist does Jesus: William Faulkner, D. H. Lawrence?

1. Jesus fictions when Jesus is off-stage

> M. Kamel Hussein, *City of Wrong; A Friday in Jerusalem*, New
> York 1966 (originally published 1959).
>   Gerd Theissen, *The Shadow of the Galilean*, London and
> Philadelphia 1987.

These are both novels, strikingly alike and strikingly different. Dr
Hussein is an Egyptian scholar and surgeon, writing in Arabic, a
believing Sunni Muslim. His fiction entails a set of imaginary events
taking place on Good Friday in Jerusalem. It is a sympathetic and
successful Islamic interpretation of both Judaism and Christianity,
and a study of how the three great high religions of the West are
inter-related. It is an interpretation that will both fascinate and
displease Jews, Christians, and Muslims, a novel, written by a non-
novelist, declaring his religious position, in which Jesus himself
does not appear.

The previous sentence can also be said of Professor Theissen's
enchanting fiction. He is Professor of New Testament at the University of Heidelberg, and his special interest is in the psychological
and sociological background of the New Testament. His book does
two things: it presents what the author considers to be the current
state of New Testament research in narrative form, on the plausible
principle that stories are easier to take than monographs; and it
uses the device of the absent or off-stage Jesus to present a portrait
that might be of use to a modern Christian. Hussein gives us a
Muslim Jesus, Theissen a Protestant (and very Green) one. Theissen
sticks pretty close to what he takes to be historically probable
events, while Hussein's narrative is nearly all imaginative embroid-
ery, with only a historical cross and a historical man who
(probably) hung there.

City of Wrong, primarily a study of both Islam and Christianity,
contains an unusual interpretation of the Jew and of Jewish
religion. The author makes two non-historical presuppositions (it
does not matter whether he knows them to be non-historical – he
probably does): that the Jews alone crucified Jesus and that Jesus'
offence was that he brought a new religion into being. These
presuppositions must not be dismissed as simply one more piece

of Muslim antisemitism. The city that 'did' the crucifying and the religious leaders that sponsored it were not only Jewish: they were all of us. All of our cities, Christian, Islamic, Jewish, are cities of wrong; we are all against the good and the new. 'Jews' are all of us, the weakness and folly of all good men and women. To say 'we are all Jews' therefore means that we are all timid traitors against the good, and also that Muslims and Christians are bound to one another by virtue of their special bond to the faith of Israel.

This interpretation of the Jew becomes especially vivid when we examine Dr Hussein's portraits of two figures of the passion week: the Jewish prosecutor and Caiaphas. The prosecutor, the one chiefly responsible for the ecclesiastical condemnation, is deeply drawn to the teaching of Jesus. For him, the God of the Jews is terrible, while the God of Jesus is love. 'They [i.e. "we"] will kill him because he has committed the crime of saying that God is love' (15).

The high priest Caiaphas is also fascinated by Jesus' teaching. What he most likes is the eschatological message about the kingdom of God. Why? Because Jesus' consistent other-worldliness solves a human problem that had always troubled him: namely, how are they to be rewarded whose virtues (of patience, humble suffering, sacrifice) are always unknown, unseen, private? Jesus' teaching provides Caiaphas with an answer. He praises the Jesus whose condemnation he consented to. This new prophet, he declares,

> apparently wanted to set conscience above religious practice. But religious people would destroy him ... He wanted to raise insignificant people to the same level as their superiors ... He wanted love for humanity to take precedence over pride of nation and race (51).

To these Jewish leaders, it seems, Jesus is almost too good, too wise to survive in an evil world. These leaders are not so much evil plotters but tired executors of worldly wisdom. It is really the mob that most desires the death of Jesus. This is how Dr Hussein deals with the issue of responsibility for that death.

The throngs made their way to the palace of the Roman governor to demand the blood of the teacher and his disciples [note this last phrase as an example of how Dr Hussein will embroider the biblical record from time to time]. Yet there was not one among them who knew any evil about him, none who sought his death out of belief or personal conviction. Thus was accomplished the greatest of the crimes of history, the crime of the condemnation of Christ to crucifixion as one who had denied God, without anybody in Jerusalem knowing who it was who wanted his death nor upon whom the guilt of this foul deed really fell (67).

This passage marks the intellectual centre of *City of Wrong*. Dr Hussein is not much interested in the traditional Islamic denial of the crucifixion of Jesus and the idea of the substitute victim. Here he is on the relevant Quranic text.

No cultured Muslim believes in this nowadays. The text is taken [properly so, he implies] to mean that the Jews thought they killed Christ but God raised him unto Him in a way we can leave unexplained . . . (222).

'God raised him unto Him': this is the author's interpretation of the doctrine of the substitute. It might remind a Christian reader of Bultmann on the resurrection: Christ is raised in the hearts of the disciples. But the Islamic 'raising' is not a redemption or a salvation but an attempt to shift attention away from the dead body to the living teaching of the man Jesus. For Dr Hussein, the Christian is one who denies the finality of the death of Jesus by living out the life and teaching. The Christian is one who takes the Sermon on the Mount seriously. That is his function in the world of religions. If for Bultmann the resurrection is the rise of faith, for Hussein it is the rise of work or action, and here he comes close to the radical vision of Leo Tolstoy. God is not vengeance but love, and love, non-violence, the significance of the poor, the demand to live by conscience alone – these make up the witness of Christians. Because the crucifixion was the murder of conscience it was 'the supreme tragedy of humanity' (4).[1]

Such an individualist and moralistic reading of Christianity implies that it has both great strength and fatal weaknesses. Two parts of the novel illustrate this. The first scene is an extended discussion among Jesus' disciples, after the arrest and trial, about the wisdom of trying to affect his escape from detention. The arguments for his release are taken seriously, but the disciples finally and reluctantly decide that Jesus' unambiguous teaching against violence means that they must take no forceful action to effect their master's freedom. This failure of the disciples, the author insists, is the 'crucial event in Christianity' (224), shaping the psychology of the Christian from that day to this. He believes that the obsessive preoccupation with sin and guilt in the Christian tradition comes from this principled but deeply mistaken refusal to rescue Jesus. In a passage of great psychological discernment, Dr Hussein explains his understanding of the disciples' failure:

> The summons to positive action [i.e,. to free Jesus from imprison-ment by the use of force] is always easier for the advocate than the summons to reflection, even if, at the hour of actual trans-lation into fulfilment, the former is more difficult. The call to abstain from action is harder to advocate but easier to obey. A positive line of action makes the spirit more assured: and brings a psychological satisfaction which controversy only intensifies. For this reason such a policy is easier and more satisfying both for him who sponsors it and for those he calls upon to follow it. The negative or inactive approach, however, puts its advocate into a position where he is suspect (111).

A second incident in the novel further illustrates Dr Hussein's compassionate Muslim critique of Christianity. A Roman soldier becomes a secret follower of Jesus. His battalion decided to take over a Jewish village mainly to demonstrate its military prowess. The village is surrounded by the Romans, but apparently there is a secret opening in the wall through which supplies are being delivered and which, therefore, renders the Roman siege ineffective. The Roman soldier accidentally discovers this secret entrance, but instead of reporting it to his superiors (and thus assuring the village's fall and a Roman victory), he chooses instead to return a wounded Jewish defender to his own people. He felt obliged to save a human life even if it meant depriving his battalion of success. The soldier is tried, convicted, and brutally killed for the treason which his faith had mandated. Again, the Christian faith looks loving, decent, but also weak, wrong, and even dangerous when confronted by occasions when force is necessary. This is the basis of Dr Hussein's conviction that Islam is better suited than Christianity to the ordinary life of natural man in society.

City of Wrong is, in fictional form, a sophisticated Muslim reading of Western religion and psychology. More than just a Muslim reflection of Christianity's strengths and weaknesses, it is a fictional essay in intellectual history that offers a unique interpretation of the relationship between Judaism, Islam and Christianity, and a serious claim that of the three great religions of the West, Islam is best able to hold together the three essential dimensions of the spiritual life: physical vitality, reason and conscience.

Apart from his critical New Testament work, Professor Gerd Theissen of Heidelberg has recently written two general theological books: *On Having a Critical Faith*, London and Philadelphia 1979, and *Biblical Faith: An Evolutionary Approach*, London and Philadelphia 1985. In these works he sets out the christological position that forms the background of his narrative or novel, *The Shadow of the Galilean*, London and Philadelphia 1987. Let us look briefly at this christological background.

In the earlier book, Professor Theissen asks what are the reasons for being a Christian today, even as he admits that Christianity itself is historically conditioned. He begins his answer by setting forth his position on the traditional problem of the historical Jesus.

1. Even though we cannot say what is historical and what is not, the text of the Gospels gives us a picture of Jesus (history or kerygma, it doesn't matter) that carries a truth that can change human life. Here, Theissen seems to finesse the whole problem of historical scepticism, and to end up with a position very much like that of Paul Tillich, who, at the end of his life, declared that the only historical entity he required for faith was the historical existence of the text of Mark's Gospel.

2. Further, Theissen argues that Jesus and the 'christological poetry' he inspired are irrevocably connected to the apocalyptic tradition of first-century Judaism. Unlike Schweitzer, Theissen does not conclude from this apocalyptic presupposition that we cannot use the Gospel portrait of Jesus as a basis for faith. What he makes

of the apocalyptic matrix is the fact that Jesus met needs in his own century. He may also do so in ours. Faith need not, should not, be wholly grounded in historical fact. Thus Theissen in *On Having a Critical Faith*.

So it is not the historically inaccessible Jesus that defines the Christian's faith, but rather the 'christological poetry' and symbolism Jesus generated. That poetry is validated because it illuminates for the believer a series of religious and human needs: it provides a way to express the natural sense of wonder or the holy; it illuminates our understanding and need of love. That is, Jesus' human love defines ours. This christological poetry finally places us under a profound moral obligation. Jesus himself (Jesus in the Gospels' texts, not 'as he really was', remember) spoke against the use of force, the inflicting of suffering, inhumanity and insensitivity to others. Christians are bound to that same protest.[2]

Professor Theissen argues that a decision for Christianity is a decision to follow this Jesus in these senses. It is not the only truth, but it is the necessary Christian truth.

> ... we have to reject those elements in the New Testament which limit resonance [his own word for the human experiences of awe, wonder, transcendence] and love, e.g. all the beginnings of discrimination against other people on the grounds of ethical and religious measures, no matter whether these are Gentiles, Jews, heretics, other believers, homosexuals or women (93).

We do not need to find the historical Jesus. The demands of resonance and love enable us to see in the Gospel record a figure to follow and a principle by which the inauthentic and false in both scripture and tradition can be rejected. This figure represents a truth from which Christians cannot withdraw.

In his 1984 *Biblical Faith*, Gerd Theissen seems to depart from the insouciance he displayed about the historical Jesus in the earlier book. He now reflects a more conventional post-Bultmannian optimism about what we can know about the Jesus of history. He has moved from Paul Tillich's Kierkegaardian carelessness about history to the modest historical confidence of a Bornkamm or a

Dodd. In this book, we seem to have enough historical Jesus to base a working christology on: we have Jesus the prophet, the teacher, the poet and the martyr. *Biblical Faith* ends up with the same ethically sensitive obedience to Jesus as the earlier book, but the conceptual journey to that end is a little different.

Jesus was a prophet, but in the apocalyptic mode. Salvation is coming through the Son of Man, and there is still time for repentance. Jesus as teacher speaks to this repentance time; the ethic is a guide to repentance. Love for God and man is the content of Jesus' message, but his love delivers an astonishing freedom. The family is relativized, the disciples' longing for power is repudiated, the last shall be first, and tradition is both radicalized and relativized, as in Matthew 5. The poetry of Jesus lies in the parables, and they are stories about prevenient grace.

So far, Theissen's *Biblical Faith* sticks pretty close to European post-Bultmannian orthodoxy: what we know for sure about Jesus was that he was a prophet of eschatological renewal who had good things to say about love and grace. Indeed, his theology was remarkably like ours.

We can construct a bridge between the two theological essays and the 1986 novel (or 'narrative exegesis', to use his rather academic label for what he does), and the bridge comes in his discussion of the fourth trait of the historical Jesus – what he calls Jesus as martyr. He does not mean martyr in the technical sense: he does not imply, for example, that Jesus – like Socrates – deliberately chose to die. The cry of dereliction would then make no sense. But he does mean that Jesus, at least toward the close of his brief career, did willingly enter into the conflicts of Palestinian society, conflicts that finally destroyed him. These conflicts are the main subject of his novel. 'Martyr' is Theissen's word for the political Jesus, the Jesus dangerous enough to deserve capital punishment at Roman hands. Apocalyptic grace and love would have gotten him into no trouble at all.

Theissen's martyr Jesus was in partial sympathy with the Zealots. (I think that this affirmation is one that Theissen believes is justified by the historical evidence). Which is to say that God must finally rule where Romans now rule. The only difference between Jesus and the Zealots is that the Zealots believed that violent human action would be necessary, while Jesus believed the Romans would be destroyed by God's direct action. The martyr dies (quite properly, and not by a perversion of Roman justice) because he made it all too clear that the emerging kingdom of God meant the end of Roman rule and Roman values. The martyr dies because his polemic against the rich (and blessings upon the poor and the sinners) threatened both the secular and religious authorities. And finally, the martyr dies because his clear words directed against the Temple are rightly seen as a declaration of war against the priestly-Roman concordat that maintained an uneasy peace in the troubled land. The poetic teacher of grace and love (whom no one would think of killing) dies because he dared to define, to exacerbate, and to defy the tensions unlying the unstable Palestinian peace.

These are the christological reflections with which Gerd Theissen comes to his 'novel'. Two conventions shape *The Shadow of the Galilean*. Each chapter in the novel is preceded by a letter from the author to an older academic mentor, and this device permits him to deal explicitly with the methodological problems in his venture. The novel itself is narrated in the first person by a young well-to-do Jewish grain merchant who is in effect on a spiritual pilgrimage through all the religious and political options of his time.

I have already drawn attention to the apparent contradiction between Theissen's untroubled historical scepticism in *On Having a Critical Faith* and the traditional post-Bultmannian optimism of *Biblical Faith*. He continues to deal with these issues in the novel, and in one of the letters to his (fictitious) mentor he assures him that he makes up nothing concerning Jesus in the book, that his imaginative touches apply only to other characters and to background events. The tension we thought we found between the two earlier christological essays may be resolved in a strange and somewhat turgid remark to the professor.

The chance distribution of remains and sources about Pilate convince us that Pilate lived. What the Gospels write about him does not contradict the other sources, but cannot be derived from them. In the case of Pilate there is no doubt that the Gospels have a 'historical background' ... In that case should we not conclude by analogy that the Jesus traditions contained in the

Gospels also have an historical background? That does not mean that they are identical with historical truth (66).

Very well, if that is what Theissen means by historical, then both his scepticism and his non-scepticism can be true. 'Historical' apparently means 'possessing a historical basis'. Which is to say that we probably know something about Jesus, but we're not sure what. (Did Theissen get this from his English translator, or vice versa?) Yet Theissen can be refreshingly straightforward about what we 'know' of Jesus.

Do these sources really tell us nothing of significance? They say that in all probability Jesus was not a member of the upper classes and that it was not 'the Jews' but a Roman official who was responsible for his execution (74).

The Shadow of the Galilean does not have the literary sophistication of *City of Wrong*. The characters tend to be exemplary of points of view, and somewhat wooden. But the book is a fine one, beautifully written with both clarity and intellectual passion (traits not often found together in theological professors!).

Andreas, the first-person narrator, is a wealthy young grain merchant with friends all over Palestine. He is arrested as an innocent bystander in an attack by some Roman soldiers on a Zealot demonstration in which his friend Barabbas took part. Andreas is imprisoned, but Pilate offers to release him if he will consent to become an unpaid informant for him, studying the various religious groups in the land to determine which might be dangerous to the social *status quo*. Andreas' various visits, and his reports back to Jerusalem, become the means by which Theissen presents the current state of research on the religious background of first-century Palestine.

Andreas first attempts to visit an Essene community. He is not admitted, but he does meet a young man, Baruch, who has just been ostracized from the Essenes, and he gets some important information from him. He reports back to Pilate that the Essenes are safely other-worldly, but he does not mention that they profoundly detest the Roman occupation.

He has another friend in the service of Herod Antipas, and

through him we hear about the murder of John the Baptist. Andreas begins to pick up pieces of information about Jesus' ministry, and he is attracted by the anti-legalism it appears to contain. Theissen makes it perfectly clear that the New Testament portrait of the Pharisees is a distorted and tendentious caricature; the Jesus that Andreas begins to be drawn to is not anti-Pharisee, but anti-legalist.

The intellectual and emotional centre of the novel and of Andreas' search is the encounter with the Zealots. Andreas is asked by his Roman employers to determine whether Jesus is a security risk. This means, in effect, that he must determine Jesus' precise relation to the Zealot movement. Andreas is an old friend of Barabbas, a Zealot leader, and the novel contains several discussions between the friends. Both Andreas and Barabbas agree that the land belongs to God, not to Rome, but Andreas is not sure that he believes in violence.

Andreas clearly understands the political implications of Jesus' attack on the Temple, for the Temple is a symbol of the priestly support of the Roman occupation. He is also aware that Jesus' teaching about the kingdom of God is political and anti-Roman in its deepest meaning. So in his report back to Jerusalem he talks mostly about Jesus as philosopher and poet, but not as an apocalyptic prophet. Andreas knows, but does not report, that 'Jesus attacked state rule as oppression and exploitation' (132).

Andreas becomes involved in the events he is commissioned to report on. Here is his description of his own religious struggle, just before Jesus' death.

> Could Jesus solve my problems, problems which all arose out of the prejudices and tensions between Jews and Gentiles? Didn't I live in a no man's land on the frontier? Somewhere between Pilate and Barabbas? Between Gentiles and Jews? In this frontier area I had found myself in humiliating dependence on the Romans. And wasn't it precisely the point at which Jesus encountered me – as a free man who remained faithful to himself and his people (140).

It is reasonable to assume that Theissen is presenting something of his own struggle in his portrait of Andreas. How could Andreas not be tempted to the Zealot belief in the use of force to overcome injustice and tyranny? How could any twentieth-century Christian – especially, we might add, a politically sensitive German – not acknowledge that evil does not always succumb to prayer and fasting? Theissen is simply setting forth, through Andreas, one of the classic dilemmas of the Christian today. How can we take Jesus seriously and still deal effectively with the entrenched evil in our world? There is an eloquent passage in one of the author's final letters to his mentor that speaks to this problem of the 'relevence of an impossible ethical ideal'.

> I have come to the conclusion that these demands [i.e. the Sermon on the Mount] should indirectly determine our political action. A society should be run in such a way that the experiment of radical discipleship is possible. A society only becomes human . . . when it allows a demonstration of love of one's enemies. It is only human if it contains outsiders who can exist without cares. Political action cannot use the Sermon on the Mount directly as a criterion, but it can provide conditions in which individuals and groups can use it as a criterion by which to take their bearings (164).

In another letter, Theissen expresses his own interests in such a way that we know how Andreas' pilgrimage will end. Why, Theissen asks, do our great modern theologians care so little for Jesus of Nazareth? Partly, he admits, because of the difficulty (which he faces with candour in his own work) of establishing a credible portrait. But it may also be that these theologians know that as soon as one admits a historical Jesus into one's discourse 'one admits a proclamation aimed at changes not only in the church but also throughout society' (95). Theissen's final Jesus is fully apocalyptic, radical and political.

The same will be the case for Andreas' Jesus. After Jesus' arrest, along with the arrest of three Zealots, including his friend Barabbas, Andreas tries to persuade Pilate to manifest his political sophistication and personal security by using the power of amnesty. Pilate thinks this is a fine idea, and he decides to free Barabbas, not Jesus. Jesus is killed, and Rome is primarily responsible. The Romans knew he was almost certainly harmless, but they loved order more than justice.

Andreas is in despair after the crucifixion, and he partly blames himself. He meets his old friend, the ex-Essene Baruch, who has just joined the emerging Christian movement. He also hears from Barabbas, who thanks him for his role in effecting his release. Somehow, Andreas feels, there must be room for both Baruch and Barabbas, both Jesus and the Zealots, both eschatology and politics. Andreas' despair begins to break apart when he reflects on Jesus' 'words':

> for I was hungry and you gave me food,
> I was thirsty and you gave me drink,
> I was a stranger and you welcomed me,
> I was naked and you clothed me,
> I was sick and you visited me,
> I was in prison and you came to see me.

If Andreas does come to Christianity, it will be through the gate marked Matthew 25. 31–46. We may assume that Theissen has already walked through that gate. It is as good a gate as there is.

It is not hard to see what Dr Hussein and Professor Theissen were up to in their fictions. Hussein offers a careful, fictionalized study of Good Friday, a profound Islamic interpretation of the Jewish faith, Jesus' teaching, Christianity and Christians. Theissen sends his narrator through the religious and political options available to a sensitive first-century Jew, and concludes that political responsibility and radical discipleship were both possible in the first century – and are so in ours.

2. *Journalists and other amateurs on Jesus*

The excellence of the novels of Dr Hussein and Professor Theissen should not blind us to the sad fact that some of our twentieth-century fictions about Jesus will turn out to be mediocre or worse. I wish to look at this soft underbelly of the fictionalized Jesus in our time. My first five titles can be subsumed under the category of 'The Americanization of Jesus'.

Advertising copywriters generally write well, but they have

nothing to say. They write neither to enlighten nor entertain, but to persuade the reader to undertake some form of economic activity. America's greatest advertising man, Bruce Barton, wrote a book about Jesus which he called *The Man Nobody Knows* (Indianapolis 1925). Nobody, that is, until he told us.

The book is not designed to sell Jesus, but to persuade us that American capitalism between World War I and the great depression was both worthy and biblical. Jesus, our justification – in a sense Paul never dreamed.

We need not be self-righteous about a book about Jesus as the first capitalist. If Jesus could be a community organizer in the 1960s and an anti-Roman agitator in the 1980s, why not a businessman in the 1920s? Barton's little book is important in itself, and it also helps us to understand the persistence of the tradition of Christianity as a gospel of success.

Barton says very little about Jesus' message. He is entirely taken up with his method. He doesn't care much for theology, and he is sometimes half-right in his suspicions.

> Theology has spoiled the thrill of his life by assuming that he knew everything from the beginning – that his three years of public work were a kind of dress rehearsal . . . (8).

Theology can often be uneasy with Jesus' full humanity. When Barton does talk about the message, it comes out as all joy and merriment. The disciples missed the point. They wanted an anti-Roman leader, but all Jesus wanted was a happy God who wanted his children to be as happy as he was.

Barton's Jesus boils down to four things: the executive, the outdoorsman, the sociable man, and – of course – 'the founder of modern business'.

By 'executive', Barton meant three things all certified by the Gospel record: his blazing conviction, his unending patience ('I came to cast fire on the earth . . .') and his wonderful skill in choosing subordinates (eleven out of twelve is not bad for Madison Avenue).

By outdoorsman, Barton does not try to get a hunter or a fisherman out of the record (but couldn't he have used 'fishers of men'?), but he does tell us that Jesus was powerfully built and muscular. All those hours in the carpentry shop. By 'sociable' Barton seems to mean fun at parties, and he jumps eagerly on the miracle at Cana and the saying about winebibber and glutton.

The central theme of *The Man Nobody Knows* is the author's interesting portrait of Jesus as the founder of modern business. This portrait has several facets. For example. Every good salesman knows the value of sensing a customer's objection and meeting it before it is advanced. Jesus was a master of this technique, and the evidence is the account in Luke 7. 36–50 of the prostitute at the house of Simon the Pharisee, where Jesus mysteriously discerns Simon's moralistic protest before it was spoken.

Most of all, Barton loves the parables. Every advertising man should study these advertisements for the Kingdom. They are everything an ad should be: condensed, simple, sincere (maybe ads *were* sincere in Barton's day), and repetitive. After all, Jesus saw his mission as business, not preaching, for did he not remind his mother that he must be about his father's business?

I'm inclined to think that the only really meretricious argument Barton uses in his portrait of the first businessman is what he says about service. Whoever would be greatest must be the servant of all. Of course, every business knows that.

> You will hear that discovery proclaimed in every sales convention as something distinctly modern and up to date. It is emblazoned in the advertising pages of every magazine (164).

Corporations don't boast of their wealth or size, they boast only of their service, their willingness to meet all their customers' needs.

> Manufacturers of building equipment, of clothes, of food; presidents of railroads and steamship companies; the heads of banks and investment houses – *all* of them tell the same story. 'Service is what we are here for', they exclaim. They call it the 'spirit of modern business'; they suppose, most of them, that it is something very new. But Jesus preached it more than nineteen hundred years ago (165–6).

When you are trying, consciously or otherwise, to get Jesus on your side, you must learn to exclude as well as include. Barton is no exception. Nothing about the rich young man and the kingdom of God. No Magnificat, of course, and, more cripplingly, no Passion Week. Jesus' suffering and death have always mixed uneasily with the gospel of success. Barton manfully faces his silence about the cross. It is a familiar story, he reminds us, and there is no pressing need to go over it again. The passion according to Barton is finally a parable about how to face up to failure. Everyone deserts Jesus (and, he properly reminds us, this is likely to happen to anyone who believes something passionately): his home town and family, and finally the crowds and disciples. Jesus faced this ultimate failure with an example of courageous manhood all of us should heed. He never gave up. The final words of Barton's book are not about the resurrection but about the authority shown even by the dying Jesus.

> But he, when his enemies had done their worst, so bore himself that a crucified felon looked into his dying eyes and saluted him as king (220).

Upton Sinclair, socialist, muck-raker, critic of capitalism, novelist – the perfect opposite number to Bruce Barton. His Jesus book is just as interesting as Barton's and more ambitious. He calls it *A Personal Jesus: Portrait and Interpretation* (New York and Philadelphia 1952). It is a mixture of conscious fiction and conscious non-fiction: Jesus up to the age of thirty, all fiction; Jesus' ministry, Sinclair on the Gospels' 'inner truth'; and a final section in Sinclair's best liberal Episcopalian muck-raking style on Jesus' influence.

The fictionalized childhood section is able and uneventful, except for the author's suggestion that Jesus may have been a hunchback (he got this from Josephus). Otherwise, the child was kind, wise, and very religious. Here is Sinclair on the ministry:

> The worst that could be said about him was that while he preached love, he sometimes became irritated and used bitter language; that, and the fact that he disregarded the Sabbath, so important to the Jews. He had the worship and the love of God guiding him and determining the whole of his life. He had no other idea and no other interest; nothing was important, compared with the wonder and righteousness of God, whom he

referred to as his 'Heavenly Father'. God had created this world in six days, and He might destroy it all in six seconds, and the only thing of consequence was that you should believe in Him, honour Him, obey Him, in order that in the Day of Judgment you would be among those who were selected for immortality in His eternal dwelling place (79).

A solid liberal reading of the message: no kingdom talk, no restoration of Israel. Individualistic and full of love, but not entirely ignorant of Jesus' eschatological centre, however imperfectly it may be construed.

Sinclair has no trouble at all with the healing miracles, because he is a follower of the work of that 'friendly little gentleman' Emil Coué, who persuaded millions of Americans early in this century to believe: 'Day by day in every way I am getting better and better.'

He is thoughtful on the messiahship. Jesus may not have believed himself to be the messiah; perhaps others imposed the title on him; perhaps it was a secret he wanted to withhold. Here is his demythologized and modernized Jesus.

> I am convinced he was a man, and that he did not know what was going to happen to Him; but he knew that he was in danger, he knew that he had come … to Jerusalem to challenge the powerful ones of the earth who both hated and feared him. He had come because a voice in his soul which he took to be God told him to come. We all have that voice in our souls, and whether we call it God or whether we call it conscience makes little difference (24).

This is good journalism and good preaching. His Jesus is apart from the church, and probably apart from God, miracle-worker and proclaimer of love. Not even the resurrection appearances trouble Sinclair's generous liberal spirit, for he is a disciple, not only of Coué, but of Sir Oliver Lodge!

Upton Sinclair, writing at the end of a splendidly trouble-making career during the anti-Communist cold war time in America, presents his answer to Communism: a socialist Jesus, God defined as conscience, the radical love-ethic in the best liberal Protestantism tradition, a firm belief in psychical phenomena – all together affirming that Jesus is productively alive today. A vivid portrait from one of America's most interesting popular writers in the first half of the century. (Incidentally, Sinclair is the only one in our large cast of characters who qualifies in more than one event. See below, pp. 263f., for a note on his earlier Jesus-novel.)[3]

If Bruce Barton represents a decadent Protestant urban liberalism, innocent of sin and grace, collapsing Jesus' message into an earnest, if fatuous, justification for American capitalism, and if Upton Sinclair proposes a socialist ethic of miracles and loves, the religious worlds of Jim Bishop (newspaperman) and Fulton Oursler (*Reader's Digest* editor) are something else. Oursler's *The Greatest Story Ever Told* (Garden City 1949) began as a series of radio scripts sponsored by Goodyear. Instead of a Protestant-capitalist moralism, we have here a quite different moralism associated with a very orthodox American Catholicism just before John XXIII and the acceptance of historical criticism by Vatican II.

Oursler uses the structure of the Fourth Gospel, inserting Synoptic material as required. Jesus has no real brothers; 'brethren' is just another word for 'family'. As a kid, Jesus was a superboy, unlike the rest of us.

> There was in the child Jesus from the very beginning an acute sharpness of all the organs; His were the first perfect faculties since Adam, and by them and through them He received a fullness of sensation not known to those around him (76).

There is too much of this sort of thing. If Barton shows us how religious liberalism can turn decadent, Oursler gives us an earnest orthodoxy becoming heretical. Catholic orthodoxy (before Vatican II) had some difficulty in avoiding both patripassianism (the assertion that Jesus was God, *simpliciter*) and docetism (as in the statement that Jesus had the best sense of smell since Adam). Here is Oursler on Mary. A friend of Joseph describes the first time he sets eyes on the young Mary.

> That girl is somehow different. Yes, she *is*. Can it be the expression? It is most unusual; it is, why . . . look . . . it has me stammering, man . . . it is . . . (6).

Sounds like love to me. Orthodoxy has a weakness for moralism no less than liberalism. Here is Oursler translating the radical eshatological descriptions of the life of the disciple in the new age into bland and trivial messages to put on your bathroom mirror and memorize while shaving.

> First of the rules was that a man must be poor in spirit; he must be gentle, practising humility, not heady and proud and arrogant [never use one word when three will do]; if one had succeeded in some great task, he was not to sit and gloat and brag, but must go right on, planning another job, a harder and better one.
>
> In the second rule a man must be meek; that was not to be a cringing coward but to believe in the goodness of God and in the friendliness of the universe. . . .

Incidentally, both Barton and Oursler seem to have had real trouble with Jesus and humility. Barton ignores it, while Oursler emasculates it by defining it as a belief in the friendliness of the universe, whatever that is.

> . . . even when the soul is suffering and can see no reason why it should suffer; the rule meant acceptance of God's will.
>
> To mourn, too, would be a third blessing [watch how Oursler squirms to avoid the otherworldliness of the original beatitudes], but happiness would come, not in feeling sorry for ourselves so much as in feeling compassion for others and trying to help them; a basic counsel implied in all the Master's teachings (140).

At no point is the uncritical biblicism of Oursler's book more dangerous (and this is just as true of Protestant biblicism) than in its wholesale embrace of the vicious and unhistorical anti-Phariseeism (and, at the end of the story, the anti-priestly venom) of the Gospels. Oursler's Jesus is so estranged from his Jewish context as hardly to seem Jewish at all. From the beginning, even as a teenager apparently, he is Son of God, sacrifice for sin, radical threat to the very existence of the Jewish religion.

Jesus as antisemitic Lord emerges vividly in Oursler's account of the trial and crucifixion. If Barton sheepishly skips over the death of Jesus, Oursler can't get enough of it. This, after all, is what the

Mass re-enacts. The Sanhedrin is uniformly jealous, insecure and stupid, while Pilate (and this comes from Oursler's slavish following of John) is almost heroic and certainly interesting. Here is lovable old Pilate, in Oursler's most fustian manner.

> Pilate looked down at Jesus, and this time it was a long scrutiny of the wavy brown hair that fell about the shoulders,

(a first – and a last – in twentieth-century Jesus fiction: Pilate really *loved* the way Jesus did his hair!)

> the forehead without a line in it, the dark eyes luminous and wide apart. The bruises and blood gave Pilate the creeps. All his life he had missed something, a mystery forever eluding him. Now did he see it, like a bright and wonderful light, in the face of a condemned man? Now, if he had found it, must he kill it? (265).

(You're just in love, Pilate. Sounds in the background of 'each man kills the thing he loves', with violin obligato.) But Pilate is tired, and he'd rather not have to deal with the hostility of the priests, so he consents to the execution out of a combination of boredom and exhaustion. The resurrection appearances are briefly reported at the end of the book, and old Annas, the retired high priest – slightly less nasty than the current high priest, his son-in-law – wonders if they hadn't crucified the truth after all.

Jim Bishop was famous for his series of books on important 'days' in history, so it was inevitable that this fine reporter and devout Catholic would get around to *The Day Christ Died* (1957). Its differences from *The Greatest Story Ever Told* are not just the differences between the *New York Daily Mirror* and *The Reader's Digest*, though that is difference enough. Notice the publication dates. Oursler is pre-Vatican II; Bishop is post. Oursler considers his own piety; Bishop uses both his own faith and a large amount of (largely Catholic) secondary literature. *The Day* . . . is more sophisticated and more carefully researched than *The Greatest* . . . *The Greatest* . . . made bad radio; *The Day* . . . would make a fair movie.

The Day Christ Died is not precisely named. It begins on Holy Thursday and goes through Holy Saturday, but there is a large flash-back that permits Bishop to review the birth, early life and ministry. (Several years later, he published a much less impressive expansion of the pages on the birth in this book as *The Day Christ Was Born* [1959]. It has all the marks of a publisher's gimmick.)

Now *The Day Christ Died* is not great literature, nor even great journalism. It knows a lot about what happened to Jesus than the New Testament does, but that is OK; that is why we can call it fiction. It is an imaginative recreation of the story of the four Gospels in which the author sometimes tells us when he is imagining, and sometimes not. It is credulous and unsceptical about all the words of the New Testament. And Bishop knows, as no one else but the Jewish guides today know, exactly where in Jerusalem all of Passion Week events took place. But he is candid about his point of view.

> My sole armament in this was, first, a lifelong belief that Jesus is God [there's our friend, the first heresy again] and the second person of the Trinity; secondly, an unquenchable curiosity to which I have become enslaved; and thirdly, a feeling that Jesus truly loved everyone [except, for Bishop, the Pharisees and the priests], and proved it (10).

Bishop has a curious relationship to the Gospels. If Barton doesn't like theology, Bishop suggests that the Gospels themselves need to be improved upon. Isn't that what he means here?

> None of the chronicles ever looked upon him as a man – a person of blood and sinew and bone and brain with a stupendous mission to accomplish in a very short time and in a place where the powers were alien to his cause. They saw him as God, and they longed to be present when he exterminated his enemies with fire . . . (133).

Strange, and of course wrong about the Gospels. But not wrong about how Jim Bishop feels about the Gospels. This theme – that he is underlining a fully human Jesus that the Gospels obscured –

must be read alongside the orthodoxy theme – that Jesus believed himself to be Son of God, Messiah, saviour from sin.

As Bishop moves through his reconstructed narrative to the end, we become more and more aware of its bitterly anti-Jewish tone. To Annas, Caiaphas and the Sanhedrin, Jesus is nothing but a fraud (because his self-claims were lies) and dangerous. Why? Because – and here again the imagination shows its power over the evidence – too many ordinary Jews were moving into Jesus' orbit of influence.

Bishop's orthodox Jesus, 'Jesus, Lord from thy birth', as the carol says, moves toward his crucifixion. His serenity, his final forgiveness, Bishop can handle. He has more trouble with 'My God, my God . . .' His language becomes uncharacteristically tormented.

> But Jesus has not called the prophet [i.e. Elijah]. He has called his Father. And, in his agony, which had not reached the point where the human nervous system will refuse to accept more and short-circuits itself into unconsciousness, Jesus prayed . . . (307).

Jim Bishop stops before the resurrection with a fine journalist's restraint. There is, he says, a victory in the death, even if no disciple or follower sees it. His statement of Jesus' final purpose is a fine one.

> He had come here [i.e. to the cross] to die. And he had died. He had come to preach a new covenant with his Father, and he had preached it. He had come to tell man that the way to everlasting life was love – each for the other, each for him, and his love for all – and he had proved this by laying down his life in a torrent of torment – for them (318).

This book strikes a sturdy and honest blow for popular American Catholic piety just as it is beginning to have to adjust to the new worlds opening before it through Vatican II and John XXIII.

Just what are the functions of these 're-creations'? Barton with his advertising Jesus, Sinclair and the socialist, Oursler with his spooky figure passing through history untouched, Bishop with his vigorous human Jesus helping American Catholics improve upon the shad-

owy figure in the New Testament? Why does the New Testament
record need to be supplemented? Why do we need more? Are these
books merely didactic? Isn't there a danger that the naïve reader
of these fictional accounts is likely to be deceived into a belief that
these fictions are somehow true? Or can we somehow learn to read
them as true fictions? Often, of course, those who give us a fictional
Jesus are trying to persuade us of the truth of their own orthodoxies, and they have a full right to that persuasion. Maybe the only
safe protection against individual orthodoxies contending for our
souls is the conviction that there are no orthodoxies available, and
only fictional truths. It's just that we should be wary when someone
knows more of Jesus than the New Testament knows. Perhaps we
should only trust those who know less.

But none of my American authors has written the worst sentence
ever written about Jesus in the twentieth century. That honour
belongs to the Lebanese guru-mystic, Kahlil Gibran, whose book
The Prophet reportedly rested on the bedside table of General
Schwarzkopf during the Gulf War. Here are the last two sentences
of his *The Voice of the Master* (New York 1958):

> For the breath of the Infant Jesus has filled the firmament and
> is mingled with the ether. Life, once full of woe, is now overflow-
> ing with joy, for the arms of the Infant Jesus are around me and
> embrace my soul (95).

Actually, Gibran has a book entirely devoted to Jesus (*Jesus, The
Son of Man*, New York 1928). It is a series of brief testimonials
to Jesus from his friends, his enemies, and some fictional observers
of the life. This Jesus has a face that shines like molten gold, and
is a travelling poet who talks a lot like Kahlil Gibran. Paul is an
evil theologian, Jesus is the Christ, herein defined:

> The Christ, He who was in the ancient of days, is the flame of
> God that dwells in the spirit of man. He is the breath of life that
> visits us, and takes unto Himself a body like our bodies (42).

Jesus is really neither man nor God. At the end of the book,
Gibran himself addresses Jesus as Master Singer, Master Poet,

Master Lover, Master of Light, Sky-heart, Knight of our fairer dream. 'The Princess awaits your coming in her fragrant chamber'. (214). 'The heart of the world quivers with the throbbing of your heart' (215).

> A man too weak and infirm to be God,
> A God too much man to call forth adoration . . .
> You do still tread this day;
> Nor bows nor spears shall stay your steps.
> You walk through all our arrows.
> You smile down upon us . . . (216).

And you are great for all our bedside tables.

Best-sellers: novels, lives and mixtures

Lloyd Douglas, *The Robe*, Boston 1942
Emil Ludwig, *The Son of Man*, New York 1928
Sholem Asch, *The Nazarene*, New York 1939
Gore Vidal, *Live from Golgotha*, New York 1992

There is no special interpretation of Jesus in *The Robe*. He is pretty much as the Gospels describe him, only more vapid: miracles and resurrection, but no apocalyptic urgency; gentle, innocent, dressed in white, forgiving all, even the executioners.

When the Roman tribune Marcellus looks at the man on the cross, he sees both failure and courage.

> There was nothing to show for his audacious courage. The Temple would continue to cheat the country people who came in to offer a lamb. Herod would continue to bully and whip the poor if they inconvenienced the rich. Caiaphas would continue to condemn the blasphemies of men who didn't want the gods fetched to market. Pilate would deal out injustice – and wash his dirty hands in a silver bowl. This lonely man had paid a high price for his brief and fruitless war on wickedness (Chapter VI).

Well written, and it nicely catches the flavour of a good deal of mid-century Protestant liberalism on Jesus. Marcellus was in charge of the soldiers who actually performed the crucifixion, and he won Jesus' robe with a roll of the dice.

The robe turned out to be a pretty spooky garment. In fact, it is more of a redeemer in this story than the one who wore it. *The Robe* is really a synedoche in the form of a novel.

Marcellus becomes depressed about his role in the crucifixion, but touching the robe partly cures him. He leaves Palestine for his home in Rome, and is shortly sent to Athens for a rest cure. Later, he is assigned by the emperor to go to Jerusalem to report on the young Christian movement. On his travels he picks up bits of second-hand information about what Jesus was up to, and he even meets a few of the original disciples.

What finally shakes Marcellus out of his sophisticated Stoic scepticism are the reports of the resurrection appearances, and that spooky robe. He is finally converted by his guilt, that garment, and all those stories about how Jesus could just look at you and change your life. He decides that Jesus was, and is, a God. And the Romans put him to death.

Emil Ludwig's popular biography *The Son of Man* deserves a brief notice as an unusually good example of that mixture of sentimental psychologizing and bad writing that seems to be unavoidable in so much Jesus-fiction. Ludwig inserts no fictional characters, nor does he follow the career of a minor character in the Jesus story, nor does he (as a Jew) have a particular orthodoxy to sell. He retells the Synoptic story, with a few Johannine touches.

What really interests Ludwig is Jesus' inner life. He has Jesus moving from early success to later failure.

> Gentle and imaginative, a poet by temperament, a teacher who lives to bring cheer and consolation, a compassionate physician, the more strenuous way has not seemed to him God's will, and has certainly not been his own. But the smouldering quarrel between himself and his brethren has broken into flame (206).

The almost unreadable purple prose is if anything worse than the dreadful speculations about Jesus' inner feelings. Here are some juicy passages about Jerusalem.

In great transitions, like the twilight now spreading athwart Jerusalem, in a hundred gradations of the spirit, like those characteristic of the light now fading on Palestine between the eastern hills and the sea, moves and sinks the curve of the old faiths while there looms through the gathering darkness one star of wisdom after another, gleaming down upon the world of men (55).

On top of all this there is the romantic psychologizing of Jesus. The young Jesus is perfect, noticing 'everything which may help to unlock the mystery of the human heart' (68). And what Jesus really goes for is nature. The first (not business man, but) romantic.

He was fain to safeguard the treasures of his innermost being; to escape from the cramping atmosphere of the synagogue to the freedom of the hillside where the lark came so near, where the brook was his intimate friend, where the clouds scudded overhead, and where between the clouds his vision could pierce the blue vault of heaven (71).

(All this lacks is a nightingale and music by Schubert.)

But fortunately this mood of sentimental optimism disappears. Jesus begins to withdraw from the crowds, from the disciples, and he ends, deserted, on a cross. When he sees from the cross that God does not intend to rescue him, and that the disciples have fled, he dies in despair. The sentimental young romantic ends up as a broken and isolated prophet who has lost everything.

Ludwig's Jesus story is about a young Jewish prophet too loving and too forgiving for the evil world of political and religious power. What begins as a sentimental tract ends as an angry indictment of a world who could do that to the gentlest man that ever lived. The sentimentalist turns out to have a canny sense of the world's corruption. The merry youngster that threw himself on the welcoming earth ends up without hope, friends, and God.

The Nazarene by Sholem Asch is both a 'life of Jesus' (like Emil Ludwig's) and a novel like *The Robe*. It is probably successful as neither, but it turns out to be a moving and important book for an unexpected reason.

The structure of the book is strange. There are two narrators: a scholarly antisemitic forger named Pan Viadomsky and a young Jewish student who is teaching the older man Hebrew. They live in Warsaw in the late 1930s.

It turns out that Viadomsky is quite mad. He believes that he actually was, in a previous incarnation, the very Roman soldier responsible for Jesus' death (i.e. Lloyd Douglas' Marcellus). Thus the first of Asch's three narrative devices involves the recollections of this Roman soldier. Viadomsky as the Roman soldier tells the Jesus story to the young Jewish tutor in modern Warsaw.

The soldier is first drawn to Jesus, then he is ashamed of his fascination. His Jesus is mainly a healer and a preacher of comfort. He is altogether Jewish, and not a little spooky.

> The frail and slender body seemed to expand until it became a mighty human pyramid ... Perhaps the afternoon sunlight, deepening into the fiery red of evening, imparted an illusion of immense height and width to his figure. But his voice too had taken on unearthly power; for it filled all the circumambient air ... (167).

This is pretty much Asch's Jesus throughout the book. Not entirely human; certainly not divine, fully within the Jewish tradition. The Roman soldier suspects this Jesus may be some danger to Rome.

Asch abruptly switches to a second narrative strategy. The recollections of the Roman soldier (who is really Viadomsky, remember) cease, and we are abruptly moved back to twentieth-century Warsaw. Viadomsky – the mad, antisemitic forger – shows an ancient manuscript to his young friend and asks him to read it to him. It is a lost Gospel, written in Aramaic, the Gospel according to Judas.

It is, alas, a very boring Gospel. It recounts the familiar story of Jesus up to the last visit to Jerusalem. Judas himself seems to be a troubled young enthusiast for Jesus, but the precise nature of his betrayal is never made clear.

The third and final narrative strategy is the most unsuccessful and most incredible of all. Let me try to make it intelligible. The young Jewish student in Warsaw finishes reading the Judas manuscript to Viadomsky. Viadomsky, during the reading, 'becomes' the Roman soldier once more, and the young man finds himself so bewitched by Viadomsky's illusion that he too turns into a first-century character: in this case, a young rabbinic student in Jerusalem at the time of the Passion week. This rabbinic student's recollections (who is really a twentieth-century Polish Jew) bring the Jesus story to a close.

Asch's story of the trial is designed to show that there were some Jews then who found no offence in Jesus' teaching. The crucifixion is rather stylized, and Jesus dies, forgiving and serene. The rabbinical student's recollections stop with the death itself, and he then turns back into the twentieth-century student speaking to the mad Viadomsky who still is persuaded that he killed Jesus in the first century. The old man cries out to his young friend that he has always lived under the curse of being the killer of Jesus; from incarnation to incarnation he has always been tormented by his guilt and by Jesus' terrible forgiveness. (Notice Asch's interesting point: the Roman, not the Jew, is the guilty Christ-killer.)

Viadomsky faces a crisis on the last two pages of *The Nazarene*, and this conclusion is a genuinely moving one that redeems much of the slipshod banality of the other seven hundred pages. Viadomsky speaks passionately of his bitter, eternal struggle with Jesus, which has been the foundation for his professional antisemitism. He cries out that he can fight no more, that God's will should be done, whatever that might be.

The young friend has an answer to that question. He reminds Viadomsky, as we begin to see his bitter antisemitism unravel, that the Sanhedrin at the time of the arrest did in fact agree with Jesus that the double commandment to love God and the neighbour was central. They disagreed – and pressed for the crucifixion on that basis – only on the method of achieving that dual love.

This word comes as genuine liberation to Viadomsky. If the Sanhedrin and Jesus really did agree on the central matter, then the Jew and the Christian are really one and Jesus died as a righteous Jew truly forgiving all. Viamdomsky can finally receive that forgiveness and he is at last released from his guilt-ridden torment and antisemitic anger.

The final message of this strange novel is that antisemitism is an evil that is not eternal; that it can be broken and wiped out. This is the truth that Asch's cumbersome fictional wrapping conceals. And it is a truth made almost unbearably poignant when we remember that the old man who finally receives this truth is a Warsaw Pole in the year 1939!

Gore Vidal's *Live from Golgotha* barely sneaks under the wire as Jesus fiction as we have been defining it. In an earlier article ('Monotheism and its Discontents', *Nation*, 13 July 1992) he offered a witty and eloquent attack on the three monotheistic faiths of the West. The novel is that attack in fictional form, concentrating on the Christians, much more angry, mean-spirited and phallogo-centric (functioning penises in almost every chapter).

Vidal is mainly out for Pauline or mainstream Christianity, and this reconstruction of Jesus is a very minor affair. The novel is quite mad, and it goes (in part) something like this. The narrator is Paul's associate Timothy, now an elderly bishop at the close of the first century. We are treated to some charming flashbacks about the good old days with Paul on the road. Paul is an eloquent preacher, a juggler and a tap-dancer. And during these days Timothy has a lot of unsafe sex with Paul, Nero, and assorted pagan and Christian ladies.

Into Timothy's serene episcopal life erupts, from the future, a collection of wild computer and television fanatics, largely from NBC. These twentieth-century friends have come to the past to warn Timothy that some hacker is in the process of erasing all the Gospels and all the records of Christianity. If he is successful, Timothy is advised, Christianity will not have been! These friends have several requests to make of the bishop. They want him to prepare a virus-free Gospel of his own about the life of Jesus: they want him to go back in time thirty years (they will provide the technology) to interview Mark, in case his first Gospel is wiped out. And finally, they want him to be the anchorman for an NBC special in the making to be called 'Live from Golgotha'. The technology is just about completed that will enable the network to move backwards in time to record events *as they really happened*. History really will become bunk with this new form of television.

Along the narrative way there are generous helpings of Paul-bashing, and we are almost tempted to think that our author-guide is a closet liberal Protestant out to praise Jewish Christianity and to clobber Paul. Here is how Vidal's Paul describes his Damascus road vision.

> So there I was. A hot day. Palm trees. A mirage shivering in the middle distance. A camel. A pyramid. Your average Middle Eastern landscape as viewed from the freeway. Complete with burning bush. Suddenly. HE. WAS THERE.
>
> In that silent smoky hall you could have heard an unweighted pin drop or the loosest foreskin slide back. 'Wide as He was tall, Jesus waddled toward me.' To live audiences, Saint often let this sort of detail slip out. But in his writing, never. 'That face. Those luminous eyes hidden somewhere in all that golden fat. The ineffable smile like the first slice from a honeydew melon. Oh, delight! He held up a hand, a tiny starfish cunningly fashioned of lard. He spoke, His voice so high, so shrill that only the odd canine ever got the whole message, hence the need for interpretation and self-consciousness – in short, mega-fiction' (32).

But we are in for a surprise. This 'lard-ass' Jesus that Paul thinks he sees is not Jesus at all, it is Judas. And this is explained when NBC finally gets its crew to Gethsemane. It turns out that Jesus manages to persuade the arresting officers that Judas is really the man they want. So Judas is arrested and Jesus escapes.

Now Jesus escapes to the twentieth century where he becomes a computer genius named Marvin. He is, in fact, the hacker engaged in erasing all the records of historic Christianity. Why? Because he was never a Pauline Christian at all; he was *really* (I am almost sure this is what Vidal is saying) a Jewish revolutionary so horrified at what Christianity had become over the years that he wanted to wipe it out, and then to return to earth in 2001 CE and wipe out the earth as well.

Back to the garden and the 'real' crucifixion. Judas is bound and led to Golgotha, but some of the NBC types in the crowd manage to convince Pilate (correctly so) that the real Jesus is this Marvin who is standing around watching things. So Marvin, the real Zealot Jesus, is crucified. The resurrection is designed by the production staff, and it involved Jesus himself floating up into the sky, finally absorbed into the glory of the Japan sun-goddess Amaterasu. Paul-bashing ends up as Jap-bashing.

Back to 96 CE, Timothy buries his own Gospel and his reconstruction of Mark in a closet in his cathedral. When these documents are discovered in the late 1990s they are literally unintelligible (Vidal gives us a glimpse). So – the mad hacker Jesus may not have died after all. Perhaps he didn't even get to Japan with the help of the sun-goddess. Perhaps he is still working for NBC somewhere in Rockefeller Center.

A charming and useful polemic narrative, weakened only by a negative emotional intensity that almost gets out of hand.

4. *Five English lives: from belief to unbelief*

Elizabeth Goudge, *God So Loved the World*, London 1951
Dorothy L. Sayers, *The Man Born to be King*, London 1943
Robert Graves, *King Jesus*, London 1946
Anthony Burgess, *Man of Nazareth*, London 1959
A. N. Wilson, *Jesus*, London 1992

Elizabeth Goudge's life of Jesus is a devout Anglican re-telling of John's Gospel, with some inserts from the Synoptics. She has a firm grasp of the doctrines of Incarnation, Trinity and Atonement, and these doctrines shape her story, at once biblical and sentimental. The life of Jesus begins, of course, with God.

> To save man from this death [of sin] the great love of God chose to do two things, to show himself to man all over again in his eternal beauty and to lift up the great weight of sin that kept man a prisoner and carry it away, that man might be free to rise up and turn from self to God and serve and love him as he used to do in the beginning (4).

God So Loved the World is an untroubled book of serene faith, very nearly unreadable. Unreadable not because it so carefully follows the four Gospels, but because of the peculiar nature of the novelist's additions and decorations.

He could have been the finest scholar who has ever lived, the greatest ruler, politician, artist, musician, or poet. We can see his great gifts shining through all his words and deeds, yet for our sake he denied himself their full use (46).

This is not docetism. Goudge knows that doctrines of Incarnation and Atonement are destroyed by docetism. But it is untoward sentimentalism. Her human Jesus is not really like us at all, though perhaps she means that *he* is truly human, and we alas are not. Her 'life' is clearly for those comfortably in the church.

And she is as effusive with the mother as with the son.

Out of all the women who have ever lived upon this earth, or who will ever live, this village girl is the one whom God chose to be the Mother of his Son, and so we know that she was as perfect as a woman can be, lovely in mind and in spirit as well as in body, and like all lovely people very much beloved (9).

This is the kind of thing that happens when piety chooses to sit quietly before the formula of Chalcedon, not restlessly before the Gospel texts.

Elizabeth Goudge has no difficulty with Jesus' anguish at Gethsemane or with the cry from the cross, but her biblicism is severely strained when it comes to Jesus' apparent rebuke of his mother at Cana. Maybe the Greek translation from the Aramaic messed things up; maybe the author just didn't remember. Maybe what Jesus really said was something like: 'Wait a minute, mom, I'll be right with you.'

In this life of Jesus, the deep anti-Jewish bias of John's Gospel is unfortunately reflected. Jesus is killed by the hatred of the priests and the fury of the mob controlled by the priests. Pilate (as in John) rather liked Jesus, but couldn't help himself and finally gave in out of fear.

This eloquent and over-imaginative book ends with Pentecost and the resurrection of Jesus in the church, his body on earth. It is hard to like, and also hard not to admire, this presentation of a splendid Anglican orthodoxy. The book is designed to declare what it is the author believes. So are many lives, both scholarly and novelistic, and the measure of our interest in them is simply the measure of our interest in the author's faith.

It is striking to turn from Elizabeth Goudge's Anglican life of Jesus to the equally Anglican life of Dorothy Sayers. A sentence from the introduction to Sayers' set of radio plays on the life of Jesus (*The Man Born to be King*) perfectly catches the difference between the two authors: 'A loose and sentimental theology begets loose and sentimental art-forms . . .'

There is nothing loose or sentimental about Miss Sayers' theology. It is as omnipresent and imperialistic as Peter Wimsey or God. Indeed, Dorothy Sayers is easily (apart from Gerd Theissen) the best theologian among all the poets and other amateurs studied in this chapter. She declares her hostility to solemnity and sentimentality with characteristic snappishness, vigour and self-consciousness:

> I am a writer and I know my trade; and I say that this story is a very great story indeed, and deserves to be taken seriously. I say further (and here I know what I am saying and mean exactly what I say) that in these days it is seldom taken seriously. It is often taken, and treated, with a gingerly solemnity . . .

'Gingerly solemnity' is a cruelly perfect description of *God So Loved the World*.

Dorothy Sayers' theology is mainstream Anglo-Catholicism of the Eliot-Auden-Charles Williams *Christian News-Letter* variety. Even Mary herself can articulate that theology.

> I, Mary, am the fact; God is the truth; but Jesus is fact and truth – he is reality. You cannot see the immortal truth till it is born in the flesh of the fact. And because all birth is a sundering of the flesh . . . the feet that must walk this road were made of me. Only one Jesus is to die today . . . the truth of God and the fact of Mary (Eleventh play).

If one can forget the excessive aggressiveness in this passage, the shape of Sayers' confident orthodoxy becomes clear. Her radio plays are elegant narrative footnotes to a vigorous Chalcedonian christology. She knows that the Chalcedonian formula makes it unnecessary to minimize the humanity in order to celebrate the divinity. Her nearly unfailing hold on the full humanity roots her plays firmly in their human and historical context. Chalcedon is her control against the sombre, the pious, the sentimental.

Dorothy Sayers nods perhaps at but a single point. In spite of her efforts, her chief temptation (as in most orthodoxies) is docetism. Her Jesus is the only lifeless one among her many characters. He is too perfect, too wise, too pure. This is partly because she draws heavily on the Fourth Gospel, the most subtly dehumanizing of the four. But it is mostly because of a technical decision she has made as a writer: almost exclusively the language she gives to her Jesus is the language assigned to him in the Gospels. (When non-biblical language is ventured, it is formal, poetical, liturgical.) The other characters live comfortably in the invented language the author has granted them. Jesus alone is 'biblical'.

Because she is so conscious about her theological underpinnings, Sayers is always clear, always unsentimental, and only infrequently heretical. Patristic heresy was always orthodoxy shouting in an exceptionally loud voice, and Sayers does love to skirt the edge of patripassianism, as in the designation of the crucifixion as the murder of God Almighty. Sayers doesn't tweak the noses of the pious, but she is not above tweaking the noses of those less pious than she. And of course she writes like an angel.

Like so many of our poets, it is Judas who most fascinates Miss Sayers and who brings out her superb craftsman's skills. If her Jesus is a bit of a bore, her Judas is one of the best-drawn characters in all of our twentieth-century fictions. Many of the writers of Jesus fictions have Judas a Zealot, a slightly worldly revolutionary distressed by Jesus' growing death-wish. Sayers' Judas is just the opposite. He is the most intelligent of the disciples, and he sees the true shape of Jesus' ministry much more clearly than the bungling Peter, James and John. To be truly the Messiah, Judas argues, Jesus must go the way of suffering and death. Here is Judas in the fifth play:

> . . . so he laid our burden upon us . . . sorrow and humility and torment and shame, and poverty and peace of heart. God's salvation. And we were filled with a strange happiness.

But somehow Judas begins to suspect that Jesus might be tempted to reject the martyr's way (Judas' way for Jesus, that is) for the way of political revolution. This mistake is the beginning of Judas' moral undoing. He goes to the high priest and sets up the process of arrest, trial and execution so that Jesus will be forced back to the martyr's way, and away from the Zealot option. He betrays in order to force Jesus to affirm redemption through suffering when he suspected that Jesus was being tempted to reject it.

Judas soon discovers that Jesus was never tempted by anti-Roman activism, and that he never intended to repudiate the Messiahship of suffering and death. Judas' problem was that he couldn't handle the fact that Jesus agreed with him without asking his advice. He was intellectually correct about what Messiahship should entail, but he was spiritually too proud to accept the fact that Jesus never acknowledged Judas' wisdom. Here is Sayers on Judas.

> . . . the itch for suffering that was only an inverted cruelty; the refusal to believe in innocence that was rooted in the envy and hatred of innocence . . . (notes to the tenth play).

Judas' intelligence is superior, his pride immense, and his repentance complete and authentic.

> I was in love with suffering, because I wanted to see him suffer. I wanted to believe him guilty [of following the Zealots' way], because I could not endure his innocence. He was greater than I, and I hated him. And now I hate myself . . . Do you know what hell-fire is? It is the light of God's unbearable innocence that sears and shrivels you like a flame. It shows you what you are (tenth play).

This sounds like a true and earnest repentance. If there had been no suicide, would not Judas have had a fair shot at sanctity, or – at the very least – an authentic faith in Jesus? Whatever the unforgivable sin might be, it is not spiritual pride.

Robert Graves was a superb love-poet, and a writer of some fine historical novels. *King Jesus* is not one of them. It is a strange book, but not boring. It is not a defence of a particular belief about Jesus (as with Goudge and Sayers), nor is it a secular word of praise for Jesus (as with Burgess). The author plays the clever schoolboy who has amassed thousands of 3"x 5" cards and who dumps them all into his text and into our laps. If there is a purpose to the novel it is to have fun and to tease the pious, both perfectly permissible goals.

Graves has invented an interesting narrator, one Agabus, writing in Alexandria at the close of the first century. Agabus has two sources that he uses in his story: Alexandria is the centre of gnostic Christianity, and so the narrator can draw on a pile of occult and apocryphal material about Jesus, which he freely uses along with material from the canonical Gospels.

But Agabus has his own point of view not fully defined by Alexandrian gnosticism. He is deeply sympathetic with the Ebionite movement (sometimes called Nazarene). It appears that the novelist Graves is using Ebionitism as a weapon to criticize traditional Christianity. The Ebionites were a very early pre – or non-theological movement, as much Jewish as 'Christian', interested in Jesus as Messiah and teacher, and deeply suspicious of gnostic speculation and Christian attempts to co-opt it. For example, Graves adopts the Ebionite suspicion of Pauline Christianity and is critical of the ways Gentile Christianity shaped the passion narrative in an anti-Jewish, pro-Roman direction. The Jesus of Agabus and Graves is virtually a Pharisee in the tradition of Hillel. It was Rome who crucified, aided by the anxiety and timidity of the Sadducees and priests.

After the death of Jesus, he continues on earth as a spiritual presence, calling for obedience to God's will and true repentance until the kingdom finally arrives. During his lifetime, Jesus had married Mary of Bethany, but because of his hatred of sex the marriage was never consummated. Indeed, as a husband, Jesus was both indifferent and cruel.

What Graves doesn't like about the Ebionites is their hostility to women, because this entails finally hostility to Graves' beloved pre-Christian goddesses. The Ebionites represented a pure patriarchalism, and their Jesus was quoted as saying: 'I am released from the jurisdiction of the Female; I have come to destroy her works' (256).

But Graves' Jesus is more than the Ebionite teacher and prophet of repentance. He is a king, literally. Jesus of Nazareth was the son of King Herod, Mary's first husband, and he therefore has a legitimate claim to the throne of Israel. He refuses his claim, wanting only a spiritual kingship.

Graves' Jesus, with his mother and step-father, stayed in Egypt twelve years while Archelaus was still on his throne. In Egypt, Jesus is both an epileptic and a dreadful prig. He caused the death of several of his playmates, and his persistence and self-righteousness as a student caused the death by heart-attack of one of his teachers. On his way back to Nazareth, he put in a year's graduate study at an Essene monastery.

The actual ministry of Jesus is rather traditionally presented. A few more miracles than usual because of the use of material from the apocryphal Gospels, but mostly ethical teaching, prophetic and kingly claims. His interest in outcasts does not indicate any special virtue on their part. It is just, Jesus said, that since synagogue Judaism takes excellent care of the devout, someone should be instructing the outsiders in God's will. Here is Graves' excellent summary of Jesus' mission and message.

> As a sacred King, the last legitimate ruler of an immensely ancient dynasty, his avowed intention was to fulfil all the ancient prophecies that concerned himself and bring the history of his House to a real and unexceptionable conclusion . . . His resolute hope was to defeat Death itself by enduring with his people the so-called Pangs of the Messiah, the cataclysmic events which were the expected prelude to the coming of the Kingdom of God; and his justification of this hope was the prophecy in the twenty-fifth chapter in Isaiah: 'He shall destroy Death for ever.' In the Kingdom, which would be miraculously fertile and perfectly pacific, all Israelites would be his subjects who acknowledged him in his threefold capacity as king, prophet and healer, and under his benignant rule would live wholly free from error, want, sickness or fear of death for no less than a thousand years (284).

Graves is not embarrassed by eschatology. The time of its full arrival is known only to God. Then comes the thousand-year reign and last judgment and general resurrection.

Graves doesn't have a great deal to add to the passion story. He does have Jesus asking Judas to kill him. Judas refuses, and arranges with Nicodemus to have Jesus arrested both to save him from his own depression and to convince Pilate that his wisest and safest course would be to persuade Jesus to begin his actual kingship. But the Sanhedrin doesn't like the Judas-Nicodemus plan. They are genuinely afraid of Jesus' capacity to stir up a Jewish revolt that would lose them the fringe benefits they enjoy under their concordat with Pilate.

After his death, Jesus' influence continues. Graves admits that even though he was a boorish cold fish, he had some impressive pedagogical skills. But the Jesus of *King Jesus* must finally be rejected, because through him Christianity developed its damaging and dangerous rejection of the female and the goddess. Graves' Jesus is finally a harmless and amiable eccentric whose function is to serve as a critical literary and religious springboard for a wily novelist.

Anthony Burgess' *Man of Nazareth* is a novel, not a life of Jesus, because it has a narrator. His name is Azor, and he writes stories and does odd translations, which means he is really Burgess himself. We are capitulated into this alluring Jesus story in a striking way. Azor begins with a vividly detailed description of a crucifixion, and he remarks that a world that countenances crucifixions is a world with good and evil in permanent encounter. Such, Azor states, is the first-century world he intends to describe.

We discover – implicitly from the narrative and explicitly in the epilogue – that Azor (Burgess) is not a Christian but is a serious admirer of Jesus. The narrator admits that he suspects that the Creator, if there is one, made and still supports the world as a diversion, that life is properly read as a game. But in this game we are still forced into obligations, and Jesus' statement that the proper name for these obligations is love is as wise as any that has been proposed.

But Christians, the narrator continues, not only play the game, they all too frequently enjoy persecuting others who play differently. Jesus' love, says Azor, means that life is not to be taken too seriously, and that the kingdom is a game requiring the skills of tolerance, forbearance and affection. He likes Jesus' love as a way of becoming liberated from what he calls the kingdom of the serious (or of Caesar).

Thus, Burgess' Jesus story is not so much a search for Jesus as an affirmation about him. It is designed for all who have, like the author, a mixture of humour, half-belief and admiration for a form of love that can lead to irrelevance and failure. Burgess takes the New Testament record as he finds it, Synoptics and John together, fills some gaps, and adds some characters and lots of interpretation – often wise, often funny, often outrageous.

On the matter of Jesus' birth, he not only gives us a miraculous conception, but he hits us in the face with it. Joseph is impotent after a piece of equipment in the shop fell on his crotch and Mary had already sworn herself to virginity before she'd ever considered marriage. God the comedian is behind it all: 'It is God's humour that his son and the prophet of his son should be conceived where conception is impossible' (30).

As a kid, in talking over his vocational plans with his cousin John, Jesus had decided that he hated respectability more than anything and that if there was a ministry in his future it would have to be among non-respectable sinners.

On miracles, Burgess is cool and tolerant. There is practically no explaining away of the healings. Angels, unusual births, the raising of Lazarus, the resurrection – all are treated as historical events because the New Testament so treats them. (This is the advantage, incidentally, of having the first-century Azor, rather than the twentieth-century Burgess, as narrator.)

With the nature miracles, Burgess does play a few modernizing tricks. The stilling of the storm is no big deal; it is just that Jesus knew enough meteorology to be able to predict when the storm was likely to break. On the wedding at Cana (an event equally beloved by both pious and impious poets) we get the full Burgess treatment. It is the twenty-year-old Jesus' own wedding that is taking place. (His wife, Sarah, is killed in an Arab-Jewish street brawl in Jerusalem five years later.) The wine runs out. Jesus murmurs some magic words over the stone water jars and in effect adds: 'This is an unusual transformation I am pulling off. For sinners – fornicators, debtors, gossips – the wine will look and taste like water. For the virtuous and devout, the liquid will be ruby red and will taste like Greek nectar.' And it worked. Burgess' Jesus is a miracle-worker in more than one way.

Burgess makes very interesting use of Jesus' loss of his wife. He imagines a moving dialogue between Jesus and God on the problem of undeserved suffering.

'My beloved is snatched away in the flower of her youth. You, who know all, knew from the beginning of time that this would happen. Why did you let it happen? Why, cursed father, did you not prevent it?'

Do not curse, son, though I take the word as but the purulence of human grief. I gave men free will, which means power to choose between good and evil. If they could not choose evil they could not also choose good. If they were always good they would still be in Eden. But there is no Eden, since Adam and Eve chose, in their God-given freedom, that that blessed garden be denied to them, and hence to their children.

'But you, the all-knowing, know what men will do. You know they will do evil. If you know this, they cannot be free, since all their acts are pre-ordained. Therefore you will the evil they do. I cannot call you a God in love with justice.'

Call me a God in love with man. Do not ask why. My passions are not to be explained. To ensure that man is truly free – and this gift is the measure of the greatness of my love – I choose not to foreknow his actions. I choose, remember, I discard omniscience. But when man's acts are once performed, then I have, as it were, a sudden memory of my own foreknowledge. For man, I render myself less than perfect.

'For man,' Jesus said, 'you become man.'

You have hit it. And now, though it may be small comfort in your tribulation, take your scriptures and read the Book of Job (105).

He gives his Jesus a lovely word on the special nature of married love.

For the love of a parent is, as it were, the very marrow of the bone, while the love of husband and wife entails a discipline. One holds oneself back from railing or counter-railing, one learns not to utter the bitter word of resentment, one learns to be grateful for the proffered pleasure, the companionship. Despite the marriage vow, one is free not to love, yet one chooses to love. I have to teach love as choice, as the one weapon against evil. I must, I think, start to get myself ready (106).

These examples show what Burgess is doing in his fictionalizing. He is not trying to shock, or to tug at our heart strings, or to defend a denominational orthodoxy. He uses his fiction of Jesus' brief life as a husband to raise real issues and to enrich the portrait of the Jesus he is presenting.

Burgess sees Jesus' ministry falling into two parts. Not early success and later failure. But rather: love without eschatology, and eschatological tension and vision. Love is the single theme that ties together the whole of the life and death. Here is young Jesus speaking to his dying father.

. . . you have been the best of fathers. In the earthly dispensation, I should say. You have had a son's love, and you will always have it, for, since love is an aspect of our heavenly father and cannot die, so the loved and lover must also live forever (95).

Love is radically unsentimental in Burgess' Jesus. It is learned slowly; it must drive out the demons of custom and the easy road. It is not easy to learn, but the kingdom of God requires the difficult way of love (147–8). Burgess ties his understanding of love to the world of the carpenter's shop.

I do not expect love to gush unbidden from your heart to enfold them that are, in truth, most unlovable. I call love rather a craft a man or woman must learn as I, in my youth, learned the craft of carpentry. Love is the tool, we may say, that shapes the hard rough dull knotty splintery wood of the hearts of our enemies into the smoothness of friendship (213).

But as the ministry developed, the language of love came to seem insufficient, even if still necessary. In showing Jesus trying to go beyond love, Burgess takes seriously the apocalyptic nature of the message. It soon became clear to Jesus that Israel as a whole must be saved, that both the Roman occupiers and the compromising priests had to be confronted, that in fact 'kingdom' was not just another word for a love that is willing to be unconventional, but a call to a transformation of all present injustice. How long will such a transformation take? I may have to return to the world to complete it, Jesus answers. When will this change, this 'coming' take place? Jesus' answer is elegant:

> In a thousand, a million years. Does it matter? Time is not a Roman march, time is a children's dance. Men are men. Time is nothing in the eyes of your heavenly father who made time for his world to dance in. But there will be signs of the end, and it may seem to some that the signs are always there – wars and rumours of wars, nation rising up against nation. Famines and earthquakes. Many shall stumble and deliver up one another and hate one another. Iniquity shall be multiplied, the love of many shall grow cold (263).

Burgess here finds a bold and lofty language to express the eschatological centre of Jesus' proclamation of the kingdom.

He is also interesting on Jesus' idea of the kingdom. At the beginning of the ministry, some may have felt that Jesus was interested in dethroning the Romans. But he was never so interested, Burgess insists. He was never a danger to Rome, because he never believed that the world could be improved by changing its leaders. (264). Jesus is often in serious and friendly debate with the Zealots, who deeply distrusted Jesus' word about love for enemies and who rightly suspected that Jesus' 'kingdom' was just too spiritual for their anti-Roman tastes. Burgess' Jesus teaches only love, and that love can often seem to be unjust, as in such parables as that of the Prodigal Son. Burgess' Jesus really rejects justice, and leaves it to God (222), and apparently to the world to come. This Jesus is either apolitical or Tory. What this means about Burgess I have no way of knowing.

The novelist's skill is not only linguistic. He has an acute theological eye, and knows how to look at the New Testament story and read off its meaning in a fresh and interesting way. For example, in commenting on the baptism of Jesus by John he says that they both saw then that not only the soul but also the flesh were clearly of God's making. Burgess has a good sense of one of the secular meanings of the sacraments.

Burgess plays some splendid games with the temptation in the desert. Before he gets to the three-fold proposal by Satan himself, Jesus gets some secular temptations, as a kind of dress rehearsal for the real show. His mother calls him and tells him to come back home and get a good hot meal. Some naked girls appear and Jesus says 'no thanks'. A Greek philosopher offers him rationality instead of blind faith. To all of these temptations, secular and Satanic, Jesus has no trouble in saying 'no'. This may be the only point where the author's Jesus fails in his full humanity. Couldn't we have had a little struggle? No; nothing can really tempt this powerful, wise, ironic teacher.

Judas is one of the acid tests for the novelists who would embroider the Gospel story, and Burgess does not fail the test. His Judas is, once more, the most intelligent and devoted of the Twelve. (Won't some novelist some day decree that Judas is really the stupidest, most immoral of the lot?)[4] He knows his scripture, and he knows that the function of the Messiah is to release and redeem the nation Israel from all oppression. Judas begins to suspect that Jesus' messianic goal is somehow less than scriptural. He is troubled when Jesus begins to talk about failure, redemptive suffering, and dying. He is persuaded that Jesus must be protected from such self-destructive visions and preserved to carry on his role as the eschatological prophet of restoration. So he tells a priest where Jesus can be found after the last supper and taken away to safety. But the priest tricks Judas, and interprets what Judas says of Jesus as evidence of blasphemy. He arrests Jesus in the garden not to save him but to set up his trial and execution. Burgess' Judas is not a morally depraved traitor eager for easy money but a biblical literalist anxious to correct Jesus' eccentric idea of a suffering messiah. Judas, intellectual fundamentalist.

In the trial and execution sequence Jesus really was a blasphemer from the Sanhedrin's point of view. Even as early as Caesarea Phillippi, Jesus had declared not only his suffering messiahship but his full divinity. (That is how Burgess reads 'Son of God'.) So Caiaphas only affirmed at the hearing what Jesus had already admitted. Now this does simplify the contradictory Gospel records on the trial, and there is no reason why a novelist should not impose an imaginative order not available in the primary sources. All the guilt of the crucifixion is Jewish. Pilate refuses to make a decision. His assistants finally approve the capital verdict, using a signed warrant already prepared for 'Jesus Barabbas' which had left out the patronymic so that 'of Nazareth' could easily be inserted. Caiaphas, afraid of unrest, bears all the blame.

We have found some interesting theological asides in Burgess' narrative reconstruction. But this real contribution, I have insisted, is not in theology but in language. Burgess is not at all interested in historicity, in the nicely calculated levels of probability that biblical scholars are obliged to come up with. He takes it all, virgin birth, healings, miracles, resurrection, and creates a language that almost by itself bridges the hermeneutical gulf (that properly worries all of us theological types) between New Testament times and our own. What demythologizing, and the kernel-and-husk metaphor before it, was designed to do, Anthony Burgess tries to do with the simple power of the word. Here is his post-resurrection Jesus, at the very end of this story, giving the disciples their final commission. When will you leave us, Peter asks, and when will you go? Jesus replies.

> Eventually I will go whence I came. When? For now, do not ask. I leave you, a resurrected man not unhappy to be back in the flesh again and live in the flesh – where, you ask. Do not ask that either, for I do not know. My mission is at an end, and yours must begin. What men must learn they must learn from men unresurrected. You may know, however, that I shall be on the earth, though never again with you . . . Dying is painful, but death itself is a mere nothing. Remember that – dying exists but there is no death. Remember what I said and did before my dying. The bread and the wine, God's gifts, and the word as palpable as bread and wine. The word now is yours, and the power, and the triumph will be yours, and also the agony. The way, as you have already seen, will not be easy . . . You'll start in Jerusalem. But the word is not for Israel only. You will be

driven as seed is driven by the winds of autumn – to other cities, other lands. to the islands of the Greeks and to Ethiopia, to the islands of the sea that the Romans call their sea, to Rome itself, for the word is for all men (351–2).

When Dietrich Bonhoeffer talked about Bultmann's demythologizing in his prison letter (5 May 1944), he accused Bultmann of not going far enough. It is not just the 'myth' (miracle, ascension, and so forth) that is problematic, but all the 'religious' concepts of the Christian tradition – God, faith, and the rest. Everything must be proclaimed non-religiously, Bonhoeffer cryptically wrote, and we never really figured out what he meant or how to do what he hinted at. Perhaps Anthony Burgess, in *Man from Nazareth*, has come as close to the vision from Tegel as anyone. Take the whole story, kerygma and history, miracle and teaching, Mark and John, sermons and resurrections and discover their possible meaning for our time by fashioning a language that embarrasses neither our century nor the first. Hermeneutics done by a novelist's playful skill.

In a pericope that didn't quite get into Luke's Gospel (Codex Bezae, between 6.5 and 6.6) Jesus meets some men picking grain on the sabbath and says: 'If you know what you are doing, you are blessed; if you do not, you are accursed.' I am tempted to address Jesus' words to A. N. Wilson and to his biography *Jesus*. In one way, this looks like the first deliberately post-historical fictionalized life of Jesus. In another way, the author gives the impression that he alone has finally found a way to discover the Jesus of history and to apply him to our time.

A. N. Wilson is a prolific and acclaimed novelist and biographer. He is also known as an Angry Young Prig, an English Tom Wolfe, and a Thatcherite intellectual. He has had some theological training, and has been both an Anglican and a Roman Catholic. A year before *Jesus* he wrote a splendidly angry pamphlet called *Against Religion* (London 1991) announcing rather stridently his Christian de-conversion, his attack on religion, his uneasiness with all monotheisms.

Against this background, *Jesus* can be seen as a post-deconversion, 'What's left?' essay. Who or what is Jesus, beyond religion, Christianity, God? The book does have some fustian silliness and some factual howlers. This is what he says of the Gethsemane prayer, without telling us whether he thinks Mark or Jesus was the author: 'It is one of the most superb of all literary creations, outstripping the *Iliad*, Aeschylus and Shakespeare at their most august and terrible' (201). Wow. He also assures us that 'the kingdom of God is within you' comes from John (cf. his p. 115 and Luke 17.21) and that Paul's letter to the Romans has nothing to say about the cross (cf. his p. 40 and Romans 5. 1–10; 6.3, 5, 10; 7.4; 8.34; 14.9).

Beyond this carelessness, Wilson has a weakness for charming fantasies for which there is no evidence. Example: maybe Paul was that fellow in Gethsemane that lost an ear, and so that is what he must have meant by carrying around the death of Jesus in his body (II Cor. 4.10) and by completing Christ's afflictions (Col. 1.24). Example: the young man with the towel in Gethsemane (surely a tendentious fulfilment of Amos 2.16) is really the same young man in white at the empty tomb. Or, most charming of all, the man (gardener?) at the empty tomb and the man walking with the disciples to Emmaus was not Jesus at all, but his look-alike brother James (though Wilson doesn't tell us how James was able to pull off the disappearance act at the moment of the breaking of the bread).

One of Wilson's polemic tricks is to position himself between an impossible orthodoxy and an impossible modernism, coming out better than either. But his descriptions of both camps are either caricatures, incomprehensible, or wrong. Here is what he means by orthodoxy.

> The truly orthodox Christian believer, holding that the Christ-child was the Godhead veiled in flesh, believes that all knowledge and all power and all dominion were invested in that baby boy. As he lay in the manger, Jesus knew the entire future history of the world, until the moment when he would announce that it was time for the Last Judgment. He understood all the mysteries of creation. He understood, as no ancient scientist or mathematician could have done, the mysteries of astro-physics which are as yet unknown in the most advanced laboratories of the twentieth century. He had the capacity, merely by blinking an eyelid, to bring all creation to a stop, just as it was by the will of Jesus,

true God and true Man, that creation had come into being in
the first place (73).

This is a shameful piece of rhetoric, both angry and wrong.

His description of rejected modernism is no better: murky and
false.

> The religious modernist recognizes that the New Testament is
> mythology, but would want to say that we can only hope to
> make sense of the New Testament if we submit to its own vision
> of things, and fail to apply to it our own crass historical or
> scientific assumptions (xv-xvi).

This is badly written, and the two final clauses are descriptions of
just what modernism is not.

Wilson rides through the New Testament on two different
hobby-horses. One is homiletic. He'll take a story, like the Trans-
figuration or the Feeding of the Five Thousand, and retell it vividly
with a few added imaginative touches. These re-tellings turn out
to be splendid liberal Anglican preaching. The second hobby-horse
is straight fictionalizing. It is very strange for a gifted biographer
not to know the difference between history and fiction, and not to
care about that difference. Sometimes he appears to be identifying
historical facts, while at other times he suggests that something is
true even if it didn't happen. This confusion about history and
fiction seriously vitiates this otherwise very interesting book, and it
needs further exploration.

It is quite impossible to say where Wilson stands in the contemporary debate on biography as fiction, though there is a touch of
Tory philistinism in his often-stated contempt for 'scholars' or
'pedants' or 'theologians' – all the same, apparently. Maybe he
wants it both ways: language constructs the reality it seems to refer
to, therefore all texts are fictions; yet facts discovered by historical
research are not the same as 'facts' invented by the imagination.
He seems to want to believe four things all at the same time.

   1. Wilson believes that we have a considerable amount of trustworthy information about Jesus' words and actions, but his method
is not historical, but intuitive: it just 'feels' like this really happened,
because there would be no reason to make it up.

   2. He seems quite unaware of the contemporary commonplace

that decisions on what is to be taken as historical are themselves decisions shaped by ideology. What we take to be fact emerges out of our interpretative systems.

3. Sometimes the Jesus he finds to be historical is the Jesus he needs, and sometimes the Jesus he needs doesn't require any historical fact at all apart from the actual texts of the four Gospels.

4. There is and is not a difference between history and fiction, and in any case it doesn't matter whether there is a difference or not. This kind of confusion dulls the edge of this otherwise interesting book.

Perhaps I am insensitive to the differences between creative ambiguity and intellectual slovenliness. But Wilson's self-contradictions are really too much to take. On Monday he can argue like a convinced Bultmannian that the function of history is to destroy our human self-confidence.

> The story of Christ invades history, but this does not mean that it is 'historical'. We shall never lay it bare by modern historical techniques; we can merely dismantle it beyond hope of restoration (74).

But on Tuesday, he is just as much at home on the opposite side of the street, sharing that apparently indelible English confidence that we can discover a solid historical core in the Gospels.

> Whether or not he said them all [the sayings of the Gospels], whether or not he said the actual words, there is enough here to suggest a body of teaching which draws on the riches and conflicts of Judaism (90).

Wilson can not only believe both of these positions; he can deny both of them as well. It doesn't matter. Good old Jesus breaks through the texts, finesses the follies of the pedants, and goes – wham! – right to our hearts.

How Wilson finds Jesus remains confused, but *what* he finds is vividly set down. Notice again that characteristic emotive shift from 'vivid and important' to 'Jesus must have said it'.

> . . . the cumulative effect of reading his words is to be confronted by a wholly distinctive view and voice – distinctively Jewish,

distinctively of its time, but distinctive. But it is more than the teachings of Jesus which make us blink our eyes and wish that we could adjust the focus a little more clearly on that figure who is one moment transfigured in glory on a mountainside, and the next is squatting on the ground frying some fish.

It is the fish which lures us on. It is those little details – a man irrationally losing his temper with a tree. It is someone remembering that a little girl, when she recovers from a fever, will be extremely hungry. It is the man who, after his arrest, can turn to look at one of his best friends, and make that man weep with the knowledge that he has not been loyal to the end. These little novelistic details could all, of course, have been fabricated, though it is hard to see what purpose would have been served in inventing them (68–9).

The Jesus he likes and finds comes from all the Gospels, from sayings, from miracles, from historical probabilities and from late church interpretation. And this Jesus comes, as always, in spite of the professors.

The troubled pathway of Wilson's *Jesus* suddenly leads to a luminous clearing near the end of the book, when the author – freed from his muddled methodologies – finally confesses what he loves most about Jesus; why, after Christianity and God have gone, he can never let him go. It is Jesus' *defiance*.

We could say that Jesus, in his passivity, defied not only Pilate, and the chief priests, but God himself. Jesus had come into the world and told the Jews that God was a Heavenly Father who loved his children as Jesus loved children . . . Jesus had put his trust in God and had assumed that the Day of the Lord would come, bringing justice to the poor, and healing to innocent suffering. He had put himself in the position of the poorest of the poor, making himself a slave to all, in that last ritual gesture at supper among his friends, the girding himself with the towel and washing his Disciples' feet. His reward had been arrest, torture and public humiliation. He had prayed for the Kingdom to come, and it had not come. If he did not utter the first verse of Psalm 22 as he hung on the cross, then he justifiably might have done. *My God, my God, why hast thou forsaken me?* (225).

No one who loves defiance can be all bad. In one final splendid 'perhaps' (redeeming all his earlier evasive 'perhapses?'), Wilson has his 'defiant' Jesus sadly repudiating the whole of Christianity.

> Perhaps if he had foreseen the whole of Christian history, his despair would have been even greater, and he would have exclaimed with Job, 'Why died I not from the womb? Why did I not give up the ghost when I came out of the belly? Why did the knees receive me? Or why the breasts that I should suck? For now should I have lien down and been quiet; I should have slept; then had I been at rest' (256).

It is hard finally to resist the temptation to read Wilson's *Jesus* as a coded political tract (see the admirable review of the book by Adam Gopnik in *The New Yorker*, 26 October 1992). Maybe this book is not about Jesus at all, but about Margaret Thatcher – a search for the historical Maggie. The Christian right is collapsing, and disillusion with the Anglican Jesus and with Thatcherism sets in at about the same time. So Wilson sets about to discover what can be rescued. Perhaps if fragments of Jesus can be found, maybe there is a possible politics to match. Is that what defiance means? Can one be an ex-Christian and still love Jesus? Can one be an ex-Tory and not reject politics or join the Labour Party? Answer: Jesus before Pilate.

> The representatives of religious and secular power in this world – the priests and the Procurator – would appear to have this man exactly where they want him. But, in fact, he calmly announces that their power is all illusory, that for those who follow him in spirit and in truth, such manifestations of human authority will always seem fantastical, and even in their most terrifying manifestations, absurd. *My kingdom is not of this world . . .*

> This icon, of the ragamuffin before the Roman governor, destroys them. The empires and churches and papacies which have been established in Christ's name are all revealed to be ridiculous by this text (217,218).

This is Wilson's Jesus in his finest hour. This is the Jesus Wilson found. Is it also Wilson?

5. *Three Catholic lives*

François Mauriac, *Life of Jesus*, London 1937
Shusaku Endo, *A Life of Jesus*, New York 1978 (first published in Japan, 1973)
Giovanni Papini, *Life of Christ*, New York 1923

François Mauriac was a skilled and devout novelist. His *Life of Jesus* is very pre-Vatican II in its confident orthodoxy. Mauriac assures us that he read the Catholic modernists and resisted their denials of Jesus' divinity. What can you do but patronize biblical scholarship if you have defined intellectual inquisitiveness as 'concupiscence', as Mauriac had done in an earlier essay? He uses in this life the Johannine framework (and language) and inserts Synoptic material into that pattern. He tries to steer between historical criticism and a docetic popular piety, and he may have succeeded. What we have is a pure Chalcedonian Christ, generously fictionalized; a devout defence of European Catholic orthodoxy.

But rigorous Chalcedonianism has rarely managed to be comfortable with Jesus' humanity, and Mauriac is no exception. Jesus is called 'the man-God'; he is said to be 'the man who called himself the Son of God', and his secret was love:

that is, that love is not a sentiment, a passion, but a person – someone. A man? Yes, a man. God? Yes, God (73)

Here is Mauriac's theological solution to the problem presented by Jesus' apparent repudiation of his mother and brothers in Mark 3. 31–35.

Christ had all eternity in which to glorify his mother in the flesh. Here below, perhaps [this 'perhaps', along with 'must have', becomes the novelists' favourite verbal devices for gap-filling] he sometimes treated her as he still does his chosen ones whom he has marked for holiness and who, behind their grilles, in their cells, or in the midst of the world, know all the appearances of abandon, of being forsaken, not without keeping the interior certainly of being his elect and beloved (24).

A touching tortured refusal to let the biblical text mean what is says. Jesus' humanity is turned into play-acting, swallowed up by the divinity.

'Lives' of Jesus written by novelists are usually more novel than biography, even when their authors think they are simply combining what happened with a touch of what might have happened. So it would be unfair to complain about Mauriac's sometimes eloquent fictionalizing. Judas, for example, is every Jesus-novelist's friend, for we know practically nothing about him. So the novelist, like the preacher, is bound to interpret.

> Intelligent, but short-sighted, when all was to melt away (by the fault of this fool [i.e. Jesus], he believed, who had squandered his magnificent gifts as he pleased and antagonized everybody), he did not understand that . . . the result he expected was to be unimaginably surpassed . . . Judas dreamed of a world conquered by Christ, wherein the elect or chosen would be no longer embarrassed by human sentiments (69, 72).

Mauriac has some eloquent asides concerning Jesus.

> The Son of Man buried himself deep in the abyss of his own peace. (143).

Or,

> Did not the Son of Man experience, in the mystery of his dual nature, the tender regrets felt by a mortal heart in the rays of a dying autumn sun? (146).

One sometimes gets the impression that Mauriac's rigorous doctrine of two natures in one (divine) person not only denies the humanity, but actually manages to deny the Incarnation itself. His 'church' is not only the extension of the Incarnation, it *is* the Incarnation.

> For those who saw Christ in the days when he was in the flesh, received less grace than we, who assist at the accomplishment of his promises (150).

The assured quantification of the two kinds of grace is an astonishing achievement; the definition of the Christian as the assistant in
the drama of redemption is remarkable. (However, the latter seems
to be the contribution of a translator who does not know that
'assister à' in French means simply 'witness'.)

Mauriac's ecclesiastical solution to all problems of biblical interpretation reaches a breath-taking climax in his reflections on the
resurrection. This miracle ought not to astonish us, he argues,
because Jesus is always coming to us after the death. The resurrection is validated by the doctrine of the real presence.

> This Presence [the risen Presence to Paul and the saints] is not
> the Eucharistic Presence [and then he proceeds coolly to deny
> his denial] but the little host gives an idea of it to the most
> ordinary Christian, when [and here follows an example of Maur-
> iac's genuinely eloquent and passionate prose] back in his place
> after Communion, he closes his cloak around that flame in the
> interior of his being, round the palpitation of love captive in his
> heart (269).

There are two troubling themes in Mauriac's finished portrait of
Jesus: a deep and abiding hatred of the Jews (which comes in part
from his dependence on the anti-Jewish Fourth Gospel) and a deep
and abiding hatred of the flesh. The first, of course, he can find in
the Gospels; the second he cannot. It comes from Mauriac himself.

The anti-Jewish animus is neither unexpected nor interesting.
The Jews didn't understand God – they took him only as a vengeful
Father. The Pharisees judged on appearances only, and the disciples'
slowness to understand is unfortunately ascribed to their 'Jewish
nature' (134). Jesus properly moves, in his anti-Phariseeism, from
reproach to insult to outrage to malediction. (When you have
decided to ridicule the historical scholars, this is what you are
obliged to believe.)

The anti-Jewishness is carried over into Mauriac's treatment of
the trial and crucifixion. The innocence of Pilate and the guilt
of the Jews is ordained by God.

> If Jesus had recourse to the famous words, 'Render to Caesar
> the things that are Caesar's, and to God the things that are

God's,' it was because in the drama of Calvary, prearranged from all eternity, it was not fitting that the Romans play any other part than that of executioner (215).

In the crucifixion, the Jews were the butchers and thus became guilty (nearly) for all eternity for their crime. Mauriac is strange and and terrible on the Matthaean confession of Jewish blood-guiltiness.

> The rabble cried out, 'His blood be upon us and upon our children!' It was, it is still, but the malediction is not eternal. Israel's place is kept at the right hand of the Son of David (258).

This final sentence is not entirely clear. I take it he is saying, with pardonable turgidity, that Jewish guilt will be abolished only by conversion to Christianity.

As already observed, this anti-Jewish ugliness is understandable and all but inevitable when you have decided to look at the New Testament without any historical-critical perspective. It was the rise of the historical study of the New Testament that began the process by which Christianity could – if it so wished – divest itself of its ugly antisemitic garments. But we cannot blame biblical literalism for Mauriac's sexual fixations.

Mauriac is by no means blind to the radical character of Jesus' ethic. He has some wise things to say about it, as a matter of fact.

> Charity is not enough, he demands the folly of charity: to hold out the other cheek, to leave the cloak to the thief who has already taken the tunic; to love those who hate us. Was he mad? Yes, in the eyes of men it is a state of madness which Christ asks and will obtain from his loved ones (79).

> It is a life full of snares and perils where everything is done prudently but in love (81).

But then there is that anger and fascination with the flesh. In an essay published several years before *Life of Jesus (Anguish and Joy of the Christian Life*, Notre Dame 1964, first published 1931), Mauriac makes it clear that Christianity's first and primary war is with the flesh. Sin is only sensuality. Pascal is quoted with approval when he calls marriage 'vile and humble in the eyes of God'. We are all fallen because we are born through and in the corrupted flesh. Only the mystics can be true Christians because they alone have learned denial.

This radical Catholic Puritanism colours Mauriac's whole reading of the Gospel story. Of the disciples, he can declare that 'everywhere they must preach the death of the flesh' (109). Jesus himself is dominated by the demand for sexual purity.

> The Son of Man knew that it is by purity we go to him, and that the flesh shelters the possibility of delights which, when satisfied, give to the creature the illusion of infinite pleasure – in other words he knew that the flesh is his rival (189).

Mauriac's theology betrays him here. He has replaced the doctrine of the Incarnation with the doctrine of the church, so there is no Incarnation available to ennoble flesh. The Word could never become Mauriac's flesh. The world is all flesh, all sensuality, and there is no sense (surely he could not so completely have forgotten St Francis) of creation's goodness. We all live in that city, he writes,

> when wine creates indulgence for every weakness, where scented bodies filled with corruption are . . . where the unbridled spirit scintillates, invents, seduces those who are there . . . the kingdom where one may hate, where one may desire, where one may tear another to pieces, where death spreads from heart to heart: the World (110).

God so loved the world? Hardly.

Jesus' most extraordinary victory was

> that among legions of holy women he was to substitute his own demands for the demands of their blood (155).

Jesus' greatest achievement – the nun.

But perhaps this fixation is not quite as strange as it seems. There is a sense in which the deepest things can be defined by their opposites, and Mauriac does truly believe that the heart of Jesus' message is love, and that love is lust's exact opposite.

To a world which corrupts childhood, which defies desire and satiety, which gives a god's name to every lust, Jesus had the audacity to . . . confer an absolute value on chastity, on the integrity of the heart and of the flesh (139).

And he goes even deeper. Lust is not only the opposite of Jesus' love – it is the brother, the comrade of that love. Since love is his key to Jesus, Mauriac is bound to be drawn to the Gospel prostitutes. Mauriac's Jesus sees in the prostitutes that cross his path something precious: 'her sins, which are many, are forgiven, for she loved much' (Luke 7.47). Prostitutes can come to know what true love means because they have experienced sexual love so fully. Mary Magdalene didn't need to make many changes in her life to come to Jesus. Just a slight shift of emphasis.

> Her vocation was never to refuse anything invented by man in the pursuit of the infinite, in the search for the absolute through the senses . . . Mary Magdalene remained faithful to her vocation: she continued to refuse nothing, but to God and no longer to man (100).

Mauriac's portrait of Jesus is dominated, and I would say vitiated, by his own hatred of the flesh. The central moments in his 'life' are the moments when Jesus, in all of the Gospels, confronts the prostitutes, named and unnamed – sometimes repentant, sometimes not – and praises, forgives, withholds judgment. We are obliged to admire the truth that lies concealed in Mauriac's moralistic error. Sexual love is not only the foe of faith (this is Mauriac most of the time), it is also faith's strange brother in that metaphorical world where a physical self-commitment of an absolute kind can be used to define and illumine a faith and a love for Jesus. Mauriac may have been served by his hang-up better than he knew. One who discerns, however imperfectly, the centrality of the Jesus-prostitute theme in the Gospels cannot, after all, be far from the kingdom.

Shusaku Endo's novel *Silence* (1966, English translation 1969) presents a moving description of the author's own tormented Catholicism and is a useful introduction to his *A Life of Jesus* a few years later. *Silence* is about the desperate struggle of the seven-teenth-century European missionaries in Japan. In the novel, Japan wins out over the leading character in the novel, Father Roderigo, who finally apostasizes, renouncing his faith after torture.

If François Mauriac's faith is an impenetrable suit of mediaeval armour protecting him from the seductive blandishments of Paris between the wars, Endo's faith is a necessary torment that in Japan he cannot escape. *Silence* portrays the tragic gulf between Japan and Catholic Christianity. There is, Endo argues, something in Japan that neither requires nor permits a transcendent God, a kind of swampy, pantheistic languor that leads not to passionate struggle but to acquiescence and resignation.

The key image in *Silence* is the face of Jesus. Father Roderigo speaks of his perpetual fascination with that face. He is first moved by the powerful face of the risen Christ in Piero della Francesca's *Resurrection*. Then, later, by the scourged, suffering, tormented face. In whatever form, the face fascinated and protected him. What an irony then when the symbol of apostasy turned out to be stamping on the face of an ugly picture of the crucified Christ. Roderigo speaks of that face at the moment of his apostasy.

> Lord, since long, long ago, innumerable times I have thought of your face. Especially since coming to this country have I done so tens of times . . . Whenever I prayed your face appeared before me; when I was alone I thought of your face imparting a blessing; when I was captured your face as it appeared when you carried your cross gave me life. This face is deeply ingrained in my soul – the most beautiful, the most precious thing in the world has been living in my heart. And now with this foot I am going to trample on it (258).

In *Silence* it was Jesus himself who advised, even encouraged, Father Roderigo to apostasize, to release other Catholic prisoners from their suffering, to participate in Christ's own eternal suffering. Apostasy in the novel is a dark form of faith. This is the Jesus we meet in Endo's *A Life of Jesus*.

In this splendid *Life* we find the same gulf between Japanese culture and Catholic Christianity that we found in the novel. It is this gulf that torments Shusaku Endo. Japan permits no transcendence, no God the Father. So Endo proposes to bridge the gulf by offering his readers (and himself, of course) a Jesus who radiates a maternal love.

As a Christian, Endo suffers from an inescapable alienation from his Japanese self, so his Jesus is the alienated man *par excellence*. From the beginning, his Jesus is alone, understood by no one.

> Heartbreaking loneliness carved his face in lines that made him look older than his years, and still the disciples failed to understand (73).

In a startling introduction to his account of Jesus' adult life, Endo cites the Johannine statement that Jesus was close to fifty years old. Perhaps in his early thirties he looked fifty, he suggests, with a haggard and suffering face that recalls the face that Father Roderigo remembered. Jesus' face was always tormented: 'the heart of Jesus was chronically in need'. This alienated Jesus is partly the classic existentialist hero of the past, and partly Endo himself, passionate and troubled Catholic fish in Japan's alien waters.

Endo carefully constructs his alluring semi-self-portrait of Jesus by setting down the systems of alienation within which he lived. There are seven of them.

1. Jesus was initially alienated from John the Baptist. John's God was 'Jewish', angry, Old Testament, ever the mean father. Jesus' God was like mother. Again and again, Endo cites the Beatitudes as his evidence for Jesus' mother-God. It is not clear whether he really believed he found this mother in the Gospels, or whether he imported mother-love into Jesus to please and persuade a languid and pantheistic Japanese culture.

Jesus was also anti-John in disposition and style of life. John was stern and demanding, Jesus (and Cana is of course his main evidence) is not; at Cana his 'laughing face [was] putting away the drinks' (34). Endo even finds 'the beaming *joie de vivre* of Jesus' (34). At moments like this it is fascinating to watch the novelist's legitimate apologetic enthusiasm win out over any historical desire to set down what happened or even what might have happened. When does a life of Jesus become a good novel? When a good novelist writes it. When the spiritual needs of the author demand it. When a present struggling faith requires validation from the sacred past.

2. Jesus was alienated from the Essenes and the Qumran community. Endo interprets the temptations of Jesus as temptations to a Qumran form of ministry. That community, he writes, sought earthly salvation and power, and the Gospel's Satan is an Essene mouthpiece. Endo writes: 'What was wanting in the [Essene] desert was love' (28). Not only do we not know that, we pretty well know that not to be the case.

3. Jesus was alienated from his disciples. Endo builds Peter's misunderstanding and denial and Judas' betrayal into a picture of total incomprehension on the part of the Twelve. They were, he argues, looking for someone to take over the leadership of the anti-Roman movement and to reform and renew Jewish religion currently corrupted by the compromise with Rome. Here is the novelist's imagination at work.

> The backstage maneuvering of the spies [i.e. the Pharisees] began to have its effect, little by little. Disquiet and wavering were taking root in the minds of the disciples, even though they were not as yet prepared to abandon their master (72).

However, Endo's disciples are far more than dolts. They are deeply corrupt traitors.

> So Peter and the others didn't merely forsake Jesus. To put it bluntly, like Judas, they turned traitor on him. The disciples denied Jesus to Caiaphas, who was the high priest and presiding officer of the Sanhedrin, and they made a promise never again to have any connection with Jesus. In exchange for the promise, they escaped arrest. That's how I see it (127).

Now this is a very interesting speculation. Of course we have no biblical evidence to back this harsh indictment of the disciples (and Endo knows that), but his conjecture has the merit of answering an important question: If Pilate considered Jesus dangerous enough to be killed, why were the disciples not treated the same?

In part, Endo needs to have the disciples are corrupt as possible in order to underline their post-resurrection transformation. When

Jesus from the cross refused to condemn the disciples for their deal with the Sanhedrin, they were shamed and astonished into post-resurrection heroism. Resurrection is not the central mark of Jesus' divinity for Endo. Radical forgiveness from the cross is.

4. Jesus was alienated from the crowds that followed him. Even though Endo tries to discern a growing popularity for Jesus' ministry, his portrait of the fickleness of the crowds matches his portrait of the inept and corrupt disciples. The crowds wanted two things Jesus regularly refused: miracles on demand and leadership in the anti-Roman movement. Endo reads the Sermon on the Mount, with its love for enemies and non-retaliation, as a specific rejection of overt political interest. So the crowds moved from initial disenchantment to hate. The rabbinic Judaism which shaped the people, Endo bitterly notes, had no room for love.

5. Jesus was alienated from the Pharisees. Endo, like Mauriac, accepts every detail of the Gospels' anti-Phariseeism. The few biblical scholars he mentions have not been able to mitigate his sense of a deep gulf between Jesus and his fellow Jews. Endo's Pharisees are intrusive spies, narrow legalists, sabbatarian freaks without a shred of compassion for human suffering. Lovelessness was bound to hate and fear radical love when it met it.

> Jesus came through to them as an insidious self-appointed reformer of Jewish religion, as an agitator who could eventually rouse the masses (43).

The Jews had everything to do with his death; Pilate nothing at all.

6. Jesus was alienated from the Sanhedrin (the priests). The priests read Jesus as a heretic, a denier of the Torah, and insulter of the Temple, a blasphemer, a Sabbath violator, worthy of death by stoning. They especially feared that the Jesus-movement might stir up a frenzy of nationalistic hope that would in turn tempt the Romans to a policy of total suppression of the Jews. To the priests, then, Jesus was both heretic and potential disturber of their comfortable concordat with Pilate.

7. For his project of de-Judaizing Jesus, the last alienation is definitive. Jesus is alienated from his own Scriptures, from the Old

Testament. The God of the Jews is all anger and judgment; Jesus' God is all love. The evidence against this doesn't appear to disturb Endo at all. He does not mention, of course, that the dual love commandment that he so values consists of two Old Testament passages.

Gone from Endo's Jesus-love is all apocalyptic urgency, all the grace of the parables. His Jesus is nothing but love, a love defined in terms of the Beatitudes, whose words (he rather too sweetly says) are 'like twinkling stars'. Most of all, like Mauriac, Endo turns for his decisive interpretation of love to the encounters between Jesus and the whores. Above all, again like Mauriac, to Luke 7. 36–50 and the woman who was forgiven because she loved much.

Whether or not one can do a full christology with love alone, and whether or not we ought to say, with Endo, that Jesus' love was *the* reason that brought him to the cross, Endo is good on this central theme. He knows that love has suffering in it, he knows that the Gethsemane prayer is a demonstration of God's love as participation in suffering. He also knows something of the folly, the carelessness of the kind of love that comes from Jesus. Love indeed can be futile in the world; it pays no bills, gains no praise or status. It is 'an act which in this visible world bears no direct correlation with tangible benefits' (52); it is 'forever vulnerable and helpless' (147).

There is something quite winning, even convincing, about the Jesus of Shusaku Endo. Its non-Jewishness is a terrible flaw; it may lack a certain self-consistency, but he has a good novelist's sense of what the springs of character are made of. When you remove the Old Testament, apocalyptic and first-century Judaism from Jesus, you might not seem to have anything left. But Endo sees some fragments among the ruins: the merriment of Cana, the insouciant forgiveness of Luke 7, the anguish of Gethsemane. He has both found and invented (in a mixture probably not susceptible to further analysis) a Jesus that genuinely tries to be faithful of both the warring halves of his soul – the Catholic and the Japanese.

When does a life of Jesus become a novel? When a novelist is the one who writes the life, of course. But lives are often novelistic even when perpetrated by scholarly piety. And are we not about ready to say that the Gospels themselves come most vividly to life when they are read as novels, as fictions? François Mauriac and Shusaku Endo are both men of deep and anguished faith. Each knows and fears the world given to them to work in and write for. Each makes an honest use of Jesus of Nazareth to give form to his faith and to relate the faith to the world. Mauriac's Jesus – fearing the Parisian sensuality of the author's real world – withdraws to become a mediaeval mystic, using sensual love, sublimated and transformed, to ascend to God. Endo's Jesus stays deeply immersed in the soft pantheism of a Japan uneasy with transcendence, and enjoys, suffers and forgives. In both cases the authors have fashioned a Jesus they need to help them hold on to faith. We make Jesus as our needs require, and in turn we may become – if we are lucky – like the Jesuses we make.

The power of the 'lives' of Endo and Mauriac is that the reader can participate in the authors' struggle to affirm their personal faith against an adversary culture. There is none of that struggle in Papini's long fictionalized biography. It is an over-written, fustian set of meditations on virtually all of the events of Jesus' life as recorded in the four Gospels.

Style and interpretation can best be illustrated in two character-istic passages. The first is an effusion on the Sermon on the Mount.

> Who has read it, even once, and has not felt at least in that brief moment while he read, a thrill of grateful tenderness, and an ache in his throat, a passion of love and remorse, a confused but urgent longing to act – so that those words shall not be words alone, nor this sermon mere sounds and signs, but so that they shall be imminent hope, life, alive in all those who live, present truth for always and for every one? He who has read it, if only once, and has not felt all this, he deserves our love beyond all other men, because all the love of men can never make up to him for what he has lost (86).

The second is a regrettable, and all too typical, bit of gratuitous antisemitism in Papini's meditation on the Gethsemane struggle.

> Or was it grief for that greater denial, the refusal of His own

people, the Jews, or the people from whom He was born and who now despised Him like one born out of His time, and suppressed Him like a child of shame, and did not know that the blood of Him who came to save them would never be wiped from their foreheads (305).

If Papini had been content just to write a nice biography, it would hardly have merited our attention. But he not only wrote this immensely popular book, he offered as well an incredible introduction telling us just how marvellous the book and the author really were. He is, he admits, a devout and secure Catholic believer who has successfully avoided some dreadful errors: this is not a pious tract or a nit-picking scholarly dissection of a beautiful truth. There is no Nietzschean romanticism and, above all, none of Renan's seductive aestheticism. Papini shyly admits that there have been no books on Jesus – until his – that 'give food fit for the soul' (10). His book, and here his modesty overwhelms him, is a great book 'without the affectations of professional piety and without the insipidity of scientific literature', written by a wise artist who 'knows how to hold the attention even of the hostile' (ibid.)

The book itself is harmless enough, but in the unfortunate preface the angry anti-intellectual fundamentalist shows his claws.

He who accepts the four Gospels must accept them wholly, entire, syllable by syllable – or else reject them from the first to the last and say, 'We know nothing' (11).

When self-righteousness is married to anti-intellectualism, it gives us a vicious mixture difficult to enjoy. Without the too-revealing preface, we would only be put to sleep. With it, anger arrives and one dares once again to pray that Jesus be saved from his friends.

6. Four European novels

Novel of the marginal character:
   George Moore, *The Brook Kerith*, New York 1956 (originally published 1916)
   Pär Lagerkvist, *Barabbas*, New York 1951

Novel as critique of orthodoxy:

Nikos Kazantzakis, *The Last Temptation of Christ*, London and New York 1960 (originally published 1955)

D. H. Lawrence, *The Man Who Died*, New York 1953 (originally published 1925)

The Brook Kerith, by the Irish novelist George Moore, is, I think, the finest of the fictions with which this chapter deals: more moving, more successful (to me) than the works of novelists with greater reputations like Faulkner and Lawrence. I have classified Moore, along with Lagerkvist's *Barabbas*, as a novel making use of the marginal character device, though Moore could fit just as well, with D. H. Lawrence, in the 'what if Jesus didn't really die' genre. The marginal character device dominates the first part of the book, while 'Jesus-didn't-die' shapes the second. Jesus-fictions are usually either experiments in fiction or interpretations of Jesus, rarely successful as both. Moore is.

The marginal character that Moore uses for the first portion of the novel is Joseph of Arimathea. We open on his youth, and follow his spiritual pilgrimage until he discovers, in his tomb, that Jesus did not die on the cross.

Joseph is a wealthy man's son who wishes to learn Hebrew in order to study the law and to become a prophet. But he decides to go to work for his father as a merchant of fish and grain. This doesn't work out, so he goes to Jerusalem for further study of the law. He is uncomfortable with the Sadducees, the priests, and the Temple cult, but is drawn to the Pharisees, coming to feel that true religion is nothing but love of God. He visits the Essenes and decides to spend some time with them.

In the Essene monastery he hears about John the Baptist's repentance movement and about John's follower Jesus the Essene. He decides to go back to work for his father, becomes friendly with Pilate, and begins to learn more about Jesus' mission.

Joseph seriously sets about trying to find Jesus, to see if he may not be the answer to his restless religious longings. He finally does find him near Capernaum, and becomes an ardent admirer. Joseph's first impression is that of a rather fey character, lyrical and otherworldly,

> ... his speech moving on with a gentle motion like that of
> clouds wreathing and unwreathing, finding new shapes for every
> period, and always beautiful shapes. He often stopped speaking
> and his eyes became fixed, as if he saw beyond the things we all
> see ... (101).

This early Jesus was all union with nature. The stars are God's
eyes, we live in his beautiful garden, and all we need is love. Joseph
is so overwhelmed that he throws himself upon the ground, and
prays that his experience of union with nature might last for ever.

Joseph soon discovers that Jesus is more than the first romantic.
He is also a healer and an expert decoder of the complex apocalyptic imagery of the book of Daniel. In both his mystical and apocalyptic modes he often acts mysteriously, withdrawing from the
disciples, failing or refusing to answer their questions. Both Jews
and Gentiles enjoy his miracles: Gentiles for their own sake, the
Jews as evidence of Messiahship.

Sometimes Moore just records the Gospel miracles. Sometimes
he improves on them: out of compassion he decides not to assign
the demons of the Gadarene madman to the herd of pigs, so they
are sent instead to the statues of the pagan divinities in Tiberias.
Sometimes Moore invents a really eccentric miracle of his own, as
when Jesus magically induces a sex-criminal to castrate himself.

During the period of Joseph's occasional meetings with Jesus,
certain changes take place. Jesus' physical appearance alters, and
Joseph now sees him with a lined and shrunken face, a face of
hatred, looking out on all the world with anger. But he is still
fascinated, and wonders if Jesus would accept him as a disciple
without his giving up his considerable wealth. The regular disciples
had indeed given up everything, but they seemed to Joseph a
petulant and unimpressive lot, anxious for the kingdom to arrive
so they could recoup their economic losses and have something
better to wear and to eat.

In the meantime, Joseph's father extracts a promise from his son
not to see or to follow Jesus while he (the father) is still alive.
Joseph agrees, but he cannot forget his strange longing. Jesus' life
– of which Joseph receives only occasional reports – begins to
move towards its climax. As the Sanhedrin draws up its indictment,
Jesus decides that sacrificing his life is more important than the

coming of the kingdom; that God apparently demands a victim, and that he shall be it. Jesus is asked if he is going to Jerusalem for the Passover. He answers,

> coiling himself like a diseased panther meditating on its spring, and as if uncertain he could accomplish it, he fell back into the chair . . . and then with a concentrated hate he spoke of the Temple . . . (182).

Moore's Jesus, at the close of his life, is only marginally sane, uncontrollably angry, committed to death. The mystic has utterly given way to the bitter apocalypticist.

> . . . I speak no more sweet words to anybody, but words that shall divide . . . Follow me, follow me, or else be for ever accursed and destroyed . . . (183).

Joseph hears about the crucifixion, and procures Jesus' body from his friend Pilate, burying it in his family crypt. He remains near the body after everyone else has left, and discovers that Jesus is not dead. He manages to get Jesus back to his own home without being detected. There is some evidence of severe mental disorder in the post-crucifixion Jesus, and Joseph supervises the process of physical and mental recovery. Resurrection rumours begin as soon as the empty tomb is discovered. Moore uses, of course, none of the 'appearance' tradition except the road to Emmaus story, in which the stranger is not the risen Jesus, but a wise friend.

Joseph hears that the Essene monastery has moved closer to Jerusalem, to the Brook Kerith, and he finally arranges for Jesus, after his recovery has been completed, to move to the monastery and to resume the role of shepherd of the Essene flocks that he held three years earlier before he began his ministry.

After staying with Jesus at the monastery for a while, Joseph leaves, promising to return. He never does, for he is shortly killed by the Zealots of Jerusalem. This death

> quickened in Jesus an almost dead memory, and as he sat gazing across the abyss his thoughts were that God held him accursed, else he would not have taken Joseph from him (267).

Jesus decides, in his despair, to leave the monastery grounds for the fields for

> the sight of men and the sound of men's voices were a torture to Jesus, and . . . he longed for solitude and silence and the occupation of the flock (268).

Jesus plays the shepherd in the fields for four years, and in this pastoral solitude he begins to reflect on his past and to come to terms with the trauma of his crucifixion. He comes deeply to regret his messianic pretensions, his apocalyptic, world-hating pessimism, his language of destruction and hate. Gradually the serene shepherd begins to prevail over the deluded and angry eschatologist.

> . . . signs and sounds of God's presence are never lacking on earth. As God's constant companion and confidant he had come to comprehend that the world of nature was a manifestation of the God he knew in himself. I know myself, he said one day, but I do not know the God which is above, for he seems to be infinite; nor do I know nature, which is beyond me . . . (288).

Jesus, being healed by his flocks, turned against his rejection of this world, his longing for the next; against repentance, rite, religion. Indeed, the final stage in the evolution of George Moore's Jesus involves a turning away from everything in the New Testament message, even from God himself. Moore's Essene shepherd becomes, finally, a first-century death of God theologian. God and heaven are both enemies of this Jesus.

> He who yields himself to God goes forth to persuade others to love God, and very soon his love of God impels him to violent words and cruel deeds [here we must recall that the author is an Irishman]. It cannot be other, for God is but desire, and whoever yields to desire falls into sin. To be without sin we must be without God . . . [Is not God therefore] the last uncleanliness of the mind . . . (297).

Thus the shepherd Jesus, some twenty years after his crucifixion, is finally at peace. Free of his ministry, his self-importance, his death, his Father in heaven.

In a striking, extended and breathtaking epilogue, Paul of Tarsus finds his way to the monastery where Jesus serves, looking for his young associate Timothy. He tries to present his message, with its rejection of the Jews, to the monks, and they pay him the tribute of a tolerant neglect. Paul finally meets Jesus, who hears about Christianity for the first time from Paul. Jesus does not initially identify himself, so Paul is more than a little troubled to meet someone whose life so strikingly parallels that of the crucified and risen Lord he is so actively proclaiming.

Jesus finally speaks, both to his fellow monks and to Paul, about the missing two years of his life, about his 'ministry' and non-death. Paul, hearing this story, flees in horror from the monastery. Jesus follows him, making very clear to Paul that Paul's gospel is based on a lie, a death and resurrection that didn't happen: if Christ is not risen, then faith is indeed vain. Jesus sternly reminds Paul that

> the Jesus which spoke to thee out of a cloud never lived in the flesh; he was Lord Jesus Christ of thy own imagining . . . (378).

Paul has two responses to this, his only 'authentic' encounter with Jesus: Jesus is mad, and what he says is false. Secure in his self-confidence and his denials, he leaves Jesus to continue passing on his deluded message across the Christian world. Jesus' final words to Paul sum up the theological message of George Moore's great novel. (Joseph of Arimathea had to die before the message could be uttered; it would have offended his decent, wise, but most traditional piety.)

> For many years, Paul, there were no thoughts in my mind, or they were kept back, for I was without a belief; but thought returned to my desolate mind as the spring returns to these hills . . . All things are God, Paul: thou art God and I am God, but if I were to say thou art man and I am God, I should be the madman that thou believest me to be. That was the second step in my advancement; and the third step, Paul, in my advancement was the knowledge that God did not design us to know him but

through our consciousness of good and evil, only thus far may
we know him. So thou seest, Paul, he has not written the utmost
stint of his power upon us, and this being so, Paul – and who
shall say that it is not so – it came to me to understand that all
striving was vain, and worse than vain (385–6).

If Paul ends up in terror and denial, Jesus decides for tolerance.
He briefly considered the possibility of travelling to Jerusalem to
visit the Jewish leaders and to identify himself. This would have
doubtless put a stop both to the Gentile mission and to the Jewish-
Christian establishment. But tolerance won out; why distress so
many unnecessarily? Denial and evangelism for Paul; tolerance and
serenity for Jesus. George Moore's Jesus is finally, in his mid-fifties,
truly risen, risen to a profound human compassion and love for
this world.

In *The Brook Kerith*, the function of the 'marginal' character is
two-fold. First, he is a spiritual seeker, testing all the available
forms of Jewish faith before coming to a kind of allegiance to
Jesus. Second, he is the instrument of Jesus' burial and renewal.
Barabbas, in the Swedish novelist Pär Lagerkvist's story, is also a
marginal character in the Passion story. But his function is different.
He is the man for whom Christ died. He is the embodiment and
display of – what else should we expect from Lutheran Sweden? –
the substitutionary doctrine of the atonement. Christ in his stead;
in all our steads. Barabbas himself probably does not end up
'converted': he doesn't need it. Lagerkvist's atonement does not
demand faith, it only demands a substitutionary death on the cross.
So whether the dying Barabbas, on the novel's final page, greets
death or nothingness or Jesus doesn't matter. He has already, with
or without faith, been saved on a hill outside Jerusalem on the first
Good Friday.
    The novel opens as Barabbas, just released from prison, watches
the skinny, androgynous Jesus dying on the cross. He is not exactly
driven to religious awe, but the experience does seem to bewilder
him. It leaves him scarred, changed for the worse. He does remember that he had seen Jesus once before, and that a kind of light
had emanated from him. And just before the death, there was a

strange darkness. But his response is only a zombie-like bewilderment.

Barabbas drops in at a Jerusalem bar, hears a little more about Jesus, and concludes that with that kind of death he could hardly have been the Messiah. The next day ('Saturday') he meets Peter, hears a bit more about the ministry and message, and is confirmed further in his denial of Jesus as Son of God. Peter hints at the possibility of a resurrection the next day.

So Barabbas hides behind a bush near the tomb when the Sabbath is over. He discovers the tomb is empty. A friend, a girl with a hare-lip, saw an angel at the tomb and is certain that Jesus rose from the dead. Barabbas is not persuaded; disciple theft is his best guess as to what really happened.

Barabbas hangs around Jerusalem for the next few days and he meets some of the disciples whom he finds unfriendly and stupid. They reject him when they find out he was the one who was pardoned in place of Jesus. They try to convert him by introducing him to Lazarus, but he is more disgusted than moved.

His friend with the hare-lip is picked up in Jewish persecution of Christians and is stoned to death, though Barabbas manages to break out of his lethargy enough to kill the scribe who stoned her. He escapes detection for the crime and returns to his friends and followers in the outlying hills (robbers, and probably anti-Roman activists). But he can't seem to concentrate on his work and he disappears.

Over the next twenty years, Barabbas is a slave under the Romans. He begins in the copper mines and he is shackled to one Sahak who turns out to be a Christian. Sahak is fascinated by Barabbas' strange connection to Jesus, and he tries to convert his friend, but it doesn't take. But Sahak's piety has an effect on his supervisors and it manages to get both him and Barabbas out of the mines and into the fields. Somehow both Sahak and Barabbas are granted an interview with the Roman governor on the island of Paphos. The interview goes badly for Sahak. He refuses to give absolute allegiance to Rome, and is crucified. Barabbas denies the Christian God without severe anxiety, saying only that he wants to believe but cannot. So his life is spared. The governor likes Barabbas and takes him with him when he is assigned to Rome.

When in Rome, Barabbas makes a half-hearted attempt to find

the place where the Christians are meeting. But when he goes to the Jewish catacombs outside the city, he finds no one, and the experience proves to be a terrifying one. He is driven into a kind of despair: 'alone in the endless night that rested over the whole earth, alone in heaven and on earth and among the living and the dead' (164).

Then in the winter of 63–64 CE the fire breaks out in the city. With this fire, and several pages from the end of the novel, Barabbas comes to life as a character and a man. He sets a number of buildings on fire himself. His languid inactivity is gone, and he becomes a convinced true believer. In what? He thinks he is helping Jesus. He becomes convinced that the fire has been set by the Christians, and that the end of the world is apparently at hand. Rome is doomed; the Saviour is about to return. Barabbas' faith turns out to be as false as his time-frame.

Finally, we find out how the Romans came to blame the Christians for the fire. It was Barabbas who told them so! In any case, the Romans arrest him along with the Christians falsely accused of arson. He meets Peter again in prison; the Christians in prison again recognize him and turn their backs on him. Only Peter is slightly inclined to forgive.

Barabbas is crucified along with the others.

> When he felt death approaching, that which he had always been so afraid of, he said out into the darkness, as though he were speaking to it: To Thee I deliver up my soul. And then he gave up the ghost (180).

Like Jesus had done? To whom was he speaking: darkness, death, or to Jesus at last? Barabbas' neurosis, his weak and very temporary faith, the recantation before the governor that saved his life, his fiery devotion to the arsonist-Jesus of the imagined parousia – all these became unimportant. Barabbas, there at the foot of the cross on the first Good Friday, was the one – perhaps the only one – for whom Jesus died. Lagerkvist will have us believe, I suspect, that he was truly saved. And Luther's passionate Anselmian doctrine of the atonement receives its most eloquent fictional defence.

Nikos Kazantzakis tells us, implicitly in a preface, explicitly

throughout his entire narrative, that *the* human problem is the war
between spirit and flesh. Since that is his problem, it will be that
of his Jesus. Both *The Last Temptation of Christ* and *The Man
Who Died* share a common concern with the sexuality of Jesus.
Lawrence's Jesus doesn't repudiate his pre-crucifixion asexual spiri-
tuality until he comes back to life. Kazantzakis' Jesus struggles
throughout his whole life against the flesh and wins only when he
finally denies it. Lawrence's Jesus is fulfilled by sex; Kazantzakis'
by repudiation.

The Last Temptation of Christ opens with a portrait of the
young Jesus, well before the start of his ministry. A very strange
young man he is: a virgin, a nerd, a practitioner of masochistic
self-laceration, and – by profession – a maker of the crosses used
by the Romans in their crucifixion of the Zealots. He is tormented by God: the main figure of speech expressing this torment
is that of the divine buzzard sinking talons into the top of the young
Jesus' head. He describes this divine torment in this exchange with
a rabbi.

> 'Why did you come to the monastery?'
> 'To save myself.'
> 'To save yourself? From what? From whom?'
> 'From God.'
> 'From God!' the rabbi cried out, troubled.
> 'He's been hunting me, driving his nails into my head,
> my heart, my loins. He wants to push me – '
> 'Where?'
> 'Over the precipice.'
> 'What precipice?'
> 'His . . .'
> (Chapter 10).

But this young neurotic, so often evoking hatred in others, is
given a semi-divine patina. His face and body often exude a kind
of glow, and his appearance is described in a passage characteristic of Kazantzakis' dreadful overblown prose.

> It was not a beautiful face, but it had a hidden, disquieting
> charm. Were his eyelashes to blame? Thick and exceedingly long,

they threw a strange blue shadow over the entire face. Or were his eyes responsible? They were large and black, full of light, full of darkness – all intimidation and sweetness. Flickering like those of a snake, they started at you from behind the long lashes, and your head reeled (Chapter 2).

Kazantzakis' Jesus is shaped by two secondary characters in the novel: Mary Magdalene and Judas. Mary stands for the struggle in his life; Judas for the struggle in his work. Jesus and Mary were play-fellows. One day (he was three, she was four) they took off their clothes and played doctor, or whatever they called it in those days. Each was fascinated by the naked body of the other, and neither forgot that early polymorphously perverse game. Jesus always felt that he had driven Mary to prostitution because she was for ever trying to recapture that early experience of sensual love. The adult Mary always desired the adult Jesus, and he always desired her. For some reason, Mary's bottom seems to fascinate Kazantzakis, even more than her hair or breasts; she is often called 'high-rumped', whatever that is. In any case, Mary was part of Jesus' last temptation.

When we turn to Kazantzakis' study of the life of this strange Jesus, it is important to remember that he is both fully human and fully divine from the beginning. The full orthodox doctrine of the Incarnation is a presupposition of the story.

Great things happen when God mixes with man. Without man, God would have no mind on this Earth to reflect upon his creatures intelligibly and to examine, fearfully yet impudently, his wise omnipotence. He would have on this Earth no heart to pity the concerns of others and to struggle to beget virtues and cares which God either did not want, or forgot, or was afraid to fashion. He breathed upon man, however, giving him the power and audacity to continue creation (Chapter 19).

In the temptation by the devil, we can watch Kazantzakis playing with the divine-human mixture in Jesus. Satan first comes as a snake, offering him a marriage with Mary Magdalene that would rescue her from her career. Next, as a lion he offers Jesus a kingdom of both heaven and earth (the way of Judas, as we shall see).

Finally, the tempter is an angel, tempting Jesus to become God (the very thing Jesus is in fact tempted to). Three alluring options: the way of Mary – redeeming the whore, affirming the goodness of the flesh (this temptation will return, as the 'last' one); the way of Judas, the struggle against Roman occupation; and the way of Jesus himself, becoming God, transcending both flesh (Mary) and history (Judas).

The most interesting difference between Kazantzakis' fiction and the Gospel story is that the novelist has very little interest in Jesus' relation to his own culture and land. The only drama is internal, existential; Jesus on the Jews and the Romans is quite subordinate. Indeed, Kazantzakis is not only indifferent to the relation between Jesus and his own people, he is profoundly hostile to the faith of Israel. His Jesus is hardly Jewish at all; he is much more like Kazantzakis. Here is a particularly nasty description of a Pharisee.

> A wild, throbbing Pharisee, stretched out face down on the last step of the Temple, was ravenously kissing the marble, and bellowing. Thick strings of talismans stuffed with terrifying texts from Scripture hung around his neck and arms. Repeated prostrations had made his knees calloused like a camel's; his face, neck and breast were covered with open, running wounds: every time this tempest of God threw him down, he would seize sharp stones and mutilate himself (Chapter 16).

Jesus has no special interest in the Jews; he is interested only in the salvation of all men and of all nature. He makes his first move from private struggle to public ministry as Mary Magdalene is about to be stoned. 'Let him who is without sin cast the first stone.' His first move is all love, all sweetness, no judgment.

> Jolly and compassionate, the son of Mary went from village to village . . . As soon as he lifted his foot, the ground he had trodden filled with flowers. When he looked at the trees, they blossomed. The moment he set foot in a fishing boat, a favourable wind puffed out the sail. The people listened to him, and the clay within them turned to wings (Chapter 14).

A spooky kid, this young Messiah. All you need ... Miracles abound, free for the asking.

But the time of sweetness does not last. Judas is constantly pointing out to Jesus the injustice of the Roman occupation. It is the death of John the Baptist that finally brings home to him the impotence of love without judgment. Jesus in effect becomes John, and the new message becomes more radical, more apocalyptic. There will be a new ark for the rescuing of some, the old earth will vanish and a new Jerusalem will be born.

The incorporation of judgment into love still does not bring the argument with Judas to an end. Judas is a Zealot who believes that men will be needed to overturn Roman power, while Jesus still holds that God alone can change all things and that it is only his own death as suffering servant that will bring that divine intervention to pass. Judas reluctantly agrees, and the two of them together plan the events of the final week.

Judas is to be the special instrument of redemption by giving the high priest the information he needs for a safe arrest. Jesus has chosen his death and Jews will carry it out. This plan has a curious effect on Kazantzakis' interpretation of the struggle in Gethsemane. It is not really a struggle at all. Jesus knows he is to die; he has chosen, he has willed it. His 'resistance' in the Gethsemane prayer is unconvincing, and Kazantzakis loses his hold on Jesus' full humanity in his treatment of the Passion week. This is strange, for Kazantzakis is often accused of so emphasizing the spirit-flesh struggle in Jesus that the humanity overwhelms the divinity. But his real theological problem turns out to be docetism. Jesus walks triumphantly to his death. It must be. Gethsemane is play-acting.

So we come to the last temptation. It is a dramatic and vivid device. But we are not convinced. In the earlier temptation, Mary and the flesh have already been rejected, and Jesus never doubts the divine necessity of his dying. He cries once from the cross: 'My God, my God ...' and then comes the flashback-dream. In this dream, Jesus reflects. Maybe I should have gone with bourgeois respectability, a good orgasm, and lots of children and grandchildren. In this dream, Mary Magdalene finally gets Jesus to bed. Then Paul of Tarsus kills her, and Jesus takes both the Bethany sisters as wives. God doesn't want messiahs or apocalyptic visions, he wants good carpenters living responsibly in the real world. Here is the flash-back Jesus:

> I've finished wrestling with God ... We have become friends. I won't build crosses any more. I'll build troughs, cradles, bedsteads ... I'll have my embittered mother come too, so that she can bring up her grandchildren ... (Chapter 31).

But no. Kazantzakis' Jesus rejects marriage and respectability. The flashback on the cross ends, and he offers his suffering Messiahship to God.

Lawrence's Jesus rejected his asexual New Testament ministry for sex and freedom. Kazantzakis' Jesus looked at the void of his asexual ministry and, after an unconvincing temptation, fully embraced it: 'God will be pleased with my superb sublimation. No to my beloved Mary and her high rump. No – and a slight yes – to Judas. God wants his children to die.'

D. H. Lawrence's fictional correction of his inherited Protestant Christianity – *The Man Who Died* – opens with a description of a rooster owned by a Jerusalem peasant. A Jerusalem cock, tethered by his owner to protect the hens. So this Jesus will turn into the Jerusalem cock tethered by his previous sexless-spiritual career. Jesus died sexless, but he breaks away, recovers, and finally discovers a true resurrection. After he finds his woman, he impregnates her, and leaves her: a colourless, dreary egotist clearly inferior to the evangelical Jesus he is apparently designed to correct.

The Man Who Died can be read in many ways, as another fictional study of the relation of sex and selfhood, as a pastiche of Christian and Mexican theologies, or as an attack on an inherited faith. Lawrence is probably the greatest novelist in our assemblage in this chapter, but this novella is one of his weakest and silliest efforts.

In any case, Jesus wakes up in the tomb. He is either dead or alive or neither dead nor alive. He is in pain, and for some reason he is overwhelmed with nausea, disillusion and revulsion. Why? It appears that what upsets him is the memory of the whole ministry that led up to the crucifixion. He now feels a deep hatred for humanity, particularly for humanity in authority.

Jesus, half alive, wanders into the yard of the peasant who owns the cock, who cares for his injuries and feeds him. This Jesus shows an uncharacteristic touch of compassion for this peasant couple, though he can't resist patronizing their trivial and mundane lives. So far, Jesus is a prig, an elitist, and a bore. He expresses revulsion against his former life.

> Why, then, should he be lifted up? Clods of earth are turned over for refreshment, they are not to be lifted up. Let the earth remain earthy, and hold its own against the sky. I was wrong to seek to lift it up. I was wrong to try to interfere.

Everything before the cross is repudiated: compassion, community, salvation, healing – all of it was nothing but interference in the lives of others. He briefly meets Mary Magdalene who loved him, and he manages to repudiate even her.

In the tomb, he left behind 'that noose which we call care', the whole idea of the self with purpose. Eschatological passion is translated into self-indulgent egotism. He leaves the peasant, takes the cock – his metaphor – decides that his old virginity was nothing but greed, and sets out upon a journey for a woman who might help him toward a real resurrection of the flesh; a woman who, at the same time, would be willing to leave him alone. No more of the old Protestant Jesus who saves and loves others. This is a Jesus out to save himself, a prick in every sense of the word.

He wanders about the Mediterranean world and finally comes upon a beautiful priestess in Syria who is tending a shrine devoted to Isis-in-search, and waiting for her own Osiris to come. They speak; she seems to believe that he is about all the Osiris she will get, and he finds her likely to help him on his problems. She rubs his old crucifixion scars with ointment. That helps, and he finally discovers that there is an alternative to his old virginity. Just before his virginity is lost, he looks upon the splendid naked body of the priestess and declares that *it* is the true rock, 'the soft white rock of life', upon which he will build – not his 'church', for he has no interest in anything but himself and his sexual fulfilment – his life.

Jesus and his priestess spend many evenings together admiring each other's divinity, and she finally conceives. Not surprisingly, Jesus decides that he had better move on. (Some lame excuses are made concerning the jealousy of the priestess' mother and slaves over his influence on her.) So he leaves the woman that completed his humanity, and leaves the unborn child he gave her. He rows his little boat away, promising to return, knowing he never will. This new Jesus is surely worse than the old one Lawrence left behind. Utterly self-absorbed, plenty of sex and no touch of love. Do we really have to choose between these two dreary fundamentalisms?

7. *The road not taken*

At the beginning of this book I promised myself and the reader that I would not be considering the 'Christ-figures' in the literature of our century. I partly broke that promise by including a study of Dostoevsky's Prince in my nineteenth-century chapter. I am now breaking it for one last time.

The modern English stage has apparently been drawn to a certain kind of Jesus-play. It might be called 'Jesus as the mysterious stranger'. I have in mind three plays of striking formal similarity: Jerome K. Jerome, *The Passing of the Third Floor Back* (New York 1904); J. B. Priestley, *An Inspector Calls (The Plays of J. B. Priestley*, Vol. III, London 1950); and T. S. Eliot, *The Cocktail Party* (London 1950). Each of them opens upon a small group in a room eating or getting ready for a party or meal. The members of the group are in some sort of need or distress, and to them comes a visitor, a stranger, with a successful diagnosis and cure. Often this stranger does such manifestly Jesus-like things that the reader (and sometimes even the characters in the play) comes to think of him as either Jesus himself or a Jesus-surrogate. Each of these plays is in some way a story of sin and redemption, reflecting the ideas of sin and redemption associated with the several authors and several times.

The Passing of the Third Floor Back ('third-floor back' refers to the stranger renting that room in the rooming-house; 'passing' refers to his 'passing-by' or 'passing through') is in three scenes: Prologue, A Play, and An Epilogue. The prologue presents the rather unsavoury residents of a slightly seedy London boarding-house. Mrs Sharpe is the shrewish landlady, dishonest in her financial dealings, cruel to her serving-girl. Stasia is the working-class servant, impudent, ill-clad, grimly realistic about her chances for self-improvement. Miss Kite is a woman of forty, over-dressed, over-made-up, simpering and pretentious. Major and Mrs Tomkins are an unpleasant couple, always fighting, behind in their rent, waiting for their attractive daughter Vivian to marry a wealthy and sleazy retired bookie named Wright. Mrs De Hooley is a baronet's cousin, widow of a potato salesman, and a dreadful snob. Jape Samuels is a hackneyed stage Jew that lisps ('an objectionable type of Jew' in the author's words), a con man dealing in non-existent silver mines and such. His associate is a young man named Larkcom who wishes he had stayed with his earlier desire to be an entertainer. Vivian, resigned to an unpleasant marriage to settle her father's debts, is really in love with Christopher, an artist who prostitutes his real gifts by cranking out easy-to-sell female nudes for Samuels. The world waiting for redemption.

At the end of the prologue, the stranger arrives to see about renting the back room. He has shabby clothes, a long coat, a hat and a staff. His eyes are deep, 'suggesting many sorrows', but his smile is radiant. He is simple and gentle and seems to possess some preternatural knowledge of the past lives of some of the dwellers in the boarding-house. One or two of the residents seem to 'remember' him from the past. (Pictures from a Sunday School lesson-book?)

Real personality changes begin at once, even before the prologue is over. Mrs Sharpe initially asks for £2.10.0 for the rent, but as she begins to melt under the stranger's mysterious sweetness, her greediness evaporates and she ends up by asking for £1.10.0. She is overwhelmed when the stranger refers to her as a 'kind woman' and becomes uncharacteristically nice to Stasia.

By the close of the prologue, we can begin to understand the stranger's redemptive technique. He cures or heals by lying. The lies are therapeutic, of course, and they all produce quick and positive results. But he is a redemptive liar none the less. He tells unkind shrews that they are kind when they are not, and they become so. He tells a self-hating serving-girl that she is really important – which she isn't – and she thereby becomes so to herself.

In the second scene, the 'play', the redemptive changes work themselves out. The stranger encourages Larkcom to go back to comedy; he does so and succeeds. He persuades Miss Kite to do without the fancy make-up. She does, and likes her new self much more than the old. He even persuades Wright to release Vivian to Christopher. He does so, and Christopher begins to do serious art. The Major and his wife are reminded that they used to love each other, so they start loving each other again and fight no more. Mrs De Hooley, the snob, once long ago took care of her delinquent sister. She starts doing so again, and is a snob no more. Mrs Sharpe stops cheating on her monthly rent bills, and Samuels is encouraged by the stranger not to be ashamed of his Jewishness. Samuels accepts himself, and we hear nothing about the stranger's own Jewishness (if any).

At the close of the play, Stasia is still a tough, wise, realistic serving-girl. But she has come to love herself, and in the final scene the stranger embraces her as he walks out of the boarding-house, leaving behind a quite incredible load of radiance and love. As he leaves, Stasia is suffused with redemptive sunlight.

Redemption through the therapeutic lie. How to be Jesus? Find the hidden goodness that everyone has; it is there, somewhere, in the past, in an old innocence. Touch it, appeal to it, and contemporary defences and immoralities will vanish.

Now this is not altogether hogwash. The stranger may make redemption seem too easy. Redemption is certainly tougher, and sin more intractable, than this fascinating 1903 play allows. But beyond the soap-opera silliness, something remains valid in all this. We do know that one way to make a child trustworthy is to trust, that one way to release someone's ability to love is genuinely to love that person. There may be a pre-Somme (and pre-Auschwitz) innocence about *The Passing of the Third Floor Back*. There may be some serious psychological over-simplification. But there is one way of reading the original Jesus story that suggests that Jesus himself occasionally functioned rather like the stranger. He sought out and loved the unloved and lovable. His healings took place when there was some faith in him. And he did change lives. Then and now, one might quietly add. One is tempted to say of Jerome's stranger what Kent said to Lear about his Fool: 'This is not altogether fool, my Lord' (I.iv.144).

An Inspector Calls takes place in 1912, in a comfortable dining-room in the Midlands, but it was written in 1944–45 and it is very much a World War II-home-front piece of work. Its message is quite secular, with none of the theological colouring of Jerome or Eliot. Yet the 'Inspector' does serve as a kind of Jesus, returned as judge. 'From thence he shall come to judge the quick and the dead.' Priestley's Inspector-Jesus is a remorseless judge of some complacent 'quick' in that moment of European euphoria before the outbreak of the First World War.

The Birlings are having an engagement dinner for their daughter Sheila. Also present are Gerald, the fiancé, and Eric, their younger son. Into their rather unpleasant capitalist complacency comes one Inspector Goole, asking some questions about a young woman who had committed suicide that night by swallowing poison. Mr Birling reluctantly recognizes the young woman in the photograph brought by the Inspector. It is Eva Smith, a young woman he had fired from his plant several years before because of her activity as a strike-leader.

After leaving the factory, Eva took a position in a dress shop, where Sheila was instrumental in getting her fired. Sheila had thought she had seen Eva smiling behind her back as she was trying on a dress. Sheila admitted to the Inspector that she was quite irrationally jealous of the good looks of the young woman.

Then Gerald submits to the Inspector's cool questioning. It now appears that Eva (now known as Daisy) had become Gerald's mistress during the previous year. He set her up in an apartment for a while and then broke off the relationship. Eva-Daisy, after leaving Gerald's protection, applied for aid to a charity committee chaired by Mrs Birling, who refused her any assistance. Finally, it is revealed that Eva had become pregnant by Eric, the young Birling son, and that he had been helping her with money he had stolen from the office.

With the five guilty ones at his feet, the Inspector departs with his final message, a sort of Battle-of-Britain, secular doctrine of the church:

> We don't live alone. We are members of one body. We are responsible for each other. And I tell you that the time will soon come [i.e. World War I] when, if men will not learn that lesson,

then they will be taught it in fire and blood and anguish (Act III).

The Last Judgment has taken place, and all are found guilty. But the play is not yet over. Two things shortly become known: there is no Inspector named Goole at the local police station, and no suicide has been recently received by the local infirmary. There are two quite different reactions to this mysterious news: the elder Birlings prove to be secure residents of the shame culture, and conclude that since they will not after all be found out, they have really done nothing wrong. The three young people are wiser children of guilt (i.e. 'we have done something terribly wrong, even if no one ever finds out') and do not feel exonerated by the discovery of the ambiguous existence of the Inspector and the dead girl.

These two responses to the last judgment, complacent shamelessness and serious guilt, co-exist until the final moment of the play. A phone call is received from the local police. A young woman has just died swallowing poison on her way to the infirmary, and an Inspector is on the way to the Birlings to ask some questions.

The Last Judgment came to the Midlands in the early years of the twentieth century, and – as has been the case with other last judgments – the way that leads to destruction has proved wide indeed. Yet, even so, some may end up on the right hand, some on the left.

Literary critics don't much care for the poetry of T. S. Eliot's third play *The Cocktail Party* – too much like prose – while theatre critics often find the play too West End, too well-made. I find both purists mistaken; it is a good play and Eliot has fashioned a bold and nervous and lofty language – whether poetry or prose or both or neither – that manages powerfully to say a good deal worth saying.

This is another play about Jesus and redemption. The room that receives this Jesus is a London drawing-room. The community, containing both associate redeemers and those in need of redemption, is constituted by the party guests, and the redeemer – quite properly for our century – is a psychiatrist. Jesus was accused of drinking wine; Eliot's Jesus takes gin, with a splash of water.

Act I gives us the world in need of redemption, the world *sub lege*. In the first scene Edward is hosting a cocktail party, including his mistress Celia, and trying to excuse the absence of his wife, Lavinia. The party breaks up, the psychiatrist (Sir Henry Harcourt-Reilly) remains behind. Edward does not know him, but he finds himself admitting that his wife has left him and he discovers to his surprise that he wants Lavinia back. Sir Henry mysteriously promises to take care of her return.

In the final scene of the first act, Lavinia returns to Edward, and each is still trapped in old patterns of self-absorption and bitter criticism of the other. Each feels uniquely misunderstood, sure of the other's inability to grasp the special nature of his and her suffering. Lavinia is somewhat wiser than her husband, and it appears that her departure (therapeutically designed by Sir Henry) was intended in part to help Edward come to himself. Edward, even having willed his wife's return, is still bewildered. There is as yet no glimmer of unselfishness: redemption is in the wings, not yet on stage. He says to her:

> Hell is oneself,
> Hell is alone, the other figures in it
> Merely projections. There is nothing to escape from
> And nothing to escape to. One is always alone.

In Act I we have met the redeemer, Sir Henry, and those in need of redemption, Celia, Edward, and Lavinia.

Act II brings the time of redemption. *Sub gratia* abolishes *sub lege*. The redemption occurs (or begins in earnest, for those who don't believe that things happen all at once) several weeks later in Sir Henry's consulting room. The psychiatrist has contrived a surprise meeting in his office between Lavinia and Edward, two of his patients, he tells them, with remarkably similar symptoms. They are both irritated with his ruse; they spar with each other and suggest to Sir Henry some confident diagnoses and cures. He coolly silences their presumption, and after allowing them to make fools of themselves, he begins to offer each of them an appropriate word of grace. They are two interlocking illnesses needing each other. They are to return to their secular world of cocktail parties, and there they just may learn how to locate a small glimmer of compassion, each for the other. Sir Henry judges and then gives grace. (It is a strikingly Protestant grace, an *innerweltliche Askese*, to come from Mr Eliot.)

REILLY: And now you begin to see, I hope.
          How much you have in common. The same isolation.
          A man who finds himself incapable of loving
          And a woman who finds that no man can love her.

LAVINIA: It seems to me that what we have in common
          Might be just enough to make us loathe one another.

REILLY: See it rather as the bond which holds you together.
          While still in a state of unenlightenment,
          You could always say: 'He could not love any woman';
          You could always say: 'No man could love her.'
          You could accuse each other of your own faults,
          And so you could avoid understanding each other.
          Now, you have only to reverse the propositions
          And put them together.

LAVINIA: Then what can we do
          When we can go neither back nor forward? Edward!
          What can we do?

REILLY: You have answered your own question,
          Though you do not know the meaning of what you have said.

EDWARD: Lavinia, we must make the best of a bad job.
          That is what he means.

As Edward and Lavinia leave, the judge-redeemer becomes the high priest ('after the order of Melchizedek'?), with the hieratic words 'Go in peace. And work out your salvation with diligence' ('fear and trembling' is perhaps too first-century, even for Eliot).

    Then Celia, shattered by the unexpected end of the affair, enters the consulting room. She is a far more attractive and humble patient than either Lavinia or Edward. She does not claim to know what the matter with her is, but she does speak, quite movingly, of two symptoms. An awareness of solitude and a sense of sin. This, she confesses, surprises her, because she was conventionally brought up to disbelieve in sin, and she feels that there was nothing

particularly immoral about her affair with Edward, using – alas –
that old chestnut from the culture of adultery:

> I wasn't taking anything away from her –
> Anything she wanted.

(The saintly Celia's only flaw; but we like that touch of fallibility in
our saints.) Celia stumbles, at the end of the affair, into theological
language. Why not? Jesus wouldn't have objected, and neither does
Sir Henry.

> It's not the feeling of anything I've ever done,
> Which I might get away from, or of anything in me
> I could get rid of – but of emptiness, of failure
> Towards someone, or something, outside of myself;
> And I feel I must . . . atone – is that the word?
> Can you treat a patient for such a state of mind?

I went into a forest, Celia confesses, to find a treasure that turned
out to be not there, that perhaps is nowhere, but I cannot find my
way out. Can you help such a one? she cries.

Yes, Sir Henry replies, I can. There are two ways out of your
forest. He then proceeds to describe for Celia the way he offered
to (or imposed upon) Edward and Lavinia.

> But the form of treatment must be your own choice:
> I cannot choose for you. If that is what you wish,
> I can reconcile you to the human condition,
> The condition to which some who have gone as far as you
> Have succeeded in returning. They may remember
> The vision they have had, but they cease to regret it,
> Maintain themselves by the common routine,
> Learn to avoid excessive expectation,
> Become tolerant of themselves and others,
> Giving and taking, in the usual actions
> What there is to give and take. They do not repine;
> Are contented with the morning that separates
> And with the evening that brings together
> For casual talk before the fire

Two people who know they do not understand each other,
Breeding children whom they do not understand
And who will never understand them.

Celia is unenthusiastic, and becomes quite despondent if there is no other way. Sir Henry gently sketches an alternative.

REILLY: There is another way, if you have the courage.
The first I could describe in familiar terms
Because you have seen it, as we all have seen it,
Illustrated, more or less, in lives of those about us.
The second is unknown, and so requires faith –
The kind of faith that issues from despair.
The destination cannot be described;
You will know very little until you get there;
You will journey blind. But the way leads towards possession
Of what you have sought for in the wrong place.
CELIA: That sounds like what I want. But what is my duty?
REILLY: Whichever way you choose will prescribe its own duty.
CELIA: Which way is better?
REILLY: Neither way is better.
Both ways are necessary. It is also necessary
To make a choice between them.
CELIA: Then I choose the second.
REILLY: It is a terrifying journey.
CELIA: I am not frightened
But glad. I suppose it is a lonely way?
REILLY: No lonelier than the other. But those who take the other
Can forget their loneliness. You will not forget yours.
Each way means loneliness – and communion.
Both ways avoid the final desolation
Of solitude in the phantasmal world
Of imagination, shuffling memories and desires.

Celia, without hesitation, chooses the second way and is given instructions. After she leaves, Sir Henry reports to an associate: 'it is finished.' It is, and it isn't, for the crucifixion is yet to come.

In Act III, two years later, we discover how the two journeys have fared. Edward and Lavinia are alone in their drawing-room, about to do what Sir Henry had commissioned them to do: give real cocktail parties in the real world and try to learn something about what others need. They have indeed begun to learn. They are gentle and loving with each other. Edward anxiously urges Lavinia to get some rest before the party starts.[5]

The friends from the earlier cocktail party assemble, and Celia's courageous and sacrificial crucifixion as a missionary-nurse in Africa is recounted. Both journeys, both redemptions, have been successful. Eliot's psychiatrist-Jesus has something for everyone; both Protestant and Catholic grace are served at *The Cocktail Party*.

And now, no more Christ-figures, I promise.

VI

The Poets

Up to now we have seen that Jesus of Nazareth has fascinated all kinds of twentieth-century writers of prose fiction, apart from the professional scholars of religion obliged to write about him. It has been interesting for me to discover that first-rate poetry about Jesus in this century (my examples are all from the English language, apart from one eloquent poem by Rilke) is quite hard to find. Like the prose we have already studied, some of this poetry celebrates a received orthodoxy, some wildly rebels or revises, and some lives somewhere between rebellion and acquiescence.[1]

Here is Lawrence Ferlinghetti's early poem from his first collection, *A Coney Island of the Mind.*

> Sometime during eternity
> >   some guys show up
> and one of them
> >   who shows up real late
> >   is a kind of carpenter
> >   from some square-type place
> >   like Galilee
> >   and he starts wailing
> >   and claiming he is hep
> >   to who made heaven
> >   and earth
> >   and that the cat
> >   who really laid it on us
> >   is his Dad
> And moreover
> >   he adds
> >   It's all writ down
> >   on some scroll-type parchments

which some henchmen
leave lying around the Dead Sea somewheres
a long time ago
and which you won't even find
for a coupla thousand years or so
or at least for
nineteen hundred and fortyseven
of them
to be exact
and even then
nobody really believes them
or me
for that matter
You're hot
they tell him
and they cool him
They stretch him on the Tree to cool
And everybody after that
is always making models
of this Tree
with Him hung up
and always crooning His name
and calling Him to come down
and sit in
on their combo
as if he is *the* king cat
who's got to blow
or they can't quite make it
Only he don't come down
from His Tree
Him just hang there
on His Tree
looking real Petered out
and real cool
and also
according to a roundup
of late world news
from the usual unreliable sources
real dead

It is sometimes said that the Jesus-freaks of the early 1960s were a spin-off from the first hipster generation. 'Sometime during eternity' suggests that connection, although the poet does not seem to have made up his mind about the importance of the figure he is describing. The setting of the poem has a faintly pre-existence or trinitarian colour: Jesus 'shows up' out of, or during, eternity. When he gets to Galilee he begins to wail, which suggests that he doesn't have much of importance on his mind. But boy, is he relevant! (Nothing is more irrelevant than yesterday's relevance.) He is 'hip' to God, his good old dad.

Then Ferlinghetti adds a strange and rather silly stanza about scripture. His Jesus apparently thinks that his true meaning was written down somewhere in the Dead Sea scrolls (which were not, of course, about the Jesus movement at all), which nobody, including the poet, seems to believe.

Not too impressive, this Jesus. He gets himself crucified, and then Christians begin happening, and they act pretty strangely. They 'croon' his name (hymns, presumably), and make crucifixes. Above all, and here the jazz talk takes over rather awkwardly, Christians try to get Jesus to come down from the cross and sit in with their groups, because they can't make proper music without him. But he doesn't come down. He stays on his cross, as dead as ever. Jesus never enters the human race in any way, ever again. No continuing influence. Jesus dead has a kind of dignity, but Christians are silly if they try to call on him for anything today.

If Ferlinghetti gives us the authentic San Francisco language of the 1950s, Barbara O'Brien's eloquent 'The Prophet Explains Religion' is pure New York City of the 1990s. Jazz rhythms influence both, but O'Brien's is a far more sophisticated interpretation of Jesus: she has either read Bonhoeffer's prison letters or absorbed them unconsciously from the culture. This is a non-ecclesiastical, non-religious Jesus; a Jesus with no need of God.

> OK so he don't look like a prophet but he's
> A real smart old guy. Got a place
> Over a Chinese restaurant on Broadway
> & you got something you want to ask
> Just take him some chateau la hooch & go up the back way.

Says PROPHET IS IN on the door.
        Like last night I went he was watching some cop show
        on tv I ask him man
        My old lady wants me to get religion. Whadda
        Ya think & he laughs
Religion's like getting yourself lost in New Jersey
He says, and shakes his head, like,
Man, how dumb can you get?
        I think about that. We watch tv a while.
        Then I say I don't get it & he says
        OK let me explain it like this.
Let's say you got a nice place on the west side –
        Where I say & he says nineties – nice place by the park
        & I say how about east nineties & he says
OK it don't matter. Anyhow you get in your car & cross
the George Washington Bridge & drive over to Paramus
        Man I wouldn't have no car in this city I say
He says never mind, you're rich, you got a car.
You stay in Paramus a long time,
& it's time to go home, so you
Start to drive but you get turned around
& you don't remember how you came
So you drive around, days & days
All over Jersey looking for a way to come back.
        He stopped & watched a Buick
        Get blown up on tv. The room was real dark –
        Just one yellow 40-watt bulb & the tube
        & the wallpaper greasy &
        The place smelled like burnt won ton.
        I still didn't get it & I said is that it &
He says what? Oh yeah – well
After a while you're about to give up
& quit – maybe just stay in Jersey
But then you see a road sign that says
I–95 EAST GEORGE WASHINGTON BRIDGE
        So then I go home I say
& he says No, you stop the car & get out
& bow down to that sign.

You light candles & pray to it &
Stick some flowers on it.
You notice other people praying to other signs
Like ones that say ROUTE 4 EAST NEW YORK
& you think they're screwed up.
You hear about people looking for the Lincoln Tunnel
& you think they're more screwed up.

   So when do I go home I ask
& he says you don't so long as you get religion.
You stay by that road sign & talk
About how it saved your ass.

   That's dumb I say & he laughs
   Real funny – kind of giggles.
Yeah he says, I don't know why
You'd want a damn fool thing like that.

   My old lady says it'd be good for me I tell him
Keeps some people out of trouble he says,
Makes 'em feel good for a while, but then
A lot get too stuck & it makes 'em ugly.

   So Jesus wasn't for real I say
Oh yeah Jesus was for real all right says the old man.
But he wasn't no god any more than you are –
He was just a man who saw the plain truth
Saw heaven & earth & everything else
As clear as I'm seeing you.
But he tried to tell people how they should go,
You know, to get back home themselves.
Tried to show 'em it was right under their noses
& nobody got it. They thought it meant
They was supposed to just wait around until he comes
To take 'em across the river.
Like he was a Jersey Transit bus.
Then they nailed him on a cross. Made
Another fucking road sign out of him.

   The prophet finished off the bottle.

   It was getting late – the local news was on the tube.
Does go home mean going to heaven I ask.
Sort of he says but you don't have to be dead

To get there. Go any time. You just gotta get going
& you gotta want to go more than you want anything else.
But nobody's gonna take ya, not even Jesus.
   So why don't you go I say & he
   Booms out a big laugh deeper than earth.
Shit I'm there right now he laughs
& I laugh too, cause I like the old guy.
I leave some cash on top of the tv
Before I go out. I still don't know
What he meant about going home but I decided to
Forget about religion.

The prophet instructs the poet. Jesus taught freedom and autonomy, rejecting mediators and dependency.

But he wasn't no god any more than you are –
He was just a man who saw the plain truth
Saw heaven & earth & everything else
As clear as I'm seeing you.
But he tried to tell people how they should go,
You know, to get back home themselves.
Tried to show 'em it was right under their noses
& nobody got it.

Jesus himself had it right. You have everything you need already.
No further searches are necessary. Trouble is that Christianity came
along and screwed things up: 'Made/Another fucking road sign
out of him.' Heaven is earth; kingdom is here. Dorothy didn't need
to go to Oz, since everything was already in her own back yard.
What Barbara O'Brien offers is a sermon or exegesis on Luke
17.21: '. . . for behold, the kingdom of God is in the midst of you.'

The Jesus-movement of the 1960s (whether it came from the drug
rehabilitation wing of the Bay area hippies or not) produced its
own poetry and music – the so-called white gospel or spiritual
music, very churchy and very commercial. These Jesus songs are
generally about redemption and are rarely interested in the man
Jesus or his message. Here is an exception, of no great literary
distinction. But this kind of thing is probably the most popular

Jesus-poetry around today, and it ought to be noted. It may blow the reader's mind, in ways unintended by the authors. This is 'Could He Be The Messiah?' by Michael and Deborah Smith.

Been here for days, I'm amazed at this teacher, carpenter, preacher.
Lost in the crowd, I hear him now; He's praying and He's saying,
    God feed them all.
Five thousand men, all of His friends are worried: find bread and
    hurry!
Five loaves and fish – what can He wish –
He's praying; still – He's saying, God, feed them all.
Could He be the Messiah, miracle man, part of the plan?
Could He be the Messiah, life in His hand?
I understand – he could be.
Bread for our needs, fully He feeds our minds, older and younger.
Twelve baskets more, can we ignore, He shows us that He knows us;
    Is He the Christ? God in His eyes, I realize His power, need of
    the hour.
Jesus His name, they say. He came to feed us and to receive us,
Is He the Christ?
Could He be the Messiah, miracle man, part of the plan?
Could He be the Messiah, life in His hand?
It is He, I understand, it is He.

Black gospel music is perhaps *the* most important source of poetry about Jesus in our century. The spiritual is folk music, shaped in the nineteenth century in a southern rural setting. Black gospel music came into being when blacks began to move north in the second decade of this century. They moved, for the most part, to cities, and the spiritual proved not altogether fitting to their new needs. Black gospel music is urban, based in the church, and it is composed – though the individual singer may add or take away as she chooses, which is not the case with the spiritual. The greatest of the writers of Black gospel music was Thomas A. Dorsey (1899–1993). He began by writing blues for Bessie Smith, and moved gradually to meet the new spiritual needs of his newly urbanized people. The greatest and most influential of the gospel songs is probably his 'Precious Lord Take My Hand'.

Precious Lord, take my hand,
Lead me on, let me stand,
I am tired, I am weak, I am worn;
Through the storm, through the night,
Lead me on to the light,
Take my hand, precious Lord, lead me home.

When my way grows drear,
Precious Lord, linger near,
When my life is almost gone,
Hear my cry, hear my call,
Hold my hand lest I fall;
Take my hand, precious Lord, lead me home.

When the darkness appears
And the night draws near,
And the day is past and gone,
At the river I stand,
Guide my feet, hold my hand;
Take my hand, precious Lord, lead me home.

Dorsey wrote this song in 1932, after he returned home from a trip to find that his wife and daughter had died. It is a powerful expression of the role of Jesus in the religion of Black America up to the time of Dr King and Malcolm X, and probably since. (It was sung by Mahalia Jackson at Dr King's funeral.) This is not Jesus the teacher, or Jesus the healer, or Jesus coming again at the time of the last judgment.

This Jesus is the one who always comes at the times of our suffering and despair. He brings no promise that our earthly trials will be abolished; the only promise is that he will be there, with us.

'Precious Lord' is, above all, a song about death. When we stand at the river, that boundary between suffering and darkness on one shore and 'light' and 'home' on the other, he will be there to guide us on our last journey. It is hard to imagine a more powerful expression of the consolation of Jesus than this simple lyric set to Dorsey's incomparable music.

Country and Western has recently discovered Jesus, and the reputation of both suffers. This is John Prine's not very naughty 'Jesus the Missing Years' (from the album of the same name):

It was raining it was cold
West Bethlehem was no place for a twelve year old
So he packed his bags and he headed out
To find out what the world's about
He went to France and he went to Spain
He found love he found pain
He found stores so he started to shop
But he had no money so he got in trouble with a cop
Kids in trouble with the cops from Israel didn't have no home
So he cut his hair and moved to Rome
It was there he met his Irish bride
And they rented a flat on the lower east side of Rome
Italy that is
Music publishers, book binders, bible belters,
Swimming pools, orgies and lots of pretty Italian chicks

Isn't it strange that white popular music has so utterly failed to find an honest voice to sing about Jesus, either in faith or hostility? Prine's song is almost as bad as the Smiths' 'Could He Be the Messiah?' and it doesn't even touch the hem of the garment of 'Precious Lord'. Jesus had an orgy in Italy. Wow!

Somewhere around 1909 Ezra Pound wrote the 'Ballad of the Goodly Fere' (i.e. companion). It became popular, but he didn't like it. Eliot didn't care for it either, but Yeats thought it had 'permanent value'. It is clearly in praise of Jesus; Presbyterian upbringing must have some consequences. The ballad is sung by Simon the Zealot, the disciple most in sympathy with the anti-Roman revolutionary movement. The song is not anti-Roman at all; it is the priests that bring Jesus to the cross.

Ha' we lost the goodliest fere o' all
For the priests and the-gallows tree?
Aye lover he was of brawny men,
O' ships and the open sea.

When they came wi' a host to take Our Man
His smile was good to see,
'First let these go!' quo' our Goodly Fere,
'Or I'll see ye damned,' says he.

Aye he sent us out through the crossed high spears
And the scorn of his laugh rang free,
'Why took ye not me when I walked about
Alone in the town?' says he.

Oh we drunk his 'Hale' in the good red wine
When we last made company,
No capon priest was the Goodly Fere
But a man o'men was he.

I ha' seen him drive a hundred men
Wi' a bundle o' cords swung free,
That they took the high and the holy house
For their pawn and treasury.

They'll no' get him a' in a book, I think
Though they write it cunningly;
No mouse of the scrolls was the Goodly Fere
But aye loved the open sea.

If they think they ha' snared our Goodly Fere
They are fools to the last degree.
'I'll go to the feast,' quo' our Goodly Fere
'Though I go to the gallows tree.'

'Ye ha' seen me heal the lame and blind,
And wake the dead,' says he,
'Ye shall see one thing to master all:
'Tis how a brave man dies on the tree.'

A son of God was the Goodly Fere
That bade us his brothers be.
I ha' seen him cow a thousand men.
I have seen him upon the tree.

He cried no cry when they drave the nails
And the blood gushed hot and free,
The hounds of the crimson sky gave tongue,
But never a cry cried he.

I ha' seen him cow a thousand men
On the hills o' Galilee,
They whined as he walked out calm between,
Wi' his eyes like the grey o' the sea,

Like the sea that brooks no voyaging
With the winds unleashed and free,
Like the sea that he cowed at Genseret
Wi' twey words spoke' suddently.

A master of men was the Goodly Fere,
A mate of the wind and sea,
If they think they ha' slain our Goodly Fere
They are fools eternally.

I ha' see him eat o' the honey-comb
Sin' they nailed him to the tree.

Simon is speaking after the crucifixion, but he will have nothing to say about the resurrection until the third-to-last line. The Jesus he presents is very physical – muscular, leader of men, lover of the open sea, eating and drinking.

Stanzas two and three are set in Gethsemane at the time of the arrest. Jesus was in good spirits, insisting that his disciples be spared. Stanza four drops back in time to a very non-sacramental last supper, while the fifth has Jesus vigorously cleaning out the Temple. Simon oddly notes that no book will ever be able to get Jesus right; no 'mouse of the scrolls' was he.

Then stanza seven moves back in time again to the beginning of the final trip to Jerusalem and to Jesus' prediction of his own death. He tells his disciples that if they were impressed by his miracles, they will be even more impressed by the way he will die on the cross. The death itself is briefly presented – no complaints, no cry of pain when the nails are driven in. This is indeed a death more serene, more victorious than that in any of the Gospels. 'The hounds of the crimson sky' (bloody clouds at the time of the darkness at noon?) cried out, but Jesus did not.

Then, rather awkwardly, Pound refers back to the walking on the water in Mark 6. 47–53 and to Jesus' words of assurance to the fearful disciples. A picture of great physical power over both man and nature.

Then, unexpectedly, the resurrection is affirmed. This is a Jesus, after all, too strong, too merry, to die.

If they think they ha' slain our Goodly Fere

They are fools eternally.

I ha' seen him eat o' the honey comb [Luke 24. 37–43]
Sin' [i.e. after] they nailed him to the tree.

W. H. Auden is not quite so sure as Ezra Pound that there is
something beyond the cross. His 'Friday's Child' (1958) is a strange
and troubled poem indeed, miles away from Pound's cheerful certainty. It concludes:

Now, did He really break the seal
And rise again? We dare not say;
But conscious unbelievers feel
    Quite sure of Judgment Day.

Meanwhile, a silence on the cross,
As dead as we shall ever be.
Speaks of some total gain or loss,
    And you and I are free

To guess from the insulted face
Just what Appearances He saves
By suffering in a public place
    A death reserved for slaves.

This poem about God becomes a Jesus-poem (for our purposes)
only in the last three stanzas quoted here. God's relation to the
poet is a deeply ambivalent one. (We are not used to theological
ambivalence from Auden.) He exists, probably. He also gave us
freedom to choose, but we didn't take the offer seriously. We never
really thought he'd dare to damn us, but he is apparently quite
capable of doing so. No reverence is due this God, no awe, no
religion. Why bother with him? The God of the Thomists, using
observation and the *via analogia*, is 'banal' and 'rot'. God doesn't
even know himself, and we don't know what is going on. Proofs
don't work.

So, after nine strange stanzas, singing praises to a powerless,
irrelevant God who seems to be both absent and worthless, Auden
turns – as if in desperation – to Jesus. Is the resurrection an answer
to the ambiguous God, as it was for Pound? Nobody knows,

though even unbelievers suspect they may be damned. And finally, the cross.

> Meanwhile, a silence on the cross,
> As dead as we shall ever be.
> Speaks of some total gain or loss,
>   And you and I are free
>
> To guess from the insulted face
> Just what Appearances He saves
> By suffering in a public place
>   A death reserved for slaves.

The cross is the answer? No, for it is either gain or loss, and only that ridiculous freedom given us by the old Odd Divinity is available to figure out just what the cross means, if anything. Auden speaks of the crucified Jesus 'saving the appearances'. This is of course a technical term in the history of science, and it means artificially maintaining the outward signs so as to conceal the absence of the realities those signs are assumed to represent. Is Auden using the phrase in this technical sense? He is rarely intellectually careless. If the cross is truly 'saving the appearances' is it something that Christians evasively affirm in order to conceal the grim reality of the ambivalent or absent God? Is it that Odd Divinity or is it Nothing that lurks behind that insulted face? There is no Anglican or Tillichian triumphalism here. Should we recall that Dietrich Bonhoeffer, to whom this poem is dedicated, once wrote from prison: 'Man is summoned to share in God's sufferings at the hands of a godless world'? Maybe the poet has simply brought up to date and versified the terrible and touching ambivalence of the prisoner.

Auden's alluring ambivalence about the Christian faith leads us to a final group of Jesus-poets for whom the traditional New Testament Jesus is clearly not satisfactory. Some will merely criticize; some will invent a new Jesus worthy of belief.

Countee Cullen is probably the finest Black poet America has produced. His 'Heritage' is a bitter meditation on the conflict between his African origin and his present but troubled Christian faith. The poem begins with a meditation on Africa: what does it mean to me, the poet asks. It is a 'book one thumbs/Listlessly, till slumber comes'. Yet he cannot deny his origin. In the final portion of the poem (quoted below) he sets Africa against Christianity, and watches the battle rage.

Quaint, outlandish heathen gods
Black men fashion out of rods,
Clay, and brittle bits of stone,
In a likeness like their own,
My conversion came high-priced;
I belong to Jesus Christ,
Preacher of humility;
Heathen gods are naught to me.

Father, Son, and Holy Ghost,
So I make an idle boast;
Jesus of the twice-turned cheek,
Lamb of God, although I speak
With my mouth thus, in my heart
Do I play a double part.
Ever at Thy glowing altar
Must my heart grow sick and falter,
Wishing He I served were black,
Thinking then it would not lack
Precedent of pain to guide it,
Let who would or might deride it;
Surely then this flesh would know
Yours had borne a kindred woe.
Lord, I fashion dark gods, too,
Daring even to give You
Dark despairing features where,
Crowned with dark rebellious hair,
Patience wavers just so much as
Mortal grief compels, while touches
Quick and hot, of anger, rise
To smitten cheek and weary eyes.
Lord, forgive me if my need
Sometimes shapes a human creed.

All day long and all night through,
One thing only must I do:
Quench my pride and cool my blood,
Lest I perish in the flood.
Lest a hidden ember set
Timber that I thought was wet
Burning like the dryest flax,
Melting like the merest wax,
Lest the grave restore its dead.
Not yet has my heart or head
In the least way realized
They and I are civilized.

Cullen is as troubled by his Christian present as by his African past. He willingly serves Jesus, the 'Jesus of the twice-turned cheek', the one who will not permit him his anger, while still 'wishing He I served were black'. He is troubled by Jesus' pacifism and his whiteness, so he deals with this conflict by giving him 'Dark despairing features' and 'dark rebellious hair' like his own.

The power of the poem comes from the poet's refusal to give up his Black anger in the face of what he assumes to be Jesus' disapproval. But he also refuses to sacrifice Jesus to his African fury. Jesus and that uncivilized fury are reconciled not by the victory of one over the other, and not by compromise. They are reconciled by forgiveness. Cullen colours his Jesus Black and angry so he himself can become a forgiven sinner.

The themes in 'Heritage' appear in Cullen's masterpiece, the long poem (too long to be included in its completeness here) called 'The Black Christ' (1929). The Christian-African tension is also present here.

Two brothers have I had on earth,
One of spirit, one of sod;
My mother suckled one at birth,
One was the Son of God.

But 'The Black Christ' is primarily a poem about a lynching. The poet's brother, Jim, has come to doubt a God who could permit lynchings to take place.

'Likely there ain't no God at all,'
Jim was the first to clothe a doubt
With words, that long had tried to sprout
Against our wills and love of one
Whose faith was like a blazing sun
Set in a dark, rebellious sky.
Now then the roots were fast, and I
Must nurture them in her despite.
God could not be, if He deemed right,
The grief that ever met our sight.

But the Black Christ will emerge from the experience of radical evil. The poem's opening lines set the note of faith that will be severely bent, but not broken.

God's glory and my country's shame,
And how one man who cursed Christ's name
May never fully expiate
That crime till at the Blessed Gate
Of Heaven He meet and pardon me
Out of His love and charity;
How God, who needs no man's applause,
For love of my stark soul, of flaws
Composed, seeing it slip, did stoop
Down to the mire and pick me up,
And in the hollow of His hand
Enact again at my command
The world's supremest tragedy,
Until I die my burthen be;
How Calvary in Palestine,
Extending down to me and mine,
Was but the first leaf in a line
Of trees on which a Man should swing
World without end, in suffering
For all men's healing, let me sing.

But the poet, reflecting on his people's suffering, questions the quietism of his inherited Christianity.

... this faith in one
Who in my sight had never done
One extraordinary thing
That I should praise His name, or sing
His bounty and His grace, let loose
The pent-up torrent of abuse
That clamored in me for release:
'Nay, I have done with deities
Who keep me ever on my knees ...'

At the end of the poem, the lynch mob finds the poet and his brother. The brother submits to the violence, enabling the poet and their mother to go free. The young man is then killed in their presence. The mother's faith remains firm, the poet's does not. The dead brother then appears to the poet and reminds him of that other innocent suffering on the cross. The poet, for all of his anger, finally discerns the crucified Jesus in his dead brother's face, and once again the Black anger and faith are united by the forgiveness from the cross.

If I am blind He does not see;
If I am lame He halts with me;
There is no hood of pain I wear
That has not rested on His hair
Making Him first initiate
Beneath its harsh and hairy weight.
He grew with me within the womb;
He will receive me at the tomb.
He will make plain the misty path
He makes me tread in love and wrath,
And bending down in peace and grace
May wear again my brother's face.

The anger of Malcolm X, the tough patience of Dr King, the Black theology of the 1960s – all are here in the work of this supreme poet.

In Robert Pinsky's most recent collection, *The Want-Bone*, there are two items of interest to a collector of contemporary Jesus-fiction. One is a charming and terrifying poem called 'From the Childhood of Jesus'.

One Saturday morning he went to the river to play.
He modeled twelve sparrows out of the river clay

And scooped a clear pond, with a dam of twigs and mud.
Around the pond he set the birds he had made,

Evenly as the hours. Jesus was five. He smiled,
As a child would who had made a little world

Of clear still water and clay beside a river.
But a certain Jew came by, a friend of his father,

And he scolded the child and ran at once to Joseph,
Saying, 'Come see how your child has profaned the Sabbath,

Making images at the river on the Day of Rest.'
So Joseph came to the place and took his wrist

And told him, 'Child, you have offended the Word.'
Then Jesus freed the hand that Joseph held

And clapped his hands and shouted to the birds
To go away. They raised their beaks at his words

And breathed and stirred their feathers and flew away.
The people were frightened. Meanwhile, another boy,

The son of Annas the scribe, had idly taken
A branch of driftwood and leaning against it had broken

The dam and muddied the little pond and scattered
The twigs and stones. Then Jesus was angry and shouted,

'Unrighteous, impious, ignorant, what did the water
Do to harm you? Now you are going to wither

The way a tree does, you shall bear no fruit
And no leaves, you shall wither down to the root.'

At once, the boy was all withered. His parents moaned,
The Jews gasped, Jesus began to leave, then turned

And prophesied, his child's face wet with tears:

'Twelve times twelve times twelve thousands of years

Before these heavens and this earth were made,
The Creator set a jewel in the throne of God

With Hell on the left and Heaven to the right,
The Sanctuary in front, and behind, an endless night

Endlessly fleeing a Torah written in flame.
And on that jewel in the throne, God wrote my name.'

Then Jesus left and went into Joseph's house.
The family of the withered one also left the place,

Carrying him home. The Sabbath was nearly over.
By dusk, the Jews were all gone from the river.

Small creatures came from the undergrowth to drink
And foraged in the shadows along the bank.

Alone in his cot in Joseph's house, the Son
Of Man was crying himself to sleep. The moon

Rose higher, the Jews put out their lights and slept,
And all was calm and as it had been, except

In the agitated household of the scribe Annas,
And high in the dark, where unknown even to Jesus

The twelve new sparrows flew aimlessly through the night,
Not blinking or resting, as if never to alight.

Pinsky takes off from the passage in the apocryphal Gospel of
Thomas (2. 1–4) where a gnostic infant prodigy five-year-old Jesus
takes clay and models twelve sparrows on the Sabbath. 'The Jews'
complain to Jesus's father, who chastizes his son. The son's impudent response to the rebuke is to clap his hands and watch the
sparrows fly away.

Pinsky tells this story and then adds a dark incident of his own
invention. Another boy, son of Annas the scribe, messes up a pool
that Jesus had made in the mud. Jesus is furious and causes the
boy to become withered. The boy weeps as Jesus arrogantly proclaims that he is a special favourite of God and you don't mess
around with special favourites. Then Jesus goes home and cries

himself to sleep. The sparrows – the consequences of the arrogant and creepy little kid's miracle – fly into the night, never to rest. Jesus is a cruel one, and his cruelty has consequences that never end.

The Want-Bone contains another Jesus-fiction. It is in prose, and it is called 'Jesus and Isolt'. Like the poem, it is about the imperfection of Jesus. In heaven, Jesus asked his mother if he could visit the earth again, and she said yes, and you can go in the form of a winged ciclogriff. He visited Isolde, and they became friends. He told her about the events surrounding his life and death (not yet revealing himself to her) and she told him about the joys of romantic love, which rather interested him.

> In Isolt's almost childish accounts of the effects upon her of the love potion she had swallowed, in the heedless contradictions and paradoxes of the behavior of the two lovers in Isolt's own account, the Son of Man felt something that eased the restlessness of his own double nature.

After a while, Jesus decided to reveal himself to Tristan and Isolde as their proper Lord and Saviour. He spoke to them of their sin and invited them to repent and to follow him back to heaven. Isolde listened politely to the sermon, then turned away, following Tristan down to hell. Jesus went back to heaven.

> There he looked into the mild eyes of Mary, who looked back with heavenly pity at the Son of Man, the most unfortunate of all his Father's creatures.

In the poem, Jesus' arrogant imperfections have permanent results; the sparrows fly away without landing. In the prose tale, Jesus on earth hears about a part of life he has never experienced and it makes him very unhappy.

There is another fine contemporary 'nasty Jesus' poem: 'Christ's Twin' by Louise Erdrich.

> He was formed of chicken blood and lightning.
> He was what fell out when the jug tipped.

He was waiting at the bottom
of the cliff when the swine plunged over.
He tore out their lungs with a sound like ripping silk.
He hacked the pink carcasses apart, so that the ribs spread
like a terrible butterfly, and there was darkness.
It was he who turned the handle and let the dogs
rush from the basements. He shoved the crust
of the volcano into his roaring mouth.
He showed one empty hand. The other gripped
a crowbar, a monkey wrench, a crop
which was the tail of the ass that bore them into Egypt,
one in each saddlebag, sucking twists
of honeyed goatskin, arguing
already over a woman's breasts.
He understood the prayers that rose
in every language, for he had split the human tongue.
He was not the Devil nor among the Fallen –
it was just that he was clumsy, and curious,
and liked to play with knives. He was the dove
hypnotized by boredom and betrayed by light.
He was the pearl in the mouth, the tangible
emptiness that saints seek at the center of their prayers.
He leaped into a shadow when the massive stone
rolled across the entrance, sealing him with his brother
in the dark as in the beginning.
Only this time he emerged first, bearing the self-
inflicted wound, both brass halos
tacked to the back of his skull.
He raised two crooked fingers; the extra die
tumbled from his lips when he preached
but no one noticed. They were too busy planning
how to sell him to the world.
They were too busy drinking
at the fountain.
They were drunk.
They would drown for love.

The evil twin was actually present when some of the Gospel
events took place. He enjoyed killing the swine when the Gerasene

madman was exorcised, and he apparently enjoyed teasing his virtuous brother at nursing time.

> He showed one empty hand. The other gripped
> a crowbar, a monkey wrench, a crop
> which was the tail of the ass that bore them into Egypt,
> one in each saddlebag, sucking twists
> of honeyed goatskin, arguing
> already over a woman's breasts.

This evil twin – interpreter of the true Jesus – was really a destructive little *bastard* on his own, apart from his role as fellow-commentator on the Gospel stories. He was made of the wine's dregs, he enjoyed opening the dead bodies of pigs, and he was clumsy, bored, dangerous. He got out of the tomb first and became the centre of the Christian movement, and the Christians were (and still are) too stupid to know the trick that was being played on them. Christians, at the poem's bitter close, are those who are willing to drown and kill for the love of the evil Jesus twin whom they call Jesus.

In 'I Heard Christ Sing' (c. 1925) the Scots poet Hugh MacDiarmid doesn't pause to criticize the Calvinist Christ, he simply invents a new one, very Scottish, celebrating both the spirit of man and the cross.

I HEARD Christ sing quhile roond him danced
The twal' disciples in ring,
And here's the dance I saw them dance,
And the sang I heard him sing.

Ane, twa, three, and their right feet heich,
Fower, five, six, and doon wi' them,
Seevin, aucht, nine, and up wi' the left,
Ten, eleevin, twal', and doon they came.

And Christ he stude i' the middle there,
And was the thirteenth man,
And sang the bonniest sang that e'er
Was sung sin' Time began.

And Christ he was the centrepiece,
Wi' three on ilka side.
My hert stude still, and the sun stude still,
But still the dancers plied.

O I wot it was a maypole,
As a man micht seek to see,
Wi' the twal' disciples dancin' roon',
While Christ sang like a lintie.

The twal' points o' the compass
Made jubilee roon' and roon',
And but for the click-click-clack o' the feet,
Christ's sang was the only soon'.

And there was nae time that could be tauld
Frae a clock wha's haun's stude still,
Quhile the figures a' gaed bizzin roon'
– I wot it was God's will.

    Wersh is the vinegar,
    And the sword is sharp.
    Wi' the tremblin' sunbeams
    Again for my harp,
    I sing to Thee.

    The spirit of man
    Is a bird in a cage,
    That beats on the bars
    Wi' a goodly rage,
    And fain' ud be free.

    Twice-caged it is,
    In life and in death,
    Yet it claps its wings
    Wi' a restless faith,
    And sings as it may.

    Then fill my mouth
    Wi' the needfu' words,
    That sall turn its wings
    Into whirlin' swords,
    When it hears what I say.

Hearken my cry,
And let me speak,
That when it hears
It sall lift its beak,
And sing as it should.

Sweet is the song
That is lost in its throat,
And fain 'ud I hear
It's openin' note,
As I hang on the rood.

And when I rise
Again from the dead,
Let me, I pray,
Be accompanied
By the spirit of man.

Yea, as I rise
From earth to Heaven
Fain 'ud I know
That Thou has given
Consent to my plan –

Even as the stars
Sang here at my birth,
Let Heaven hear
The song of the earth
Then, for my sake.

The thorns are black,
And callous the nails.
As a bird its bars
My hand assails
Harpstrings . . . that break!

O I wot they'll lead the warl' a dance,
And I wot the sang sall be,
As a white sword loupin' at the hert
O' a' eternity.

Judas and Christ stude face to face,
And mair I couldna' see,
But I wot he did God's will wha made
Siccar o' Calvary.

The poet is watching a Scottish country dance in which the
disciples dance a ring around Jesus who is singing in the centre.
Already, we are far from Galilee. The experience overwhelms the
poet: it is the 'bonniest sang' that ever was sung; both his heart
and the sun stood still. Indeed, as Jesus sang and the disciples
danced, time itself stood still, and eternity entered into time. This
is not only a singing Jesus, it is a genuine incarnation.

Jesus' song is about the spirit of man and its need to be free.
Jesus sings so man may be freed from his cage, and he sings also
of his own death, resurrection, and ascension as all forming part of
the liberating 'song of the earth' addressed (as if in challenge?) to
heaven.

The song ends with a strange image of destruction and danger,
and the poet offers a final reflection on Jesus' song. The freedom
of the human spirit that the song celebrates is, after all, rooted not
in human virtue or piety. It is rooted in Judas' betrayal and in the
death of Jesus on the cross. At the poem's close, the singing Jesus
and the crucified Jesus become one.

Two fine poems, one from early in the century, one contemporary,
focus on a curious theme in the life of Jesus: his critical uneasiness
with his mother. Here is 'The Marriage at Cana' (circa 1913) by
Rainer Maria Rilke (1875–1926).

How could she not have been proud of him
who, even at her simplest, made her beautiful?
Even the night, accustomed to greatness,
went beyond itself the moment he appeared.

Didn't his once overstepping himself
add, incomprehensibly, to his glory?
And didn't the wisest exchange their mouths
for their ears? And didn't the house

seem new again holding his voice? Yes,
there must have been hundreds of times
when she had to restrain her delight
from shining on him. She followed him, in awe.

But there at the wedding
when suddenly the wine ran out,
she glanced across at him, asking for some gesture
without noticing he was unwilling.

Then he did it. She only understood later
that she had rushed him into it:
he'd caused a miracle, it couldn't be
stopped, the course of his life was decided

forever. Yes, it was in writing.
But was it already prepared for?
She: she brought it about
in her vanity's blindness.

She sat at the table covered with fruit
and vegetables, taking part, oblivious
to the fact that the water of her tears
had become blood with this wine.

Rilke is not inventing the tension between Jesus and Mary. He finds it in the Johannine story. The poem speculates. How was it that Mary's proper pride in her gifted son became corrupt and self-centred? What exactly had she done at this wedding? Rilke -- departing decisively from the biblical text – is quite clear. Mary prematurely and deliberately forced Jesus into a ministry of miracle-working, against his will. She did successfully what Satan had failed to do in the wilderness: 'Do miracles and gain a following.' For Rilke, John's Gospel does indeed contain a temptation story. It is at the wedding at Cana and Mary is the tempter. He had not wanted to do it; 'she had rushed him into it.' And in the final two lines, it is suggested that not only had Mary forced Jesus into a premature act of self-definition, she had also become a cause of his death:

. . . the water of her tears
had become blood with this wine.

In 'An Old Joke', Andrew Hudgins also imagines a Jesus-Mary hang-up. And he also uses a story from the Fourth Gospel (John 7. 53–8. 11) – the woman caught in the act of adultery. Mary is not of course present in the biblical story, but she certainly is there in Hudgins' retelling.

They'd rushed so close to her, their stones
were pelting one another. Christ
pushed roughly through the crowd and shouted,
Let him without sin cast the next stone.
The crowd paused, thinking. Then out of nowhere,
out of the shuffling, silenced crowd,
one stone flew, hit the woman. She dies.
And in the joke I started out to tell,
Christ looks into the crowd and howls,
Goddammit, Mother – that's not funny!
But I have sinned enough to understand
it wasn't she, not Mary. It was the man
who still had love's scent on his flesh,
love's fragrance on his hands, as he selected
one stone, weighed it, thought twice, three times,
then threw – and baffled Christ, who thought
it was his perfect mother, correcting him.

In this revisionist version, the adulteress is already being stoned when Jesus arrives on the scene and momentarily stops the punishers with his imperious word. Then, suddenly, someone throws a stone at the woman and kills her. Without careful examination, Jesus assumes at once that his mother is the killer and shouts angrily to her: 'Goddamit, Mother – that's not funny!' But it wasn't Mary after all, it was apparently the man who had just enjoyed the woman's body. (We are not told why he had to kill her immediately after sex.) Jesus' reaction to his mistake is not penitence but bewilderment. He had assumed that his mother (as always?) was second-guessing him morally, preferring her own angry vengeance to his preferred style of radical forgiveness.

These poems make a fascinating psychological point. Jesus, with a traditionally ambiguous fatherhood, may never have had a real Oedipus complex, since there was no real father there to be killed or wished dead. No anger with a non-existent father, and therefore no desire to possess the mother. Instead, in Rilke and Hudgins, we have Jesus with an Orestes complex: the mother is formidably there – tempting (Rilke) or moralizing (Hudgins) – and she must be denied, even removed, if his own future is to have any integrity. It is from his mother, her vanity and her moralism, that Jesus must be freed.

Jesus without Mary. Not just Protestantism's uneasiness with the co-redemptrix. This is a fully twentieth-century, post-Christian Jesus. Without father, without mother, without any structure of authority over him. Just Jesus in the world, ministering without signs and wonders, offering a forgiveness without judgment.

The appropriate climax of our Jesus poetry is reached in a remarkable set of three poems by the English poet Stevie Smith (1902–1971). She cannot stand Jesus or Christianity as they are, but she cannot relinquish Jesus.

In 'Was He Married?' Jesus' full humanity is called into question.

Was he married, did he try
To support as he grew less fond of them
Wife and family?

No,
He never suffered such a blow.

'How Do You See?' is a radical indictment of Christianity in which the poet affirms that we must learn to be good without enchantment.

You say He was born humble – but He was not
He was born God –

Taking our nature upon Him. But then you say
He was perfect Man. Do you mean
Perfectly Man, meaning wholly? Or Man without sin? Ah
Perfect Man without sin is not what we are.
Do you mean He did not know that He was God,
Did not know He was the Second Person of the Trinity?
(Oh if He knew this and was,
It was a source of strength for Him we do not have)

But this theology of emptying you preach sometimes –
That He emptied Himself of knowing He was God – seems
A theology of false appearances
To mock your facts, as He was God whether He knew it or
not.

Oh what do you mean, what do you mean?
You never answer our difficulties.

In 'The Airy Christ' Stevie Smith offers a Jesus she can take seriously, a Jesus without atonement or sacrifice.

Who is this that comes in splendour, coming from the blazing
  East?
This is he we had not thought of, this is he the airy Christ.

Airy, in an airy manner in an airy parkland walking,
Others take him by the hand, lead him, do the talking.

But the Form, the airy One, frowns an airy frown,
What they say he knows must be, but he looks aloofly down,

Looks aloofly at his feet, looks aloofly at his hands,
Knows they must, as prophets say, nailed be to wooden bands.

As he knows the words he sings, that he sings so happily
Must be changed to working laws, yet sings he ceaselessly.

Those who truly hear the voice, the words, the happy song,
Never shall need working laws to keep from doing wrong.

Deaf men will pretend sometimes they hear the song, the words,
And make excuse to sin extremely; this will be absurd.

Heed it not. Whatever foolish men may do the song is cried
For those who hear, and the sweet singer does not care that he
  was crucified.

For he does not wish that men should love him more than
  anything
Because he died; he only wishes they would hear him sing.

The post-Nicene fathers, defending what they believed to be Jesus' full humanity, used to argue that 'what is not assumed is not healed'. Thus the Godhead must be said to have assumed a full human nature. Stevie Smith, in 'Was He Married?', defends the patristic saying, but argues that since the Jesus of the Gospels was not like us, he cannot redeem. He wasn't married, he never felt unwanted, he knew no fear of death as the end, he knew nothing of guilt. He never even had the joy of overcoming a weakness or a sin. Human beings go through a lot of hell, and should be praised for it. Jesus missed most of what ordinary humanity is all about.

Gods, furthermore, are things that men and women invent to help them do things they ought to do, like love. It may be a small victory that people can conceive of a god of love, but – she concludes – it will be even better when we can love and hate without needing to import any god at all to support or condemn.

'How Do You See?' is Stevie Smith's broadest and most telling confession of her love-hate for Christianity. (Her shorter poem 'Oh Christianity, Christianity' is mostly stanzas taken from this longer one.) Her arguments will be familiar to twentieth-century readers, but they have never been set in such simple and touching language. To be sure, she grants, Christianity has been and can be productive of good.

But must we allow good to be hitched to a lie? The time for beautiful fairy stories is over (a striking admission for a poet, whose function in part is surely the creation of 'beautiful fairy stories') and to call those stories facts is morally harmful. 'We must learn to be good in a dull way without enchantment.'

Then she turns to her indictment proper. She is not just opposed to morally uplifting fairy stories, she is opposed to 'the penal sentences of Christ': to all language of damnation and rejection. Smith does in a stanza what Schweitzer did in a chapter – she indicts the whole New Testament eschatological scheme as repugnant and irrelevant to our religious struggles today. Not only eschatology but atonement is repudiated. What kind of wisdom is enshrined, she asks, in

... the dreadful bargain, that God would take and offer
The death of the Son to buy our faults away ...

Her plea, both deeply emotional and intellectual, is summed up in two vivid quatrains:

> Oh Christianity, Christianity
> Why do you not answer our difficulties?
> If He was God He was not like us
> He could not lose . . .

She offers Christianity no second chance.

> Oh Christianity, Christianity,
> That has grown kinder now, as in the political world
> The colonial system grows kinder before it vanishes, are you
>   vanishing?
> Is it not time for you to vanish?

The poem's final lines deepen her anger. Christianity is not merely a harmless tale, it is dangerous and it makes its believers into dangerous men and women.

> I think if we do not learn quickly, and learn to teach children,
> To be good without enchantment, without the help
> Of beautiful painted fairy stories pretending to be true,
> Then I think it will be too much for us, the dishonesty,
> And, armed as we are now, we shall kill everybody,
> It will be too much for us, we shall kill everybody.

'The Airy Christ' makes Stevie Smith's final and decisive point. It is not just a matter of doing without, of being good without enchantment. Christianity and God may have to go; that seems clear enough. But Jesus emerges from the ashes. This is the 'airy' Christ. He has a form (he is not all air), a location (a park) and a message (he sings, but not in Scots dialect). He is strangely remote; aloof, frowning, he knows he has to die. But he sings, and we are as moved by his song as we would be by any song of Mozart or Schubert or Lennon-McCartney. The words he sings are words of love. These words probably ought to be translated into words of justice, equality and law. But the song is so persistent, so ravishing and true, that it we really listen to it we will never need to translate love into law. 'Love, and do what you like'. This is an antinomian Jesus that sings over Christianity's ruins. The singer does not seem to care that he had been crucified, and he does not want us to love him because of his sad death. In 'The Airy Christ' Stevie Smith attempts to break Christianity's persistent love-affair with death: we are saved by 'his' death, we are fully saved only when we die. Her splendid song invites us to listen to Jesus' song: love, not death, is what it is all about.

VII

Jesus Comes Back

The most difficult of all the forms of Jesus-fiction is surely that in which Jesus 'himself' returns to earth. In 'The Grand Inquisitor' Dostoevsky finessed some of the technical problems by having his Jesus remain silent. Listening, and finally kissing. I propose to conclude this round-up of twentieth-century Jesus fiction by attending to five wildly different fictional experiments, different in reach and in grasp.

William Faulkner's 1954 Jesus book, *A Fable*, is sometimes turgid and incoherent (qualities not altogether absent in Faulkner's greater works, but present here in massive doses). But the novel (if that is what it is) is partly redeemed from its ineptness, and indeed takes on considerable interest, if we observe that the corporal who persuaded a French regiment not to undertake an assigned attack on the Western front in May 1918 does not merely 'stand for' or 'resemble' Jesus: he is Jesus himself, returned to French earth, doing (what is for Faulkner) his thing and getting himself crucified once more, 'killed by the hands of lawless men', as it is written. So if *A Fable* works badly as a novel, as a piece of personal and passionate theological exorcism it becomes a work of importance.

It took Herman Melville two books to kill the evil God (*Moby Dick*) and then to praise the ineptness (and portray the dangers) of sacrificial love (*Pierre*). Faulkner does both in one. This is not all the novel is or does, but I am interested in it as a combination of indictment and affirmation of the author's tradition of, shall we call it, Mississippi Protestantism. Some words of a black clergyman in the novel come close to what I am calling Faulkner's central intent – or, if not intent, achievement. The black man is asked if he is an ordained minister.

'I don't know. I bears witness.'

'To what? God?'

'To man. God don't need me. [Which is to say, I suspect, that Faulkner don't need God.] I bears witness to Him, of course, but my main witness is to man.'

'The most damning thing a man could suffer would be a valid witness before God.'

'You're wrong there,' the Negro said. 'Man is full of sin and nature, and all he does don't bear looking at, and a heap of what he says is a shame and a mawkery. But can't no witness hurt him. Some day something might beat him, but it won't be Satan . . .' (Chapter 6).

Faulkner seems to mean here that God alone can and does destroy man.

A Fable is Faulkner settling the score with his Protestantism. It is an attack on an evil (Calvinist) God, a portrait of a strangely alluring and inept Jesus, and, finally, a deeply pessimistic portrait of human nature. Irving Howe points out that we have in *A Fable* one of the most desperate and radically bleak visions of human experience that any novelist in our time has advanced.[1] The very idea of a re-enactment is itself utterly desperate. To conceive of a Second Coming which is essentially a repetition of the original agony; to see the Christ figure as again scorned by the crowds, again betrayed and deserted by his followers, again crushed by the state; and most terrible of all, to conceive of a Christ who knows he is doomed, who offers neither hope nor a belief in the idea of hope – all this, if not heresy or even blasphemy, implies a vision of despair that completely undercuts the assumptions of both our liberal culture and of Christianity itself.

At the centre of this theological exorcism is the story of a mutiny. Three thousand men, mysteriously under a corporal's influence, refuse to make an attack that probably was intended to be a failure. The Germans refuse to counter-attack, and ultimately the British also lay down their arms. The war stops, the generals are horrified at the prospect of both peace and unemployment; but the allies and enemy finally negotiate the war's resumption, and the refusal fails of its purpose. The whole resisting regiment, including the corporal and his twelve associates, are arrested. He is killed and ultimately, after a series of ludicrous accidents, he ends up buried in the tomb of the Unknown Soldier.

Faulkner turns his mutiny leader into Jesus in two ways. He sets him in the midst of the events of Passion week, without much subtlety or conviction. And he describes his actions, his character and his teaching in such a way that we become persuaded that the corporal is indeed the Jesus Faulkner would like to believe in.

The biblical parallels are obvious. The corporal has a twelve-man squad; one betrays, another denies. He is engaged to a girl named Magda, a prostitute with – of course – a heart of gold. His friends include a Marya and a Marthe. He is captured on a Wednesday; he distributes a meal to his friends the next day, and he is killed on a Friday: shot while tied to a post between two robbers, his head finally crowned with barbed wire. His body disappears from its first grave, and ends up beneath the Arc de Triomphe.[2]

The historical setting of Faulkner's Jesus is not as interesting as his character. Here we can see the love-hate relationship between the novelist and Jesus. His Jesus is quite different from the church's Christ. In this mood, Faulkner can sound like an old-fashioned anti-clerical liberal Protestant. Both his hatred of war and his contempt for high christologies come out in a passage like this one:

> . . . the generals and admirals, the corporals and ratings of glory, the batmen and orderlies of renown, and the chairmen of boards and the presidents of federations, the doctors and lawyers and educators and churchmen who after nineteen centuries have res- cued the son of heaven from oblivion and translated him from mere meek heir to earth to chairman of its board of trade . . . (Chapter 7).

Faulkner wants no redeemer; he wants only the man of oblivion, the 'mere meek heir of earth'. (That phrase, surely, is evidence enough for Faulkner's genius.)

This is just what he has in the corporal, and the corporal is almost aware of his own true identity. A priest visits him the day before his execution (inept, of course, just as in *Billy Budd* and *The Stranger*), and he accuses the corporal of confusing himself with Jesus. He fails to persuade the corporal of the superiority of power to powerlessness, and so he takes his own life. (Not a usual response when you have failed to propagate error!)

The corporal-Jesus is illiterate, almost inarticulate. Faulkner's word about him is interesting: 'a comprehension, understanding, utterly free of compassion'. A Jesus without teaching and without love. But not without a deep commitment to the power of power-lessness, the necessity of non-resistance to evil. Faulkner makes no attempt to explain just how this single man's resistance spreads first to his squad, then to his regiment, and then to the Germans and British. He just refused, and the refusal becomes magically extended. Hatred of power, willed powerlessness: this is the Jesus Faulkner wants. We do not know if the corporal himself believed that his rebellion would stop an evil war.

The centre of this weak novel and powerful tract comes in the scene between the old general (who, it turns out, is the corporal's father-Father) and the corporal the night before the execution (Chapter 8). It is this extraordinary scene that gives A Fable its distinction.

There are two theological-biblical models for this interview between father and son. The obvious one is the temptation of Jesus by Satan (as recorded by Matthew and Luke). The general is indeed the devil, arguing against the corporal's resistance, and trying to dissuade him from martyrdom. But the dialogue is also an intra-trinitarian discourse between Father and pre-existent Son, carried on in heaven prior to the incarnation, on the nature of the incarnate life to come. The general is both devil and God; in fact, he is the evil God. Faulkner shows both admiration and contempt for this Protestant God. The general is omnipotent, yet believes in nothing; a God, powerful, corrupt, empty. The general 'no longer believed in anything but his disillusion and his intelligence and his limitless power'. Or again, the general's face was 'the face of one who long ago had won the right to believe in nothing whatever save man's deathless folly'. The general as evil God is perfectly rendered in a splendid piece of Faulknerian verbal magic. Another general said of this general:

If I were evil, I would hate and fear him. [For God judges all evil.] If I were a saint, I would weep. [Why shouldn't one weep to discover the corruption of God?] If I were wise, and both [i.e.

evil and saint] or either I would despair. [An evil God is a comfort to no one.] (Chapter 7).

The dialogue takes place at night high over the city in the ruins of a Roman citadel. The general begins by warning his son that he has only bewildered his followers, not converted them. After we have killed you, they will come to hate you and your protest will prove to have been fruitless. War, the general argues, is far too natural to man to be abolished by such empty gestures of protest.

So the first temptation of this wise, powerful, and evil father-general is the offer of escape. Take my car, drive to the coast and I'll set you up for a trip to South America or Asia. I offer you liberty, I offer you the earth, I offer life. Perhaps, he adds, you are too young to know how precious life itself is and how it is to be preferred to death.

The corporal speaks very little in this key scene. He seems impervious to both argument and emotion. The general's offer of escape and life elicits a simple response: 'No, if I did what you ask, I would desert my friends.' This response, made again and again to the general's temptations, suggests a final dimension to Faulkner's returned Jesus. He is a radical pacifist; his power over others is mystical, not pedagogical; he is without compassion, but he deeply believes that he has an absolute commitment to his friends. Faulkner's Jesus does not return as the figure from the Gospels, but as one whose hatred of war and sense of loyalty have deeply affected the novelist.

The general renews his attempt to dissuade the corporal from his movements toward death. Look, he says, I am the champion of the earth, while you are merely the 'champion of an esoteric realm of man's baseless hopes and his infinite capacity – no: passion – for unfact'.

Of course, the general's argument is specious. He has no real love for the earth; he loves only war and himself. Such gods should be ignored. The corporal stands with his loyalty. Besides, the corporal continues in his most extended response to the father, perhaps you are offering to sponsor my escape because you fear me, fear that I may be right. The general replies that the corporal may be right in his rejection of this war. But, he adds wryly, if he rejects escape he will never know whether he is right or not.

The general's final criticism of the son is theological, having to do with the nature of man and the problem of salvation. The point he makes can be summed up, I think, in this way. 'The trouble with you, son, is that you believe that man can be saved, and that only a redemptive death – yours – can save him. I know man's dark heart better than you. Man is too evil to be savable by anyone.' But, he adds, and here we come to the heart of Faulkner's book (and, incidentally, to the key that unlocks what appears to be the vapid piety of his 1950 Nobel prize acceptance speech): it is not a saviour like you that will save man or give him his eternity, it is man's own infinite capacity for evil. Man is 'saved', 'immortalized' only by his evil. Only the devil can save.

That, I think, is the meaning of this key passage in which the general, as Satanic saviour-god, claims a theological superiority over the martyr-son.

> I know that he [i.e. man] has that in him which will enable him to outlast even his wars; that in him more durable than all his vices, even that last and most fearsome one; to outlast even this next avatar of his servitude which he now faces: his enslavement to the demonic progeny of his own mechanical curiosity, from which he will emancipate himself by that one ancient tried-and-true method by which slaves have always freed themselves: by inculcating their masters with the slaves' own vices – in this case the vice of war and that other one which is no vice at all but instead is the quality-mark and warrant of man's immortality: his deathless folly.

It is important to understand what the general is saying. That someone else, some god or redeemer for example, can save man is out of the question. But man can outlast even wars; he can lay hold on immortality. How? By virtue of his radical evil, his slavery, his folly. As fool, man is immortal. This is the key that unlocks all Faulkner's language about enduring, prevailing, immortality.[3]

Now we are prepared for the final texts that will complete our portrait of Faulkner's idea of salvation that is neither his old Protestantism nor the fashionable liberal optimism of our century. It is that liberalism that appears to reverberate through the final lines of the Nobel address:

I decline to accept the end of man. It is easy enough to say that man is immortal simply because he will endure: that when the last ding-dong of doom has clanged and faded from the last worthless rock hanging tideless in the last red and dying evening, that even then there will still be one more sound: that of his puny inexhaustible voice, still talking. I refuse to accept this. I believe that man will not merely endure: he will prevail. He is immortal, not alone because he alone among creatures has an inexhaustible voice, but because he has a soul, a spirit capable of compassion and sacrifice and endurance.

This seems to be the kind of cant we have come to expect in such speeches. Let us put alongside these words the final words (except for the last goodbyes) between the father and the son. The general is speaking.

'Oh yes, he will survive it because he has that in him which will endure even beyond the ultimate worthless tideless rock freezing slowly in the last red and heatless sunset, because already the next star in the blue immensity of space will be already clamorous with the uproar of his debarkation, his puny and inexhaustible voice still talking, still planning; and there too after the last ding dong of doom has rung and died there will still be one sound more: his voice, planning still to build something higher and faster and louder; more efficient and louder and faster than ever before, yet it too inherent with the same old primordial fault since it too in the end will fail to eradicate him from the earth. I don't fear man. I do better: I respect and admire him. And pride: I am ten times prouder of that immortality which he does possess than ever he of that heavenly one of his delusion. Because man and his folly – '

'Will endure,' the corporal said.

'They will do more,' the old general said proudly. 'They will prevail.'

The Nobel address is redeemed from fatuity by reading it as it appears on the lips of Faulkner's satanic god, the old general. In 1950, Faulkner ironically offered the system what it expected. In 1954 he said what he really meant in 1950. In the address, he said that man will prevail because of his sacrifice and endurance. In the novel, these are the virtues of – the soldier. Man will endure, even prevail, because he is evil. He will last because wars will last and men will always find a way to have a war if they really need one.

God is satanic. Jesus is touching and irrelevant, powerless before the brutal reality of man's affection for violence and evil. The night before the final encounter between the general and his son, the quartermaster-general had already made explicit the link between evil and immortality – the secret of Faulkner's theological pilgrimage. Not by an inept Jesus that effects nothing, man is saved by his folly.

> Rapacity does not fail, else man must deny he breathes. Not rapacity: its whole vast glorious history repudiates that [repudiates failure, that is], it does not, cannot, must not fail . . . Because it [i.e. human rapacity, man's love and need of war] endures [sic], not even because it is rapacity but because man is man, enduring and immortal because he endures [a Faulknerian way of declaring that enduring and immortality are the same]: and so with rapacity, which immortal man never fails, [never fails to manifest, that is] immortality – the vast, the all-being, the compassionate, which says to him only, Believe in Me; [i.e. in rapacity as Saviour] though ye doubt seventy times seven, ye need only believe again (Chapter 7).

Thus the weak novel becomes a piece of fascinating and demonic theology. Or exorcism.

The first of Father Joseph Girzone's Joshua books is called *Joshua* (New York 1983). The priest is no William Faulkner; the book is unpretentious, sentimental, but deeply felt. It is a touching story capable of bringing real comfort to many readers. It is a book not to be patronized.

Joshua lives in the cultural world of, say, 'Father Knows Best'. The setting is today, in an almost perfectly virtuous small town (no untoward sex, no poverty, no crime or drugs) apparently in New York State, somewhere around Saratoga Springs.

A young man, early thirties, moves to Auburn and begins to support himself as a carpenter and wood sculptor. From the beginning he is clearly special. He looks with compassion into your soul, he has no immediate family, and he comes from a near-by town called Bethlehem. People come to know and like him. He invites the mailman to break bread with him, and it is quickly apparent that he knows Aramaic. He solves people's problems and people always leave their discussions with him with a sense of peace. He also does five or six miracles, including a stilling of a storm and two resurrections from the dead.

It is clear he has not just come to Auburn; he was 'sent', and after a few pages it is clear that this is not just a Christ-like young man, it is Jesus himself inserted into a small upstate town for a particular purpose. What is Joshua up to? The answer is, I suspect, almost entirely ecclesiological. Joshua is the mouthpiece of the author's loving but decisive criticism of his own Roman Catholic tradition.

Joshua goes regularly to synagogue, and he also visits various Christian churches in town. He gets along very well with the Jewish community, but it does seem that Father Girzone really wants Joshua to remind the Jews that their ultimate function is to convert. Joshua says, unfortunately:

That Jesus was born from the Jews is an honour that can never be taken from them. They still share that glory [is their only glory the fact of Jesus' Jewishness?], a glory that they will one day realize (83).

When they become Christian? This is perhaps less than antisemitism; it is, of course, a kind of naive Paulinism.

The Jews love Joshua, except for one synagogue member who angrily accuses him of not taking seriously the history of Jewish suffering. Joshua's response to this is to embrace the man, who thereby falls apart, weeps, and begs for forgiveness. Joshua is very good at effecting these swift personality changes from naughty to nice. There is a nice Methodist minister, a mean-spirited Presbyterian, a pompous Episcopalian priest, and a splendid Black Pentecostalist. The local Catholic priest dislikes Joshua, but his young curate – decent, but bibulous – becomes his best friend.

This is a sinless small town. No, that is not quite right, for otherwise Joshua wouldn't have been sent there. There is sin in

Auburn – it is ecclesiastical arrogance and denominationalism. That sin is mostly Catholic, and it is this sin Joshua has been sent to exorcize. He ultimately fails.

This function may explain the nature of Joshua's message, which has some odd and unpleasant prejudices about it. It is a message critical of the arrogance of scientists, it believes the United Nations to be a 'pack of vultures' (166), and it is angrily contemptuous of those who believe that the Christian message has an interest in changing society (165). This strain of uncharacteristic hostility in Father Girzone's Jesus suggests perhaps the author's own anxiety to distinguish his criticism from that of the liberation theologies.

Joshua's gospel is mostly about love, and would have passed as liberal Protestantism in the 1930s. Religion is in the heart, not in buildings or hierarchies. Jesus fought organized religion, and he opposed priestly arrogance. Joshua himself criticizes Catholic teaching on priestly celibacy, marriage, and divorce. (But he has nothing to say about abortion or birth control, though that may be because there is no sex in Auburn.) Here is the kind of thing that Joshua says, over and over again. It is the core of Father Girzone's message to his own church.

> Jesus was free and preached to people that they are God's children and that, as God's children, they are free. They are not slaves. Jesus also intended that his leaders be humble men and allow people to enjoy being free. Unfortunately not many religious leaders feel comfortable with people being free but enjoy more exercising their authority over the people (170).

The style may be unpretentious, even ungainly, but there is surely something of the New Testament Jesus here, and the author's anti-ecclesiastical message, however gentle, still has the capacity to give offence to the powerful. Whatever does that cannot be patronized.

There is a touching scene in the story that encapsulates the combination of intellectual carelessness and pastoral wisdom that we find in this book. Joshua is speaking before a group of blind people in town. He makes some rather vapid (and very Platonic) remarks about how the real world which they cannot see is really not real, but only illusion. What their hearts can see alone is real. But following this heretical repudiation of the Christian doctrine of creation, Joshua adds some pastoral remarks of great sensitivity and wisdom on how one can productively bear suffering and limitation. One senses both a naive polemic courage and a very wise pastor in Father Girzone.

If the author gives offence to religious authorities, it is because Joshua does. He is haled before the local bishop, and ends up being sent to Rome to be examined by some Vatican cardinals. His sweetness impresses some of them, and he even manages a miracle at the hearing when the cardinal-chairman has a slight stroke which is immediately abolished by Joshua's touch. But they are evil priestly authorities, after all, and they condemn his teaching by a vote of six-to-one. When a group seeks out Joshua in his Roman apartment to inform him of his condemnation, he has, of course, disappeared, leaving only his sandals behind. No crucifixion, no resurrection. Ascension only; back to heaven.

Ordinary people will remember him, while the conservative Catholic laity and almost all the ordained clergy in Auburn are glad he is no longer around. Father Girzone's Jesus is interesting: very unsophisticated, individualistic, American. All there is to him is freedom and love. But for all its limitations, this is still a Jesus capable of giving offence to power and authority, and that can never be done enough.

Some thirty years before he wrote his 'Life' of Jesus (see above, p. 149–51), Upton Sinclair wrote a brief 'Jesus comes to our town' novel called *They Call Me Carpenter* (New York 1922). As with his 'life', the novel is about Jesus the socialist, and it is written with his accustomed passion and skill.

The narrator bears the admirable name of Billy and he is a wealthy 'clubman' (what ever happened to that grand old noun?) who ends up, in the fiction, as the rich young ruler who cannot bring himself to sell all for Jesus. Anyway, Billy is beaten up by a gang of anti-German, anti-Bolshevik thugs as he leaves a movie theater showing 'The Cabinet of Dr Caligari'. The year is 1921, the city is a New York City look-alike called Western City. Groggy and bloodied, Billy stumbles into St Bartholomew's Church to recover. Suddenly the white-robed Jesus in the stained glass window over the altar comes down to him and offers comfort and healing. It is time, Jesus tells Billy, for him to leave the church and enter the world. *They Call Me Carpenter* is a fictionalized secular christ-ology, and it is a tragedy.

This Jesus turns out to be somewhat bewildered by the city. He speaks almost entirely in biblical quotations or paraphrases, and he decides he had better learn something about the city before he sets about saving it. He falls in with some of Billy's friends, includ-ing an outrageous movie producer who wants to sign Jesus to a contract and a famous star named, of course, Mary Magda, who finally becomes converted to Jesus' way. There is poverty and unemployment in Western City, and Jesus is drawn to the outsiders and the poor. He performs a few modest healings, but he mainly turns out to be a non-violent political and economic radical with a fascination for speaking in public whenever he gets a chance. 'I broke the Roman Empire,' this Jesus declares, 'and I can break the corrupt power of the capitalist.' He proves to be mistaken. Here is a sample speech, and after a few more like this one, he manages to get into real trouble with right-wing mobs and police. 'My people,' he said, arguing against the wisdom of the oppressed killing their oppressors,

> what good would it do you to kill these wretches? The blood-suckers who drain the life of the poor are not to be killed by blows. There are too many of them, and more of them grow in place of those who die. And what is worse, if you kill them, you destroy in yourselves that which makes you better than they, which gives you the right to life. You destroy those virtues of patience and charity, which are the jewels of the poor, and make them princes in the kingdom of love. Let us guard our crown of pity, and not acquire the vices of our oppressors. Let us grow in wisdom, and find ways to put an end to the world's enslavement, without the degradation of our own hearts. For so many ages we have been patient, let us wait but a little longer, and find the true way! Oh, my people, my beloved poor, not in violence, but in solidarity, in brotherhood, lies the way! Let us bid the rich go on, to the sure damnation which awaits them. Let us not soil our hands with their blood! (70–71).

It turns out that Western City is the site of a conference of war veterans, and this Jesus is getting some bad publicity as a rabble-rouser and a red. He spends most of his time either with the poor or with officials of the labour movement and the Socialist Party. The vets in town decide that they have heard enough of his revolutionary politics. (Jesus' language, remember, is almost entirely biblical – both Old and New Testament – rendered somewhat less eschatological than the Gospels permit. Sinclair is a master of biblical interpretation by paraphrase.)

Jesus manages to assemble a group of associates, people with names like Mark and Matthew and Luke and John and Peter and Mary Magda. He also gets a betrayer. There are the evil cops (the Jews) and the mob of paranoid vets (the Romans). They almost tar and feather Jesus, but he manages to escape capture. Billy follows Jesus as he escapes into St Bartholomew's. Once inside the church, Jesus returns to his origin in the stained glass window, while Billy sinks into a pew, exhausted. Wow. The whole Jesus thing turned out to be a dream, a bad dream. Billy in the church had just escaped from the thugs who tried to beat him up as he left the movie theatre. Jesus had not *really* left the church for the world, after all.

A charming tale, and a dark one. If Jesus ever should decide to leave the irrelevant church for the real world of American capitalism, and should he decide to say what was really on his mind, he'd be killed in a couple of days. So it is back to his pretty window, and let radical politics remain secular. Jesus came to Western City; he was nearly lynched, and he returned to the irrelevant church where he has remained to this day.

In A. J. Langguth's comic novel *Jesus Christs* (1968), we are in the presence of a narrative experiment, a joke, and probably even an interpretation of Jesus of Nazareth. The novel is built like Pascal's *Pensées* – fragments short and long, often with little connection – and it often reads like Joseph Heller. In the novel, Jesus keeps coming back to earth again and again, sometimes to the first century, sometimes to the twentieth, sometimes to an unspecified time. Apparently he 'comes' (or, occasionally, is 'sent') to improve on, or criticize, or deny, or laugh at his 'first' coming. As an example of the sheer non-tendentious playfulness of the book, one of the longer fragments is a riotous rewriting of the Fourth Gospel in which Peter is arrested, tried, and crucified, and Jesus goes free.

Apart from the exuberance, there appears to be a serious theological passion in *Jesus Christs*. It is probably silly to characterize the theological agenda, if any, but it's worth a shot. I think that besides having fun, the author is engaged in trying to describe what a serious half-belief in Jesus might look like. One of the extracts, in its entirely, goes like this:

Jesus: Guess what's more debasing than to believe in something that never existed.
Simon: What?
Jesus: To stop believing in something that never existed.

This is what I mean by half-belief. The same point seems to be made in a note that Jesus posts on the disciples' bulletin board.

Doubt is the coffee break in faith's routine.
Doubt is the black root of an angel's blond faith.
Doubt is the knot in faith's muscle and the cramp from faith's plenty.
Doubt is the runt in faith's litter.
Doubt is the one reward faith can ever offer.

Something like a serious half-belief is most touchingly expressed in one of the long fragments in the novel, a dialogue between an imprisoned Jesus and a guard, apparently prior to some sort of execution. The guard is thoughtful and intelligent, and Langguth places on his lips some of his most thoughtful criticisms of New Testament Christianity. The guard is speaking to Jesus.

The guilt you have managed to breed in any man or woman or child fool enough to give you a hearing. The guilt and sense of failure that you've raised to a level of perfection that has never been matched. You've found a way to strike at even the best men – if they live a blameless life, you condemn them for their thoughts. It was your God that shackled men to their lusts. Then, knowing they couldn't change, you came to demand that they free themselves. You examined the nature God gave men and called it base, but you made your complaints to men, not to God. Once you praised the lilies of the field. But if a man manages to live as he has been formed to live, you threaten him with eternal fire.

This is an indictment both intellectually and psychologically honest. The guard continues, confessing at the same time that he is speaking to a Jesus he cannot escape.

> I believe in nothing you teach . . . I know that only emptiness surrounds me, and that when I die the void will claim me. I know and accept that. But deep in my wretched memory your lying promises have lodged themselves, and as I prepare myself each day for death, your words seduce my arguments. In some weak corner of my brain, I think: Perhaps I will be spared.

Even if it is rash to identify the guard's words with those of the author, the words describe a kind of half-belief that is both common and convincing.

If this novel is, among other things, a description of half-belief, an early fragment in the book takes on a special importance. There are two Jesuses, one a man being strapped in an electric chair, the other an inept priest trying to offer consolation. The prisoner-Jesus is serene in the presence of death; the priest-Jesus is confused and is grateful to the prisoner for his example of courage. A Jesus to blame and a Jesus to praise. *Jesus Christs* is about both.

Let us look first at some of Langguth's blame. His blameworthy Jesus is often self-righteous, occasionally cruel and short-tempered, and sometimes even a stupid klutz.

> 'I have come to die for your sins,' Jesus told a stooped figure passing him on the road.
> 'Then what am I to die for?' the old man asked.
> Jesus took a small notebook from his pocket and copied the question. 'If I may have your name and address,' he said, 'an answer will be sent to you.'

This is the klutz Jesus who doesn't even understand a doctrine of the atonement when it is staring him in the face.

Jesus is discussing with Pilate his personal strategies in picking disciples. I want them, he says, really dumb, weak, and unhappy, so there is no chance they will ever be as virtuous as I am. Having dumb disciples is very good for the self-esteem.

Sometimes Langguth's Jesus sets a very low value on human life. At one point he described his own crucifixion as a welcome escape from a rotten world, and the resurrection as a dirty trick forcing him back into it.

Jesus, critical of the virtue of tolerance, angrily slashes the tyres of a yellow convertible belonging to a fashionable clergyman. In another fragment, he lists his faults:

Demanding
Self-righteous
Proud
Moody
Suspicious
Filled with doubt
Tend toward arrogance

Altogether, a fair description of half of this Jesus.

In an important longer fragment, Langguth faces the problem of theodicy in a discussion between Jesus and God. God is watching Jesus as he is inflicting various natural disasters on the world. In the discussion, God is the cruel realist who knows that undeserved suffering is inevitable and inexplicable, while Jesus comes on as a compassionate but inept believer that faith and hope can cure anything and wipe away all suffering. God is cruel, Jesus irrelevant. Jesus is later instructed by a courageous woman who calls him on the phone.

> 'I don't believe . . . that we have the right to ask for health or money or happiness. Tom [her dying husband] might not agree with me. You know he's never done much praying, and when he comes out of the anaesthetic tonight, he might ask you for an end to his pain . . . I'm not asking for courage either. If I can do my part while he's in the hospital, it's because you gave me the strength long ago . . .'

This wise woman, while grateful to Jesus, is still closer to the realism of the cruel God than to the Jesus as sentimental optimist.

In one strange fragment Jesus practises non-resistance to evil with the animals in the forest, and he is killed by a bear for his pacifism. But if the pacifist Jesus is irrelevant, he is also to be admired, and this leads us from the Jesus blamed to the Jesus praised.

Jesus is touching and non-priggish on sex. He wonders why he has been excluded from one of humanity's deepest needs. Has his ministry been vitiated by this un-asked-for exclusion? He knows the importance of sex, but decides not to criticize himself too sharply. Then he wisely adds:

I have stayed a priest's hand raised against a prostitute. But the other misuses of their sex I have attacked with righteousness and ignorance. If ever again I am made sure about my message and myself [Langguth's Jesus is always anxious about himself and his function, as we all are], I will ask to be given that one last link with mankind. I will see if, with it, I can remain the Son of God.

Langguth's most interesting and ambiguous word of praise for Jesus comes in an extended fragment on war and pacifism. Earlier, in his encounter with the black prince, Jesus had confessed that he hated killing. In this fragment, Langguth sets up a war between the disciples (led by Jesus and Judas) and the aliens or traitors. Jesus' pacifism is absolute, and Langguth seems to find this both admirable and foolish. Let us try to sort things out.

The disciples are busy with their war. Mary Magdalene brings news about a projected alien attack. Her information, properly used, would mean the aliens could be ambushed and defeated. Jesus gets Mary's information, and decides not to use it against the enemy. Why? Since there were no orders from headquarters and no word from God, Jesus himself had to make the decision, and he decided not to fight even when victory was assured. God would have approved the killing, but he either does not exist or doesn't care, so Jesus had to go with his own pacifist instincts.

God watched the aliens murdering farmers, setting fire to the rice crop, torturing prisoners to make them betray their country-

men. God watched, and if he was God, he would not ask
godly men to let an alien plague destroy their land.

That is, God – if there were a God – would approve the killing of
the evil enemy.

> But if there was no God [and for this Jesus there was none],
> then Jesus would have to listen to his own soft instincts, to the
> numbness that crept across his body saying, No more killing.

Judas is Jesus' second-in-command, and he knows that the aliens
cannot be vanquished without doing some killing. He also knows
that killing is wrong: 'I know it's wrong, even when it must be
done.' Judas is wise, honest, protective of his comrades. Jesus is
like Judas in one way, he knows he is wrong in refusing to kill,
but he refuses none the less. Jesus both refuses to kill and refuses
to warn his comrades of the aliens' attack, and his double refusal
causes their destruction and defeat.

> It is not just. I must live in the world, but I will be judged by
> scholars, who have avoided life [why are scholars always
> assumed to have avoided life?], writing for children who have
> not begun to live. Something is lost. Life is lost. The cry of my
> body is lost. And a generation of children will sneer or spit when
> they speak my name.

Langguth's Jesus prayed to God to tell him not to kill and to justify
his refusal to give out the information about the aliens' attack.
Jesus expected no response from the empty heavens, and got none.
    The Jesus of Langguth's half-belief is flawed but courageous. It
is not clear that the author is proposing that such a Jesus is to be
'followed' or even 'believed in'. For all his faults, and for all the
damage he may have done, there is a splendid mad courage in him.
Such a Jesus cannot be ignored or forgotten. Even in his folly, he
may have something for us.

There is one more ingredient I want to add to our twentieth-
century stew. It doesn't fit smoothly into any of my silly categories.
It is, I think, charmingly heterodox; it is also very funny and will

remind readers of *Jesus Christs* without the 'Jesus comes to our century' device as dominant. The book is called *Jesus Tales* (San Francisco 1987), by the American playwright Romulus Linney.

It is a marvellous bit of writing and, whether the author wants it or not, a neat if not serious interpretation of Jesus. The tales will remind some readers of the apocryphal gospels from Christianity's early years in which new personalities and events about Jesus were invented for specific ideological purposes: to take him (and his movement) look a bit more gnostic or Alexandrian or Essene. Linney invents all kinds of new personalities for Jesus, for no discernible reason. For the hell of it, presumably.

But purposeless or purposeful, what he does is surely interpretation and even (horrors!) theology. For example, Linney's Jesus is dangerously unsound on monotheism. Here is a dialogue between a young Jesus and a teacher. The teacher speaks first.

> I said, You want to know how many old Gods, who could be so terrible, can now exist in one good God. Am I right? Jesus said, For the first time this morning. And I said, The old Gods, separate, held only separate powers. God, until he was recognized as one God, was not all powerful. When he became one God he became all powerful. And Jesus said, What does that have to do with it? and I said, Since we now know God to be all powerful, we understand him better. Jesus said, We do? I said, of course. We see now that God can be all good even when he may seem to be partly evil. And Jesus said, Or all evil even when he may seem partly good? I saw it was no use. I said, Do not mock the prophets, child. And Jesus said, Wasn't it the prophets who said God was a jealous God and a loving God and a God of happiness and revenge all at the same time, just exactly like the old gods, with only one difference, now that he's just one God if you do anything wrong anywhere in your life he can get you for it? And I said, Exactly. That is what makes God God. And Jesus said, No, it doesn't. That only makes God like my father. That is the worst idea I ever heard. You are a god damned fool (38).

Elegantly written and funny. And naughty. This Jesus kid is arrogant, unable to suffer fools gladly, a critic of all theodicies, furious with the idea of one God and with the idea that the one God should be called Father. It is about time that someone understood the dilemma of people with unhappy father-experiences (either of having or being) and their consequent terror over the idea of the Fatherhood of God.

But Linney's Jesus is not only a post-Christian theological critic with a nose for orthodoxy's soft underbelly. His Jesus is mainly a funny man, a humorist, the first of the borscht-belt comics. Now this may constitute a criticism of the New Testament Jesus. Not many really good gags there. Anthony Burgess gave Jesus the wife the Gospels denied him, and Linney gives Jesus a sense of humour, and comedian's skill, which the Gospels also deny him. Not that his Jesus couldn't be sad.

> He did not look like a very happy man. He was sitting there staring at nothing, sifting sand through one hand. Peter wondered about a man who was so idle, and sad.
>
> Of course the Lord was there for his own reasons, thinking thoughts not always cheerful, since life is hard on everyone, especially him, with that painful cross waiting for him there at the end (60).

But humour was this Jesus' main gig, and the humour depends on our remembering that *other* Jesus that *this* Jesus is so different from.

Linney's first tale is typical. Jesus, walking with Peter in Spain, meets a farmer whose wagon had tipped over, spilling its contents all over the road. But the farmer didn't get mad. He prayed to Jesus that he was a sinner and that he probably deserved the accident. Jesus saw all this, and passed the farmer by, doing nothing.

Soon they came to another farmer whose wagon had tipped over in a ditch. The farmer was cursing. Jesus stopped, knocked the man down, pulled the wagon out of the ditch and miraculously returned the scattered contents to the wagon. Peter couldn't figure out what Jesus was up to. 'Try,' said Jesus. 'Well,' Peter said, 'maybe it means that a decent man's curse is better than a shifty man's prayer.' 'Maybe,' Jesus seemed to reply. But, Peter reminded

Jesus, the first farmer wasn't shifty and the second wasn't decent. Jesus didn't answer Peter and the question remained unanswered.

Now this tale would be good enough to get published in an obscure regional literary quarterly if the leading character's name was Claude. But it wasn't Claude, it was Jesus, and that is what makes the story funny, or funnier. The joke is mainly in the tale's contrast with the joke-free New Testament.

To ascribe humour to Jesus is to suggest uneasiness with moralism and didacticism. And this is what we find. Honour your mother, Linney's Jesus says at one point, but don't overdo it. Linney's Jesus must not be tamed. He does not teach by humour, or heal by humour. He does comedy in place of teaching. His comedy does not instruct, or stimulate to further reflection. It confuses, and is meant to.

Linney knows a lot about Jesus and about humour. He knows humour can be thoughtless and insensitive. Jesus, in one of the tales, tells Peter that he decided not to heal his crippled daughter because if he had, he might have stayed home with his family, and not joined him and made him laugh. Jesus' need for laughter is more important than healing some kid.

These tales ask both to be enjoyed and to be figured out. These, along with all our Jesus fictions, say something about the authors, about the readers, and about Jesus.

I wish to close with a fiction of my own.

Epilogue

Jesus Comes Back:
Between the First and the Second

As God slowly departed from the seat whence he had controlled the universe and its order of values, told good from evil, and given a sense to each thing, then Don Quixote came out of his mansion and was no longer able to recognize the world. In the absence of the supreme arbiter, the world suddenly acquired a fearsome ambiguity. The single divine truth decomposed into myriad relative truths shared among men. Thus was born the world of the Modern Era, and with it the novel – the image and model of that world – sprang to life.

(Milan Kundera)[1]

I know what happened, but I'm not sure how or why. I was alone on the beach, just before dawn, on my regular walk: part exercise, part reflection, letting the recurring waves exercise their healing powers. I wasn't flirting with anxiety. there was no inarticulate cry of help, no waiting for the heavens to open. He came alongside me as I was watching a heron fish in the shallow surf.

'May I walk with you?'

An unusual request, I remember noting. Beach walkers usually leave one another alone. 'Certainly.' He was somewhat younger than I, dressed the way everyone dressed for a morning beach walk. It was too early for anyone to be selling beach-front property. At this point I was merely perplexed. We walked together in silence for a while. 'Are you looking for someone?'

'No,' he replied, warmly.

'Can I do anything for you?'

'I was about to ask you the same thing.'

His comment signalled a shift in my understanding of what was going on. I wasn't sure what to say in response, and a sense of something strange began to steal over me. Things like this do not happen to me. I am non-mystical, non-para-normal. I've never been out of my body, and I can't understand what Shirley MacLaine is talking about. I've never even been hypnotized. I decided to be venturesome rather than cynical. 'Have you been sent here?'

'Probably, but not necessarily to you. We don't have much more than an hour.'

I decided to resist any reasonable explanations that might account for this young man's gentle but persistent presence: escaped patient from a near-by minimum security mental hospital, avant-garde drama school experiment conducted by a disciple of Grotowski? . . . so I pushed ahead.

'I recently read this in Tolstoy's diary. What do you make of it?

The Christian doctrine cannot be lived. Then, is it nonsense? No, but it cannot be lived. Yes, but have you tried? No, but it cannot be lived.

'Neither nonsense nor relevant. That does interest me.'

'Except that Tolstoy finally became persuaded that only he knew how to live it properly.'

He didn't reply immediately, and I suspect he was deciding to test me just as I had been mildly testing him.

'There may be something in what came to be called Christianity that makes people priggish or arrogant or dangerous. But I'm really not interested in seminars.'

'I'm not interested in exchanging reading lists, so you don't have to worry. The Tolstoy passage came to mind when you offered to be of use because I saw in it an anguish I share about the Christian faith today, so impossible, so inescapable.'

'I promise that I will offer no short-cuts to either belief or unbelief.'

I thought carefully before entering the world he was proposing. I wasn't clear about what he might want, or, for that matter, what I might want. I assumed he'd laugh at silly New Testament questions like 'What made Judas do what he did?' I decided, somewhat nervously, to try to say something about myself, without falling into a boring autobiographical monologue.

'I'm a rather ordinary non-heroic man of my times. I live here at the end of this terrible century. It's been quite properly called the century of death, for death-dealing is the thing we've proved to be best at. Communism is dying in the streets of Eastern Europe; capitalism is dying in the streets of most American cities; and Christians and other monotheists are killing each other all over the world. Should I persist in my already tenuous religious affiliation? Perhaps if I knew who you really are – or really were – '

'You don't want much in a short time, do you?'

'Everyone who has written you up – even the Gospel writers in the beginning – has come up with a deeply self-interested portrait that suspiciously resembles the author. Is that all there is?'

'I may be able to help in answering your problem, though your touching confidence that there is something somewhere – out there or in here – that "really" is the case may be a problem. But before we play with your question, I have a question for you. You see, two things have to happen: you are asking for something from me, but I also need something from you. Who is it that is asking this question?'

'Fair enough, though my dislike for yet another encounter group is at least as deep as yours for a religious seminar. What are we supposed to be to one another: is it to be teacher/student or doctor/patient?'

'I am perfectly comfortable, in spite of the oddness of this whole experiment, with a dialogue between friends who have something of importance for each other.'

'I am grateful for my liberation from the couch. I can say a little about myself without descending into autobiography. I am interested in, though not particularly worried about, the matter of my possible religious affiliation. Religion has always meant two things: a way of articulating the mystery that surrounds us, and a way of defining the most productive way of being in the world. A collapse of the serious forms of Christianity would mean that the climate of mystery is unexplained, or has to be explained in a new way. It would also mean that the conscience that you have so largely shaped must be reshaped and redefined.'

'How would you say I have shaped the conscience?'

'I believe I have learned, from you and from those who have learned from you, that in this world we are obliged to live beyond our pleasures. Religion is not what we do with our solitariness, either mystical or sensual; it positions us somewhere – in *this* world, beside our neighbour in need. I might further mention that I have come to be impressed by the great fragility of the civilization I live in . . . I know what I might do to help you locate me. I carry around in my head some odd pieces of poetry and prose that have come to mean something to me. Why don't I put them before you as a way of meeting your request? Here are two that belong together that say well what I have just said badly.

Th' abuse of greatness is when it disjoins
Remorse from power.

'The function of literature is to remind the powers that be, corrupt as they are, of the forces they have to control.'

'Very nice. Two weapons against the corruptions of power: literature and forgiveness.'

'There is another passage that belongs with these: "I came to cast fire upon the earth; and would that it were already kindled." You were reported to have said that.'

'If I didn't I should have. Of course that fire was both metaphorical and apocalyptic.'

'Here is another ingredient for the stew. The fight against evil is both necessary and dangerous; dangerous because such fighters often ascribe all wisdom to themselves and thus become part of the evil they are trying to fight. Here is Oliver Cromwell.

I beseech you, in the bowels of Christ, think it possible you may be mistaken.

Is this of any help? Shall I go on?'

'Of course; I am fascinated.'

'I have sat willingly at the feet of a number of modern poets. They've tended to do better than our moralists.

And life is the destiny you are bound to refuse until you have consented to die.

This gently reminds me of my own mortality, and helps me to befriend it. And again:

The intellect of man is forced to choose
Perfection of the life, or of the work,
And if it take the second must refuse

A heavenly mansion, raging in the dark.[2]

I've always been fascinated by Yeats' "choice", perhaps because I have never been entirely satisfied with my own work and so I needed a justification for that dissatisfaction. Maybe one never really chooses between these perfections. One just looks back and finds that the choice has already been made, almost inadvertently. I think I probably chose "life".'

'This has been a fascinating introduction.'

'May I add one more, rather silly, comment? "The Wizard of Oz" is one of the great movies, and one of the most influential myths of my time. Dorothy is taken to Oz, the land of her dreams, and finally, with the help of friends, finds a way of returning home. This is what she says, at the end of the movie, about what the journey has taught her.

> ... if I ever go looking for my heart's desire again, I won't look any further than my own back yard; because if it isn't there [I think this means 'if my heart's desire isn't in my own back yard'], I never really lost it to begin with.

This may be gibberish, though Miss Garland spoke the lines with great beauty. But if it isn't gibberish, it is wrong and I'd like to tell you why I think so. I don't think anyone should stay in his own back yard. (I'd still be stuck in a boring suburb if I took that advice.) One should take wild and mythic journeys to places like Oz or Ithaca or San Salvador ... But I've given you all you need about me. I have some questions for you. Are there any ground rules for this part of our discussion?'

'I think there ought to be. How about something like this? I will not let you treat me as a vulgar bibliographical source for questions about God or heaven or the New Testament. I will be reluctant to offer any responses that would create a dependence or limit your freedom or give you some absolute assurance that you'd be better off without.'

'Do I take it that when our time is up I will still be living in uncertainty?'

'You certainly will – just like my disciples in the old days. They handled that uncertainty, you may recall, with varying degrees of success.'

'But after your death, Peter and then Paul were hardly tentative or uncertain. We don't ordinarily go to them for their wise tolerance of ambiguity or their negative capability.'

'That may be, but don't forget, that was after my time.'

'I've got it: "accepts no responsibility for Christian self-righteousness". Speaking of your time, do I need to know about what you know about what happened after your death?'

'Don't worry about that. I know at least what you know. I want to return to your first question to me, the question about what I really was or am.'

'Let me explain why I am willing to put you on the spot. I am living in the time of the collapse of the kind of Christian faith that means – or meant, that is the issue – a great deal to me. I cannot wholly escape that faith, nor do I want to. And since I have you here, I'd like to know what a new relationship to you would be like.'

'Let me tease you a bit about your desire to know who I really am. Isn't that desire just another form of that old disease – the longing for an unshakable truth better than anyone else's unshakable truth? I keep telling you that you will get no liberation from uncertainty from me. What do you really want? A promise that I'll be there to meet all your needs? A kindly mentor that will hang around to approve of what you were planning to do anyway?'

'I recall your old evasive ways with the disciples. They wanted to pin you down: signs, definitions of your status, instant liberation from the Romans. And you gave them nothing.'

'I'm not sure I like "evasive". I respected their freedom to choose or not to choose to follow me. Same with you.'

'No "Jesus as he really was", after all?'

'If there were such a thing, it would turn any religion based on it into one more authoritarian system. There is enough of that already in place and I have no intention of adding to it.'

'You've cleverly refused to answer one question, trying to convince me it is in my own interest. Let me put my question another way, and then I can watch you shoot that one down as well.'

'Just don't assume that my ultimate function is to meet your needs.'

'You did manage to meet some very real needs, long ago. The broken, the sick, even the disciples.'

'Yes, but that was indeed a long time ago. I said many things then that are of absolutely no use to you now.'

'I assume you're speaking of that apocalyptic baggage; the immediate end of history, demon-possession . . .'

'Those things involved the best my age had to offer. Compared to your own time, my time was wrong on many matters. I was wrong. Albert Schweitzer had many of the details wrong, but on the main point he was right, and still is. Whenever scholarship tries to drag me into the twentieth century, I slip away and return to the first. I was a child of my own time – what else could I have been? You are a child of your time. I have no desire to turn you into a child of my time, and I'm sure you don't wish to make me a child of yours.'

'I suppose I have cherished a secret hope that you might turn out to be a gentle left-liberal revolutionary, correct on women and the environment. Have you really just come to this beach to tell me that the gulf between us is unbridgeable?'

'It is theoretically unbridgeable, I suspect. No more hermeneutics. (You see, I have picked up some of the new words.) But practically, in the realm of action, I think we can set a relationship in motion, a friendship as we have been calling it, and avoid the rather authoritarian flavour of Schweitzer's ultimate "follow me". No more longing for certainty, and a willingness to take some risks.'

'What do I do without? You've already liberated me from both demonology and eschatology. How about God the Father? Much of your old teaching is based on that. Is God part of the dispensable first-century baggage?'

'I'm not going to pronounce on that one. What you will want to figure out is what function the idea of God performed in my world, what sense of wonder it articulated, what it meant as a pointer to the undeserved character of much of the goodness that comes our way. These functions are important, but the use of the term is up to you. I've no language test for orthodoxy to propose.'

'This is certainly proving to be an unusual friendship. What have I so far learned from you? "Live with uncertainty." "I am largely irrelevant." How about ethics? Also irrelevant? I've been taught to manifest a touch of anguish about the relevance of your impossible ethical ideals.'

'Give up your anguish and be content with the irrelevance. After all, a great many of what you call my ethical principles were really invented by the early church for their own purposes of self-defence. My so-called pacifism, for example.'

'I have a minor concern before we get down to serious business. Will you take a question about the New Testament?'

'Yes, I will take it. I may throw it back, but I promise not to be offensively evasive.'

'It has to do with the parable of the Prodigal Son.'

'I know what you are referring to.'

'I understand the broadly anti-Pharisaic function of those three parables in Luke 15, and that Luke needed to make you into an enemy of the Pharisees for his own reasons. I'm not interested in his rather silly attempt to show up the Pharisees as less interested in forgiveness than you.'

'It looks like your question may be more interesting than I had expected. What's the problem?'

'I've always been distressed by the parable's treatment of the elder brother. He was neither spendthrift nor sensualist, but no party was arranged to honour his decent bourgeois behaviour. The younger brother was a creep. I've never been convinced that he had an ounce of contrition. I suspect he came to see one day that poverty and hunger weren't fun any more so he decided to try the repentance game as a way of getting his old room back, rent-free. His dumb father bought the trick, and the party had been going on all day when the older son comes in from the field, looking forward to a shower and a beer. Of course he was mad; he should have been. You can't allegorize him into a self-righteous Pharisee; he'd simply been treated unfairly. The parable illustrates one of the sickest sides of popular Christianity: sinners enjoy committing sins and God enjoys forgiving and things couldn't be more satisfactory for both parties in the game. Is the true message of this story that we should give up all bourgeois virtues in order to be acceptable?'

'Is that all?'

'Don't put on your irony hat; I'm almost completely serious.'

'Exactly. The trouble is you're too serious. I am not taking responsibility for any of the "lost" parables in Luke 15. You've properly noted how they reflect Luke's rather nasty anti-Pharisee-ism. But they're just stories, and you shouldn't read them so moralistically. I probably agree with your affection for the elder brother, and I certainly have no complaint against your defence of bourgeois virtues and values: loyalty, keeping your word, telling the truth – these cannot be patronized, however unheroic they may seem. Both modernism and post-modernism seem to have a sick affection for the criminal. My serious reaction to your mini-sermon on the elder brother is this. You still take the Bible far too seriously as a source of reliable historical information. Just as there is no "me as I really was", so there is no certain sense of the meaning of the Gospels. They simply do not deliver my inner meaning, whatever that means. Their stories are fictions; all the stories about me are, even those that pretend to be histories.

Fiction is all you have, and you must be playful, not earnest, with fiction. They teach as art teaches, not history. In part what you get from fiction is what you bring: your own passion and sorrow and need. If your century (or the next) manages to move beyond history to literature as its key to the New Testament, it will be a worthy achievement indeed. The nineteenth century gave us the historical experiment, and it was an experiment of priceless value. But many expected that it could produce something to depend on, and it didn't do so. That is what I am inviting you to take your New Testament less seriously so you can make it work for you in new ways in your time.'

'Thank you. I am beginning to understand how you have decided to treat me in this meeting. You don't really answer my questions directly, but you're not really evasive either. What you seem to be doing is to answer the real question you think I should have asked rather than the silly question I did ask and which you refused to answer.'

'We're beginning to get somewhere. I was beginning to think I'd mislaid my pedagogical skills. I now need to understand you a little more precisely. I enjoyed your half-playful monologue with the bits of prose and poetry. Let me move closer to your concern about the present viability of the Christian faith. Certain obvious forms of that concern don't interest me: can one "believe" in

God? or can one "be" a Christian? I really don't know about those things. But in place of answers to those silly questions, we are trying in our limited time to set up a relationship with each other that can become the basis of your continuing reflection. Is that your understanding of what we are up to?'
'Yes. That was a non-ironic, non-evasive, and very helpful location of our present position.'

'Here is what I want you to try to answer for me. If the systems that have promised absolute religious certainty have broken down, what is left among – let us say – the Christian fragments lying at your feet that still seems to you important, something you'd rather not do without? Even if I have promised not to meet your needs, it would be useful for me to know what those needs might be that I won't be meeting.'
'I think I can respond to that. I have, over the years, come to value three themes in your recorded actions and words that I do not care to dispense with. I cannot easily demythologize them away. Without them, I could manage a fairly easy escape from you. And I don't even know if these themes are "yours".'

'Your old historical anxiety again. If you found them in the record, they are there. What are they?'
'The attack on anxiety; the attack on judging or radical forgiveness; and anger or the criticism of religious and political power. If you like: Matthew 6, Luke 7, and Mark 11. There are problems with all three.'

'You are asking if these are part of the first century that can be jettisoned, or whether they can be put to work in your world.'
'Take the analysis of anxiety in the Sermon on the Mount, yours or not. No one can read that today without knowing that it is impossible not to take thought about what we eat or wear or earn. Our uncertain futures always impinge on our presents, often making those presents impossible to enjoy. It's really not fair. You had an easy time of it: a wandering prophet living off the land, unmarried, no family to care for. So of course you could tell your friends not to worry, that God would take care of everything.'

'Why not forget it?'
'Because there is something in that attack on anxiety that I find infinitely attractive. These are words that I "need". Again and again I find that my over-zealous concern about the future empties the

present of any meaning. I am up-tight. I get to the airport a full hour before take-off. I would be a much better person if I could borrow some of your splendid carelessness and freedom.'

'I am sure the cultural differences between us are formidable, but I don't see why you can't attack your particular anxiety-systems as radically as I attacked mine. I really don't think that because I was agrarian and you are technological and urban makes all that much difference. What is it that constitutes your inability to take delight in the present? What makes you postpone present enjoyments for a future that may never arrive? Think about the wisdom of the very ill and the dying. They tell us that their shortness of time leads them to value each passing moment with a special intensity. Instead of complaining about transiency and mortality, accept them and you may find that your present can be returned to you. It's not a matter of cultural difference; I think it is attitude, and I am sure your nervous and well-meaning Protestantism is a mild affliction that can be cured by taking thought. Make every day function as if it were both your first and your last. I think "my" attack on anxiety is true because it can lead you to mount "your" attack on yours, even though "my" answer may not be like yours at all.'

'Another one of your non-answers; no, answers I didn't expect. I should have learned by now not to expect a traditional answer.'

'Which would have been – what?'

'Oh: Matthew 6 is irrelevant to the modern world, like demon-possession and the three-story universe. Or – prayer will take care of everything if you have enough faith.'

'You should have discovered by now that I have little interest in either liberalism or biblicism. Let's move on. What do you mean by radical forgiveness?'

'The recorded incidents of your ministry that have fascinated me the most – and presented a moral demand very difficult to respond to – are those strange stories, all somehow connected, in which a woman, usually disreputable, moves into a group with you and other respectable people. And you do something that offends the respectable and frees the woman. Usually an act of forgiveness or a refusal to judge. It is sometimes argued that this is where you gave most offence to your fellow Jews: you seemed to forgive without requiring words or deeds of repentance.'

'I don't want to get into another discussion about what I really meant, but such a debate won't be necessary. I've never felt that I differed much from the Pharisees of my day. I got along well with them, and learned from them as well. They generally offered forgiveness after repentance, while I may, from time to time, have begun with forgiveness and followed up with a severe moral injunction, such as "neither do I condemn you; go, and do not sin again" – as to the adulteress about to be stoned. No vast gulf between me and the Pharisees. The church later found it necessary to blow up that minor divergence out of all proportion, practically depriving me of my Jewishness. That's why your Gospels have always made me a trifle uneasy.'

'I have two problems with radical forgiveness and the refusal to judge. A moral life which is only forgiveness is a life devoid of moral discrimination. There is a courageous resistance to tyranny that risks one's life and there is a sycophantic service to the tyrants. (You must remember that my generation, old enough to fight in World War II, experienced German, Italian and Japanese Fascism as unforgivable systems of evil.) So I'm afraid of any forgiveness that prohibits judgment. How am I supposed to take this: "Judge not, that you be not judged. For with the judgment you pronounce you will be judged . . ." For one thing, I can't make use of the Last Judgment as part of the argument. For another, I'm afraid that all careful distinctions between true and false, courage and fear, beautiful and shoddy – all these seem to disappear in the pious fog of "no judgment at all".'

'That is nicely stated. I may have been responsible for the strain of ever-smiling pious sentimentalism ("have a nice day" expanded into "have a nice life") that can be found in some of the traditions emerging from my life and death. I have no interest in attacking the need for discriminating intellectual and moral judgments. We need as much of this as we can get. I would hardly have taken on the priests and Pilate – at some personal cost – had I believed that there was no serious difference between good and evil. But I do believe that forgiveness must inform the whole fabric of our lives. We need to offer it, because we need to be offered it. Relationships of great importance get broken, and they can be repaired. Forgiveness is the name of that slow, painful process of repair. It's not a glib "forgive and forget". On what you call my attack on judging: what I want is an attack on egotism, an attack as appropriate to your century as to mine. What bothers me about "judging" – and this means mostly the judging of people – is that the judger usually elevates himself and demeans the one being judged. Judgment as a weapon of ego domination; this is what I dislike. Censoriousness, gossip – this is what the prohibition of judging prohibits. No one is good enough to judge in my sense, and none of us is without the need for forgiveness.'

' "Father, forgive them; for they know not what they do." What if "they" had known? Would the forgiveness have been requested?'

'Probably not.'

'You see, I live in a corrupt and evil time. Greed and stupidity dominate our public lives and suffering caused by that greed multiplies. I am sometimes tempted just to withdraw: silence, exile, and cunning. So, you see, I was more than a little afraid that your "forgive everyone, judge no one" might feed that temptation. I see that it need not do so.'

'This brings us around to the third fragment from my work that you want to preserve. My words about forgiveness and judgment can hardly be accused of feeding quietism (your "silence, exile, and cunning") since I did, after all, finish out my life in open opposition to the timid priests and corrupt Roman bureaucrats who had concluded I was a public nuisance, or worse. If you want support for your generous anger from me, you've got it – from the disturbance in the Temple down to the trial and crucifixion. To be sure, I didn't invent any new political or religious forms, but I did as much as I could to embarrass the old ones.'

'And to force them into an act of retaliation that profoundly damaged their credibility.'

'That can always be done – fighting the corrupt structures you inherit, even when you have no promises of success.'

'That reminds me of another piece of prose floating around in my head: ". . . to realize the relative validity of one's convictions and yet stand for them unflinchingly is what distinguishes a civilized man from a barbarian".'

'You cannot do everything; you must not expect praise or success. But you can, you must, keep on doing the one or two things that you have learned to do well. A lot of free-floating anxiety can be abolished. Simplify your life; your desires themselves can be the enemy; yet avoid asceticism; welcome transiency; kill the postponement demons. Each day as it comes can be taken as a gift. You may find your discovery of forgiveness (for others and for yourself) and avoidance of judgment genuinely liberating. There will always be time and room for a generous anger not over-sure of itself.'

'Did I discover all this in the records of your life and death?'

'You did; but notice that I have not required of you any slavish imitation of those records.'

'That is so, and I am grateful. You have truly been of help – can I dare to say that you have met some needs? – without requiring a debilitating dependence on you or those records. I suspect I would not have a sense of something new, the beginning of a journey, without your willingness to listen and to speak.'

'Even though I have thoroughly cured you of your initial desire for the real me?'

'You have almost persuaded me that what I have found was some-thing I already had. "You would not seek me . . ."'

'Our hour is nearly over. I really don't have anything to say about your problem with Christianity. I didn't see all that coming. After all, for me history was about to be wrapped up, and I was wrong. There is one more thing I wish to speak about, and that is my death. The Gospel records must be used very carefully, for they all exaggerate Jewish responsibility and underplay Roman involvement. The first Christians wanted a non-political prophet; they couldn't find one in memory or history so they invented one. But that kind of thing doesn't matter. I died in part because of my own decision to take one last trip to Jerusalem to engage the Roman usurpers and their priestly defenders. That was an engagement I had to carry out, and I set it in an apocalyptic context which was the only context available to me. I "really" did pray in that garden to be spared the death I saw coming. I "really" did complain from the cross of the abandonment by God. I should remind you of what you already know in case you expect reward for whatever consequences in your life our meeting might bring. I don't know what enemies you might come to make, or who will be the object of your anger, or who may be upset by your forgiveness and refusal to judge. But if your world is at all like the one I (with some reluctance) left behind, you should expect discomfort, or worse. Remember, I did not come into the first century to settle your twentieth-century problems.'

'Yes, you have said that more than once. And saying that has become the basis for the way in which you may have indeed begun to solve some of those problems.'

'There is still something for you to use, apart from the outdated eschatology and its ethic. I didn't really say it myself; someone else put it on my lips, but I have always liked it. Let me leave you with these words: "as you did it to one of the least of these my brethren, you did it to me." '

Then I was alone. The sun was just becoming visible at the horizon, as dawn began to turn into morning. I walked along the beach for a while, and decided to resist any attempts to verify the experience just past. Were there footprints alongside mine? Did anyone we passed on our walk see someone with me? I had no desire to set aside the encounter as an hallucination or a brain lesion. I decided to take it as real; or rather, to assume that something really did happen, and that it would receive whatever validation it merited not by tape recorders and cameras, but by what took place in my life and work in the months to come. I was both troubled and moved, but not afraid. At least I didn't take him for a gardener.

Notes

I Beyond Belief

1. I am comfortable with Shakespeare's definition of the poet as one who sees what isn't yet there:

   The poet's eye, in a fine frenzy rolling,
   Doth glance from heaven to earth, from earth to heaven;
   And as imagination bodies forth
   The forms of things unknown, the poet's pen
   Turns them to shapes, and gives to airy nothing
   A local habitation and a name
                                    (*A Midsummer Night's Dream* V.i, 12–17).

2. I am citing the version of Rushdie's lecture that appeared in *Granta* 31, Spring 1990, 97–111. The quoted passage is from pp. 102–3. More recently Rushdie has called this 'dispute' into question by re-defining, much less ambiguously than in this address, his own relationship to the Muslim faith.

3. Nathaniel Hawthorne, *The Scarlet Letter*, ch. 17.

4. Rushdie, *Granta* (n.2), 104.

5. Charles Davis, *Cross Currents*, XXXII.13, 1982.

6. Todd Gitlin, 'Hip Deep in Post-Modernism', *New York Times Book Review*, 6 November 1988, 35.

7. E. P. Sanders, *Jesus and Judaism*, London and Philadelphia 1985, 159f.

8. A. Schweitzer, *The Quest of the Historical Jesus*, London and New York ³1954, 396.

9. Ibid., 401. There are some unresolved problems in this notable passage. He 'comes' to us, but he is not known in his coming. The move from ignorance to knowledge is neither intellectual nor ecclesiastical. It comes in the world of action. The anti-theological Schweitzer has almost refashioned the doctrine of the incarnation in such a way that the Word becomes *our* flesh.

10. John Kent, *The End of the Line*, London 1982, ix.

11. John Bowden, *Jesus – The Unanswered Questions*, London 1988 and Nashville 1989, 32. Geza Vermes, *Jesus the Jew*, London and Philadelphia 1986, 225, says that we can know that Jesus was a just man, a helper, a teacher and a healer. But we cannot add much flesh to those bare bones. Bowden's principle does of course rule out the modified historical optimism of scholars like Dodd and Bornkamm and Küng, who claim that we do know enough to make out Jesus' message, and this knowledge is necessary, but not sufficient, to faith.

12. Two recent remarks about ideology have impressed me. Erik Erikson, *Young Man Luther*, London 1959, 22, defined ideology as 'an unconscious tendency underlying religious and scientific as well as political thought: the tendency at a given time to make facts amenable to ideas, and ideas to facts, in order to create a world image convincing enough to support the collective and individual sense of identity', and Vaclav Havel, 'The Power of the Powerless', in *Open Letters*, New York 1991: 'Ideology is a specious way of relating to the world. It offers human beings the illusion of an identity, of dignity, and of morality . . .'.

13. Richard Rorty, 'The Contingency of Community', *London Review of Books*, 24 July 1986, 14.

II Jesus: 'These fragments I have shored against my ruins'

1. T. S. Eliot, 'The Waste Land', line 430, in *Collected Poems*, London ²1974, 79.

2. Shakespeare, *Henry V*, II.iii, 18–21.

3. References will be to Dietrich Bonhoeffer, *Letters and Papers from Prison*, The Enlarged Edition, London and New York 1971.

4. Dietrich Bonhoeffer, *Christology*, London and New York 1966.

5. Bonhoeffer, *Letters and Papers* 13–14. The remaining references to the prison material will be given in the text.

6. Today, we might wish to add that the suffering of God is also caused by the religious world, the world *with* God.

7. Graham Shaw, *God in Our Hands*, London 1987.

8. Lewis Carroll, *Through the Looking-Glass*, VI.

9. Graham Shaw, *The Cost of Authority*, London and Philadelphia 1983.

10. Ibid., 233.

11. He has one elegant comment on christology: 'christological claims are only disguised forms of clerical self-assertion' (ibid., 288).

12. James Baldwin, *The Fire Next Time*, New York and London 1985, 41, 57.
13. Jens Glebe-Möller, *A Political Dogmatic*, Philadelphia 1987.
14. Ernest Hemingway, *For Whom the Bell Tolls*, New York and London 1941, Chapter 3.

III How to Invent a Political Jesus

1. E. P. Sanders, *Jesus and Judaism*, London and Philadelphia 1985, 159–60.
2. J. L. Segundo, *The Historical Jesus of the Synoptics*, Maryknoll 1985.
3. L. Boff, *Passion of Christ, Passion of the World*, Maryknoll 1987. Page references to quotations from both these titles will be found in the text.
4. Is this the reason why 'Casablanca' still exercises so powerful a hold on the moral imagination of my generation – that is, those old enough to have fought in World War II? (Hence the rule of thumb, 'Trust no one born after 1926'.) 'Casablanca' is a world of sublime moral simplicity: either fight the Fascists or become one. Some of this old moral Manicheeism may still live in the Third World today. It is not much help in the First World.
5. Sanders, *Jesus and Judaism* (n.1), puts the current exegetical consensus simply: '. . . those who presumably know the most about Judaism, and about the law in particular – Jewish scholars – do not find any substantial points of disagreement between Jesus and his contemporaries . . .' And, 'I find no substantial conflict between Jesus and the Pharisees.' By contrast, Boff and Segundo need the major blame for the trial and death of Jesus to go to the Jews.
6. Sanders' powerful conclusion to *Jesus and Judaism* is the best antidote to Boff's polemical anger: 'The setting of Jesus' work within Judaism, therefore, is not to be understood as one of polar opposition between a man of good will and men of bad intent. It is not reasonable historical explanation to say that Jesus believed in a whole list of non-controversial and pleasant abstractions (love, mercy and grace) and that his opponents denied them. It is not reasonable to say that he sought the will of God and that they intended only to play with Scripture to turn it to their own advantage' (339).
7. If one could only insert 'hegemony' and 'hermeneutics of suspicion' into this sentence we would have almost all the cliché theological wisdom of our time in one tiny, useful container.
8. The depth of Boff's anti-theological animus should be noted: 'My own position is that when faith, in the reverence of mystical silence,

has said, "Jesus is God," it has said all there is to say. After that, silence alone is adequate. Anything else that will be said will be vacuous, superfluous, or redundant. We cannot go on with constructs upon the reality enunciated. We have said all we can. It is the part of theology and of faith simply to demonstrate that the proposition that Jesus is God is not self-contradictory. Neither theology nor faith can then seize upon God as a fixed, stable, rational datum and make deductions from this datum. God would no longer be the God enunciated in the formula, "Jesus is God." God would be an idol, something you can make deductions from' (113). This is an astonishing obscurantist definition of the role of theology, worthy of the wildest Social Gospel activists of the early twentieth century. Boff's docility before the heretical patripassianism of 'Jesus is God' is particularly interesting in view of his angry rejection, in this very essay, of Moltmann's crucified God.

9. Segundo is so anxious to have Jesus agree with him that he can actually claim – with pardonable vagueness – that Jesus recommended atheism. 'I am talking about the acceptance of atheism as a serious possibility vis-à-vis Jesus of Nazareth because it is a concrete, historical demand that he himself makes' (14).

10. This identification of the political with the religious is the key to Segundo's search for a political Jesus. There is, of course, a deep connection between the two worlds, and eschatology overlaps both. But Segundo's simple identification is really the absence of thought. Another strange element in his argument is the description of the political structure of first-century Palestine as 'theocratic'. Both Pilate and Caiaphas would have smiled.

11. J. L. Segundo, An Evolutionary Approach to Jesus of Nazareth, Maryknoll 1988, 122.

12. Milan Machoveč, A Marxist Looks at Jesus, London and Philadelphia 1976.

IV Four Nineteenth-Century Studies

1. D. H. Lawrence, Studies in Classic American Literature, New York 1971, 2.

2. Fyodor Dostoevsky, The Notebooks for The Idiot, edited by Edward Wasiolek, Chicago and London 1967.

3. Dostoevsky's wife described the effect of the painting on her husband: '. . . he could never forget the sensation he had experienced in the Basel museum in 1867: the figure of Christ taken from the cross, whose body already showed signs of decomposition, haunted him

like a horrible nightmare. In his notes to *The Idiot* and in the novel itself he returns again and again to this theme.'

4. IV.7. There is only one other moment in the novel, apart from this one, where Myshkin departs from his normal innocent passivity. Ganya attempted to strike his sister after she had spat in his face, and Myshkin restrained him with an untypical word of judgment: 'Oh, how you'll be ashamed of what you've done' (I.10). This is Jesus casting out demons, not recommending non-resistance to evil.

5. Twenty years later Nietzsche (*The Anti-Christ*, 18) will pick up the theme of God as spider, and in a hundred years Ingmar Bergman will use the metaphor in the climactic scene in 'Through a Glass Darkly'.

6. *Correspondence*, Vol. I, edited by Culmann-Levy, Paris 1961, 157, the letter to Baroness von Wizine.

7. M. Gorki, *Reminiscences of Leo Nikolaevich Tolstoy*, 1920, 5.

8. This formulation of the law has the curious effect of neutralizing Jesus' uniqueness, since it was known not just 1800 years ago (the Sermon on the Mount), but five thousand years ago, presumably in Hebrew scripture. This may explain the fascinating footnote from Aylmer Maude, the translator of *What I Believe*, which he appended to Chapter VI: 'The only contribution the present translator can make to the matter is to record the fact that, some fifteen years after *What I Believe* was written, he asked Tolstoy whether he still held to the interpretations he had advanced when dealing with the Gospels. Tolstoy replied that he had ceased to attach special importance to precise words attributed to Jesus, and admitted that, in his anxiety to counteract the bias he detected in the "Orthodox" translation, he had sometimes overstrained the sense too much in a contrary direction . . .'

9. The struggle in Lenin between culture and politics is painful to observe. See especially 'Leo Tolstoy as a Mirror of the Russian Revolution', in *Selected Works* XI, London 1939:

On the one hand we have the gifted writer who is not only able to draw an incomparable picture of Russian life, but is able to produce first-class world literature. On the other hand we have the landowner wearing the martyr's crown in the name of Christ . . .

Tolstoy is great as the expression of those ideas and moods which arose among the millions of the Russian peasantry with the advance of the bourgeois revolution in Russia. Tolstoy is original because his views, harmful as a whole, express in their totality precisely the

distinguishing characteristic of our revolution, viz., a peasant-bour-
geois revolution.

10. I have been helped by three studies of Mrs Stowe's religious thought:
Ellen Moers, *Harriet Beecher Stowe and American Literature*, Hart-
ford 1978: Gayle Kimball, *The Religious Ideas of Harriet Beecher
Stowe*, Lewiston, New York 1983; and Charles H. Foster, *The Rung-
less Ladder*, Durham 1954.

11. James Baldwin, *Notes of a Native Son*, New York 1963, 17.

12. It is natural for us today to be uneasy with this description of the
Black character. It is especially poignant when we remember that
this Black passivity is created by the very Protestant faith that Mrs
Stowe is trying to shape as an alternative to a Calvinism too docile
before slavery's evil.

13. D. H. Lawrence, *Studies* (n. 1), 119.

14. Nothing shows Mrs Stowe's idea of the redemptive power of the
Black mother more vividly than her frequent and beautiful descriptions of the preparation of meals. Here is unselfish maternal love in
action, and each of the meals in *Uncle Tom's Cabin* is a sacrament
offered up by the Black mother as the loving and redeeming Jesus.

15. After Eva's death, Tom prays the dying St Clare into salvation. He
assures the dying man: 'I's willing to lay down my life, this blessed
day, to see Mas'r a Christian' (XXVII).

16. My study of Emily Dickinson has been helped by two admirable
books: a psychoanalytical essay by John Cody (*After Great Pain:
The Inner Life of Emily Dickinson*, Cambridge, Mass. 1971) and a
literary-theological interpretation of great power by Cynthia Griffin
Wolff (*Emily Dickinson*, Reading, Mass., 1988). The citations from
the letters come from the standard edition: *The Letters of Emily
Dickinson*, edited by Thomas H. Johnson, Cambridge, Mass. 1958
(3 volumes; citations will be in the text, by volume and page number).
The poems are also cited in the text by poem number, according to
the standard edition: *The Complete Poems of Emily Dickinson*,
edited by Thomas H. Johnson, Boston 1960.

17. John Cody, *After Great Pain* (n.15), 55.

18. In John 17. 9–10, which is reflected in the final words of this passage,
Jesus is referring to his disciples in this world as 'his', not to dead
children he has transferred from earth to heaven. Passion may make
a kind of truth, but it sometimes makes lousy exegesis.

19. Cynthia Wolff, *Emily Dickinson* (n. 15), 265.

20. John Cody, *After Great Pain* (n. 15), 434, shrewdly comments: 'One

of her favourite ideas is that one can only appreciate a thing when one lacks it . . .'

V Novelists, Journalists, Playwrights and Others

1. This should not be too tough a nut for modern Christians to crack. Just as we have been enjoined to take the resurrection seriously but not literally, so Hussein takes the crucifixion in the same way.

2. For example, Theissen includes Jesus' protest against Pharisaic legalism as part of his Christian ethic without needing to believe that anti-Phariseeism was historically part of Jesus' teaching. He suspects it was not. The point is that the anti-legalism is in the text, even if not in the history.

3. Reading Sinclair and some of the other great muck-rakers, one senses the deep affinity between the muck-raking movement and the Social Gospel, an affinity that surely honours both parties. The muck-rakers seem powerfully drawn to Jesus as the anti-theological prophet of justice and love.

4. Several themes regularly fascinate the Jesus-novelists. One is Jesus' love-life. Another is Judas: what did he betray and why? This may be the place to mention an essay by Jorge Luis Borges in *Labyrinths* called 'Three Versions of Judas'. He reports on the work of the Swedish scholar Nils Runeberg who argued (1904) that Judas, the wisest of the disciples, betrayed Jesus in order to force him to reveal his divinity and to stir up an anti-Roman rebellion. This has been a fairly common speculation, both in fiction and theology, and even Karl Barth has suggested that Judas bears a redemptive function. In a later book (1909) Runeberg went much further. Now, Judas is no longer a helper in the redemptive drama, he *is* that drama. God became man – in Judas, taking the form of the most despised and sinful of men to rescue all men from their sin. Borges writes of the consequences of Runeberg's final Judas-theology.

> Drunk with insomnia and vertiginous dialectic, Nils Runeberg wandered through the streets of Malmö, begging at the top of his voice that he be granted the grace of joining his Redeemer [i.e. Judas] in Hell.

Tim Rice, the lyricist for Andrew Lloyd Webber's *Jesus Christ Superstar*, used Judas as the key to his drama. The musical's opening number, 'Heaven on Their Minds', is a solo by Judas in which he expresses some uneasiness about Jesus' integrity. He fears that Jesus is in danger of believing all of the theological superstructure that people are beginning to erect around him, and that his life will be endangered when the ordinary people come to see that he is really only a man, not a Messiah.

5. Many years ago, I was talking to W. H. Auden about *The Cocktail Party*, and he happened to mention, quite off-handedly, that Lavinia is pregnant at the beginning of Act III. I laughed my denial, confident of my mastery of the text. 'Where do you find that?', I asked. Auden gently replied, with more than a faint smile, 'Tom told me.' Never tangle with icons.

VI The Poets

1. References for the poems cited here:

Lawrence Ferlinghetti, *A Coney Island of the Mind*, New York 1958.

Barbara O'Brien, 'The Prophet Explains Religion', *The Sun, A Magazine of Ideas*, issue 195, Feb. 1992, 12–13.

Michael W. and Deborah D. Smith, 'Could He Be the Messiah?', Meadowgreen Music, Nashville, TN.

John Prine, 'Jesus The Missing Years', Weona Music, BMI.

Ezra Pound, *Collected Early Poems*, New York 1976.

W. H. Auden, *Collected Poems*, ed. Edward Mendelson, New York 1976.

Countee Cullen, *On These I Stand*, New York 1925.

Robert Pinsky, *The Want Bone*, New York 1990.

Louise Erdrich, *Baptism of Desire*, New York 1989.

Hugh MacDiarmid, *Collected Poems*, New York 1967.

Andrew Hudgins, *The Never-Ending*, Boston 1991.

Rainer Maria Rilke, *The Unknown Rilke: Expanded Edition*, translated by Franz Wright, Oberlin 1990.

The Collected Poems of Stevie Smith, ed. James MacGibbon, Harmondsworth 1985.

VII Jesus Comes Back

1. 'Thirteen Who Mutinied: Faulkner's First World War', *The Reporter*, X, 14 Sept. 1954.

2. More than once, Faulkner had expressed his fascination with the idea that the Unknown Soldier might be Jesus himself, returned and re-crucified. If he came again, he remarked, it would be just like it was the first time.

3. I am writing this during the air-bombardment phase of the 1991

Gulf War, America's most recent attempt (to use Faulkner's bitter language) at self-immortalizing.

Epilogue   Jesus Comes Back: Between the First and the Second

1. Milan Kundera, 'The Novel and Europe', *The New York Review*, 19 July 1984, 15.
2. The sources of the 'fragments' are as follows: *Julius Caesar*, II.i, 18–19; R. P. Blackmur; Luke 12.49; a 1650 letter to the General Assembly of the Church of Scotland; W. H. Auden, 'For the Time Being: A Christmas Oratorio'; W. B. Yeats, 'The Choice'.

Acknowledgments

The author wishes to thank the following for permission to quote copyright material; every effort has been made to trace sources, and if any material remains unacknowledged the author wishes to apologize; the omission is quite unintentional.

Artellus Ltd, for selections from *Man of Nazareth* by Anthony Burgess. Copyright by Anthony Burgess 1959. Augsburg Fortress Publishers for excerpts from *A Political Dogmatic*, by Jens Glebe-Möller. Copyright Fortress Press 1987; and for excerpts from *Jesus and Judaism* by E.P. Sanders. Copyright in the United States Fortress Press 1985. Bantam Doubleday Dell, for extracts from *The Greatest Story Ever Told*, by Fulton Oursler. The Ecco Press for 'From the Childhood of Jesus', from *The Want Bone*, by Robert Pinsky. Copyright by Robert Pinsky 1990. Faber and Faber for extracts from W.H. Auden, 'Friday's Child', in *Collected Poems*, ed. Edward Mendelson; T.S. Eliot, 'The Waste Land' and *The Cocktail Party*. GRM Associates, Inc., agents for the estate of Ida M. Cullen. Selections from 'Heritage' from *Color* by Countee Cullen. Copyright 1925 by Harper and Brothers; renewed 1953 by Ida M. Cullen. Selections from 'The Black Christ' from *The Black Christ and Other Poems* by Countee Cullen. Copyright 1929 by Harper and Brothers; renewed 1953 by Ida M. Cullen. Harcourt Brace for excerpts from T.S. Eliot, 'The Waste Land' and *The Cocktail Party*. Harvard University Press, for selections from *The Letters of Emily Dickinson*, edited by Thomas H. Johnson, Cambridge, Mass., The Belknap Press of Harvard University Press, copyright 1958, 1986 by the President and Fellows of Harvard College. William Heinemann Ltd, for selections from *The Brook Kerith*, by George Moore. Houghton Mifflin Co, for 'An Old Joke' from *The Never-Ending* by Andrew Hudgins. Copyright 1991 by Andrew Hudgins. Ignatius Press, for selections from *The Man Born to be King*, by Dorothy L. Sayers. Little, Brown and Company, for selections from *The Complete Poems of Emily Dickinson*, edited by Thomas H. Johnson. Copyright 1929, 1935 by Martha Dickinson Bianchi; renewed 1957, 1963 by Mary L. Hampson. Macmillan Publishing Company, for 'I Heard Christ Sing', from *Collected Poems of Hugh MacDiarmid*, copyright 1948, 1962, by Christopher Murray Grieve; for an extract from *For Whom the Bell Tolls* by Ernest Hemingway. Copyright by Ernest Hemingway, 1940 and Mary Hemingway 1968; for extracts from *The Brook Kerith* by George Moore. New Direction Publishing Corporation for extracts from Stevie Smith, *Collected Poems*, reprinted by permission, and for 'Sometime During Eternity', from *A Coney Island of the Mind* by Lawrence Ferlinghetti. Copyright by Lawrence Ferlinghetti 1958. The New York Times Company, for an extract from 'Hip Deep in Post-Modernism', by Todd Gitlin. Copyright by The New York Times Company 1988. Orbis Books, for excerpts from L. Boff, *Passion of Christ. Passion of the World*, and Juan L. Segundo, *The Historical Jesus of the Synoptics*. Peter Owen for extracts from Shusaku Endo, *Silence*. Penguin Twentieth-Century Classics and Mr James MacGibbon, for selections from *The Collected Poems of Stevie Smith*. Random House UK Ltd, for excerpts from *A Fable* by William Faulkner. Reed International Books (Sinclair Stevenson), for excerpts from *Jesus*, by A.N. Wilson. Copyright 1992 by A.N. Wilson. SCM Press for extracts from Dietrich Bonhoeffer, *Letters and Papers from Prison*; John Bowden, *Jesus, The Unanswered Questions*; John Kent, *The End of the Line*, E.P. Sanders, *Jesus and Judaism*, Graham Shaw, *God in Our Hands*, and Gerd Theissen, *The Shadow of the Galilean*. Taplinger Publishing Company, for excerpts from *Silence*, by Shusaku Endo. Copyright 1969 by Monumenta Nipponica. Yale University Press, for excerpt from Freud's *Moses*, by Yosef H. Yerushalmi.

Index

.